ATTACHMENT AWARE SCHOOLS COLLECTION®

The Attachment Aware School series

Book 1   The Key Adult in School

Book 2   The Senior Manager in School

Book 3   The Key Teacher in School

Book 4   Team Pupil in School

Book 5   The Parent and Carer in School

Attachment for Teachers

Attachment in the Classroom

Better Play

Conversations That Matter

Inside I'm Hurting

Little-Mouse Finds a Safe Place

Overcoming Barriers to Learning

School as a Secure Base

Settling to Learn

Teaching the Unteachable

Teenagers and Attachment

Temper Temper!

What About Me?

What Can I Do With The Kid Who...?

You Think I'm Evil

Conversations that Matter

Dr Margot Sunderland is Director of Education and Training at The Centre for Child Mental Health London, and a Child and Adult Psychotherapist with over thirty years' experience of working with children, teenagers and families. Margot is the author of over twenty books in the field of child mental health, which collectively have been translated into eighteen languages and published in twenty-four countries. Her internationally acclaimed book, *What Every Parent Needs to Know* (Dorling Kindersley) won a First Prize in the British Medical Association Medical Book awards and has been voted as one of the best brain books of our time by The Dana Foundation. Dr Sunderland has been studying the neuroscience of adult-child relationships for seventeen years.

Dr Sunderland is also founding Director of The Institute for Arts in Therapy and Education, a Higher Education College and Academic Partner of University of East London. The College runs Masters Degrees/Diplomas in Child Psychotherapy, Child Counselling, Parent-Child Therapy and Therapeutic Play. Dr Sunderland was also a member of the Early Years Commission, Centre for Social Justice, Westminster and co-author of the cross party advisory report *The Next Generation* (early years intervention).

Conversations that Matter

Talking with children and teenagers in ways that help

Margot Sunderland

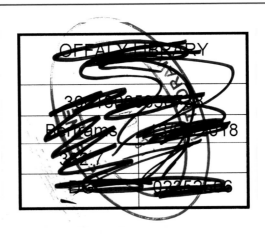

First published 2015 by Worth Publishing Ltd

www.worthpublishing.com

© Worth Publishing Ltd 2015

Reprinted, 2017

Printed in Great Britain by TJ International Ltd., Padstow, Cornwall

British Library Cataloguing in Publication Data

A catalogue record for this book is available from the British Library

ISBN 978 1903269244

Design, layout and illustrations by Stephen Hall

Front cover image © Image Source

Acknowledgements

I wish to thank some of the key people who have influenced my work and thinking over the last 30 years: Professor Jaak Panksepp who has so generously given his time and patience over many years so that I can ensure that the neuroscience I refer to is accurately presented; Dr Dan Hughes whose brilliance in conveying empathy to children and using his voice as an opioid activating musical instrument have been inspirational; Bessel Van der Kolk because his prolific work and research on trauma in children and teenagers is breathtaking; Professor Leslie Greenberg for his deeply moving and evidence based research on therapeutic change; Professor Martin Teicher for his research on the impact of adverse parent-child interactions on the brain; Dr Paul Wachtel for his writings on therapeutic communication; Professor Jean Decety for his research on the neuroscience of empathy; the late Sue Fish, founder of Humanistic Child Psychotherapy, who not only opened my mind to the work but also my heart; Jay Vaughan and Roz Read who have taught me so much about the needs of fostered and adopted children; Julia Bird and Lynne Gerlach who have taught me so much about the developmental needs of troubled children with their stunning intervention Thrive (www.thriveapproach. co.uk) which helps thousands of children to thrive; my children Amelie and Eloise who have taught me how to help under-fives to speak about difficult feelings and who teach me daily about the power of relational play for bonding and brain development; all my child and teenage clients over the years who put up with my mistakes and were the best supervisors, and finally my editor Andrea Perry whose attention to detail, intelligence, rigour, a wordsmith par excellence, stickability and humour through a hugely long and winding process of getting this book ready for publication has been a delight.

NOTES ABOUT THE BOOK

1   To protect the confidentiality of individual children, young people, carers, parents or professionals, names and autobiographical details have been altered in every case discussed. Case examples are composite and drawn from a number of similar examples known to the Author from her experience over many years of working with children and adolescents.

2   To simplify the text, either gender is used to represent the experience of children, young people or adults. No prejudice is implied by this.

3   To simplify the text, the word 'child' has been used on occasion to represent both children and young people. The strategies described are relevant to both children and young people unless stated otherwise, recognising that the emotional age of a young person may also be less than that of their chronological age.

4   To simplify the text, the word 'parent' is used on occasion to represent those now proving primary care to children and young people. The term will therefore include adoptive parents, kinship carers, foster carers and other family members. No prejudice implied by this.

5   If proper acknowledgement has not been made in respect of any material included in this book, the publisher would appreciate advice of this so that the deficiency can be made good in future editions.

6   Child and adult drawings have been reproduced to preserve confidentiality. Illustrations of sandplay are indicated by the following symbol:

Preface: Why this book is needed

My purpose in writing this book is to provide child professionals, parents and carers with the tools to help children and teenagers to talk about their feelings, and to engage them in meaningful conversations about their lives.

So when a child or teenager is troubled by painful feelings, you will know how to respond, what to say, and how to say it. As a result of their relationship with you, and the meaningful conversations you have together, the child or young person will develop the capacity to reflect on and successfully work through whatever life throws at them. In this way they will thrive, rather than grow up with a load of 'emotional baggage' to blight their lives.

People often fail to take on board the fact that children suffer from troubled feelings just as much as adults, and that *'childhood is rarely the happiest period in someone's life'* (Sinason 2008). Moreover, despite our best efforts and often passionate desire to protect our children, they *will* experience painful life events: friends who don't want to be their friend anymore, sibling rivalry, parents arguing or getting ill, separating. Many children will also suffer from all manner of profound losses, shocks, trauma, abuse, neglect, hurts and disappointments. Such painful feelings always need to be talked about and 'worked through' with an adult, who can help a child or young person make sense of their experiences, empathise, soothe and understand, and in so doing, modify the pain.

It is vital that negative life events are talked through at the time. If not, children and young people can all too easily develop neurotic symptoms such as obsessions or phobias, anxiety or low self-esteem, or some kind of body-based problem, for example, difficulty with sleeping, eating or bedwetting. Other children communicate their distress and discharge their troubled feelings through challenging behavior and violent acts. In addition, all too often, the emotional baggage surfaces in later life in the form of depression, problems controlling anger and impulses, blighted relationships or addictions.

There can sometimes be the misconception that difficult life events leading to debilitating emotional problems happen to only a minority of children. Sadly, this is far from the truth. Let's look at some of the statistics:

- Half the people with mental health problems in the UK had their first symptoms by the age of 14 (*No Health Without Mental Health*, HMG/DoH, 2011)
- In 2013 there were more then 50 million prescriptions for anti-depressants. Even taking into account repeat prescriptions, this is a huge number, as there are around 60 million people in this country. (Health and Social Care Information Centre 2013, http://www.hscic.gov.uk)
- One million children grow up without contact with their fathers. (*Fractured Families*, The Centre for Social Justice, 2013)
- One in two 16-year-olds will experience family breakdown. And with no-one to help them talk about their experience, they are more likely to experience behavioural problems, perform less well in school, need more medical treatment, leave school and home early, report more depressive symptoms and higher levels of smoking, drug and alcohol abuse during adolescence and adulthood. (*Fractured Families*, The Centre for Social Justice, 2013)
- 80% of people in prison have had a conduct disorder as a child. (*The Chance of a Lifetime: Preventing early conduct problems and reducing crime*, Sainsbury Centre for Mental Health, 2011)

If we don't help children and teenagers to talk about their feelings and in so doing, enable them to successfully work through what life throws at them, we will continue to see these epidemic levels of mental ill-health and human misery.

In addition, major cuts in the provision of NHS mental health services for children and teenagers leave so many other non-medical child professionals, particularly school staff, dealing with mental health problems in pupils. As the House of Commons Health Committee: Children's and Adolescents' Mental Health and CAMHS, November 2014 report states:

> There are serious and deeply ingrained problems with the commissioning
> and provision of Children's and Adolescents' Mental Health Services. These
> run through the whole system from prevention and early intervention.

So this book is designed to be a vital resource for all those child professionals and parents who feel de-skilled, out of their depth or anxious about helping children and teenagers who are in a miserable state, locked in destructive anger or suffering from some other mental anguish. We don't just need more child counsellors or child psychologists. We need to empower everyone who lives and works with children and young people in the art of how to listen and talk with children: how to have healing conversational times together.

In short, my hope is that this book will help any caring adult to have conversations that really matter with the children and teenagers they live with or work with, making that crucial difference to their long term emotional well-being. All too often, books say what children and teenagers need in order to be well and happy, but don't actually provide the wherewithal to bring about such positive changes. In contrast, this book, packed with tools, techniques and a myriad ideas for *what to do, how to be and what to say*, is intended as a vital support for adults to make those connections with children and teenagers that can change their lives for the better: and sometimes, even save them.

Contents

Section 1   Why conversations matter   1

    Introduction   3

 1   Why it's good to talk   13

Section 2   What to say   29

 2   The art of empathic listening   31

 3   The three key stages of empathic listening   43

 4   Different ways of conveying empathy   69

 5   Empathy troubleshooting   107

Section 3   Deepening the dialogue   117

 6   How to say it   119

 7   Getting to the painful stuff   161

 8   Dialogue deepening interventions   173

Section 4   Talking about feeling through creative media   211

 9   Using puppets and sandplay to ease conversation   215

10   Twenty creative techniques for conversations that matter   231

11   Talking about feelings through story   289

12   What to do when a child doesn't want to talk   315

    - bringing it all together

continues ...

Contents (continued)

Appendices

I   Mental health in the UK, and the links to problems in childhood   349

II   Conversations that matter between parents and children   353

The Adult to Child Responsiveness Checklist   378

III   Common themes for painful childhood experiences   382

IV   Conversations that matter in the classroom   386

V   Key psychological messages   405

VI   The Feeling Rooms   412

VII   Recommended therapeutic stories   414

VIII   Useful contact details and addresses   416

Bibliography   419

Index   428

Conversations that Matter

Why conversations matter

Introduction: How this book will help you have conversations that matter

In **Section One**: **Why Conversations Matter** with children and teenagers, I'll cover the vital reasons why children and young people need adults who can provide healing conversations and help them make sense of their lives. I'll address the awful toll on mental health and well-being when a child or teenager has no such adult in their lives: or when children go to adults with their emotional problems, and the response they get is to be talked at, questioned or lectured, instead of being met with empathy, compassion, and the sincere desire to understand what's happening from the child's perspective.

Of course I am very much impacted by statistics: as I mentioned in the Preface, half the adults with mental health problems in the UK have their first symptoms before the age of 14 (*No Health without Mental Health,* DoH 2011); one in two 16-year-olds will experience family breakdown (*Fractured Families*, The Centre for Social Justice 2013); one in five young people aged 16 to 24 in the UK have reported some symptoms of anxiety or depression and one in eight 10 to 15-year-olds are being frequently bullied in the UK (*Measuring National Well-being - Exploring the Well-being of Young People in the UK*, Office for National Statistics 2014). There are more equally shocking statistics in Appendix I. In light of such information, I am passionate to spread the word that so much misery experienced by children and teenagers could be prevented if far more people were able to offer healing conversations, and I hope the book will be a vital resource for anyone engaging in this task.

In **Section Two: What to say: How to listen, enquire and comment** we'll explore how to master the art of listening, enquiry and comment in ways that really connect with the child or teenager. We'll consider how to listen, when to question, when not to question, and then how to express empathy; then I'll take you through the three key stages of empathic listening. I'll provide different ways to convey empathy of particular relevance to children who are highly defended or mistrustful, and who 'spit out' or reject your attention and concern. I'll talk about this more through highlighting the need for *indirect expression* of empathy as well as *direct expression*, so that you have both possibilities in your tool box. This section ends with essential troubleshooting for those tricky situations we will all encounter from time to time, particularly with hard to reach children.

In **Section Three**: **Deepening the dialogue** - we will look at how to deepen the dialogue in safe and healing ways to help children and teenagers work through the profoundly painful stuff that's really blighting their lives. As psychotherapist Leslie Greenberg (2014) says, *"We cannot leave the place* (the painful stuff) *until we have first arrived"*. This section is also about 'finding the words to say it.' All too often people living with or working with children have such wonderful compassion and concern but when faced with a child's distress or pain, find themselves tongue-tied or using words they think are crass or inadequate. So I'll help you with what to say and how to say it, right down to some of the words you can use. It's like needing stabilisers on a bike for a while, until one day, you're off! So I'd like to give you those stabilisers: not by putting words into your mouth, but in the form of vital examples of key vocabulary, tone of voice, expression, and more, all of which can really help you connect with troubled children and teenagers.

In **Section Four: Talking about feelings through drawing, play and stories,** we start by acknowledging the fact that for many children and teenagers, their best way of expressing themselves is not through telling but through showing. So I'll give you a really good repertoire for easing and facilitating the best conversational flow with techniques using sandplay, puppets, art and drawing. Then there's a whole chapter on using stories, ones you find as well as ones you make up, and I'll take you through how to do this. And finally, in this section I'll address what to do when a child doesn't want to talk.

In the **Appendices**, you'll find a lot more statistical information about the current situation for children and adolescents in the UK in terms of their mental health and well-being. There's a section on having *Conversations that Matter* in a group context within school, and a section for parents. You'll find some of the key charts I refer to throughout the book, and finally, some resources to help you either find help, therapy or counselling for a child, young person or yourself, as well as where you can go to if you feel that having *Conversations that Matter* with children and teenagers is something you'd like to do professionally.

The key things to bear in mind whilst reading through the book

- Conversations that matter with children and teenagers can happen in all manner of situations - from formal settings such as child counselling or therapy, to time together on the stairs, on a park bench, in a classroom or corridor, in a child's room before they go to sleep at night. Hence I've used the expression 'talk-time'.
- In light of this, the book is designed for all kinds of readers: parents and child professionals, social workers, foster carers, adoptive parents, school staff, counsellors, therapists, GPs, psychologists, psychiatrists, YOTs teams, PRUS, family support workers.

- I am well aware that relationships with children and teenagers take time in terms of trust and psychological safety, and so sometimes the most powerful life-changing conversations will only happen after frequent talk-times.

- I will repeatedly emphasise the importance of ascertaining from the start whether a child or teenager wants to talk directly about life events or whether this is too much for them, or too shaming, and they need you to work more indirectly, for example through story or metaphor.

- I will repeatedly emphasise the vital importance of holding in mind *at the same time*, the child's 'play story' and 'life story' and noting what emotional themes are common to both. I strongly disagree with the practice of 'working blind' - starting work without finding out what has already happened in the child's life. In other words, the more information we have about the child's history of trauma, loss, relationship pain and so on, the more effective we can be, and the more potent our empathy.

- The book is mostly about one-to-one talk-times, but you will find a section on conversations in groups at the back of the book (Appendix IV).

- The book is heavily informed by the latest neuroscience, to prevent opinion based interventions. So here you'll find both the Art and Science of healing conversations: in other words, creativity-based healing conversations that matter, informed by brain science.

- And finally, I wish to stress the importance of confidentiality. The child needs to know that what they tell you is confidential: and that if they tell you something that means that they or another person is at risk, you would have to tell someone, but you would let the child know first. This of course means referral to appropriate educational staff or child protection people if you are concerned that the child's emotional or physical well-being is at risk.

How to use this book if you're a parent

Intimacy, like everything else, requires art.

Thomas Moore 1994, p.115

Key skills in conversations that matter between parents and children

When parents and children have conversations that matter, when our children openly share their worries, hurt, anger or delights with us, and when we as their parents really listen, empathise and attune, the relationship between us is deepened and strengthened, often in profound ways. The Office for National Statistics 2014 study entitled *Measuring National Well-being* found that child well-being was highly linked to children knowing that they could talk to their parents about important things, and that their parents would listen well.

Of course as parents we know this, and we're naturally relieved when our child comes to us for help. With my own children this often happens at bedtime, or over cooking supper or some other relatively unrushed time: *"Mum, I sometimes don't understand sums, but I'm too scared to put up my hand"*: *" Mum, it felt like no-one wanted to play with me at school today"*: *"Mum, I had that bad dream again last night .."*: just three examples of recent approaches from my daughters.

Sometimes things go well: our child feels we have really listened, and as a result he or she may be able to change something in their life. At other times, it can be more difficult, particularly if our own pain gets triggered by hearing about their pain, and/or because we lack the skills of how to be and what to say in such conversations. And we all know it's not easy with all the pressures of being a parent, to move out of 'quick-fix mode,' of pacifying with swift advice, rather than taking the time to really think about what our children are telling us in ways that enable them to feel truly understood. The Childline/NSPCC report 2013 *Can I tell you something?* found that many children do indeed feel they reach out to adults and parents for help with difficulties, but when they do, it seems that many of them often feel that it doesn't work, because they don't feel understood.

In many cases, things go wrong because we parents, so naturally wanting to take the pain away, are sometimes too quick to tell children *what to do* rather than listen to *what they feel*. At other times our children and teenagers exasperate us, because when they don't have the words, they *behave their feelings*. When faced with all manner of strops, sulking and melt-downs at the tiniest thing, the last thing you can feel like doing is to empathise. I know that when faced with challenging behaviour, I often find myself at a crossroads. A part of me would love to get angry, walk away or other such 'reptilian behaviour' (*see* p.33) but whenever I have taken myself by the hand, so to speak, and tried empathising, it has been very moving and has, without doubt, strengthened the bond between me and my child. I remember once when both my girls were in a state of exhilaration on the trampoline. My older daughter hurt herself and burst into tears. My other little girl found herself suddenly alone, all the adults tending to her hurt sister. When I went out to see her, she was crouched in a furious huddle. She shouted, *"Go away"*. Most of me wanted to say crossly, *"Fine then, if you feel like that I'm gone."* But after willing myself to resist that childish impulse in myself, I went and sat next to her. *"Wow, that must have felt horrible. There you were, having such fun with your sister and suddenly there was a big crash. Your sister was hurt and you didn't know how badly, so perhaps that was frightening and then all the grown-ups were gone and you were left all on your own ..."*

Now of course, children won't say *"Thank you Mummy for helping me process my feelings"* but they will show you. Her body melted, all the anger left her and she let me carry her back into the house.

The other 'pull' with the enraged child is to move into facts or advice. When faced with the screaming toddler, for example, it's all too easy to say *"No you can't have the chocolate biscuit before lunch"* rather than responding in ways that will help both calm her body and develop her own reflective skills. *"You want the chocolate biscuit. You are so cross with Mummy that I am not giving you one. You wanted one so badly."*

Here is an example of a conversation between a parent and a child where the parent is really trying to help, but has moved into advice before empathising with a teenager's painful feelings.

Teenager: *Mum, I feel so miserable about taking my exams, I might fail. It feels just too much to learn and I really don't understand a lot of the maths. I'm so scared of failing, letting myself down, feeling I'm a failure.*

Mum: *Never mind. Look, what you need to do is just keep up that revision. Discipline yourself to do an hour every night - no TV or Facebook for that time. I will help you.*

Teenager: *OK* (the child walks away feeling even more sad and alone)

Let's try it another way:

Teenager: *Mum, I feel so miserable about taking my exams, I might fail. It feels just too much to learn and I really don't understand a lot of the maths. I'm so scared of failing, letting myself down, feeling I'm a failure.*

Mum: *Ah, sorry to hear you are feeling so wretched about the pressure, all those subjects must sometimes feel like a huge mountain to climb, you're worried about failing, and you're feeling just awful at the moment.*

Teenager: *Yes I am* (and thinks, Mum understands)

Perhaps after that Mum will suggest ways of accompanied learning with her child, and help her to take things step by step: but it's been vital to empathise with the child's worries and fears *first*.

Throughout this book, in your vital role as parent, I hope you'll find all kinds of ideas and thoughts about how to communicate with children that you can use at home. Here's a list of some key sections in the book that should really support you to have the best relationship with your child.

Firstly, I think that the chapters on empathy are a must as there are lots of examples of how to convey empathy in ways that strengthen parent-child bonds. In particular, may I suggest you read,

Chapter 3: The three key stages of empathic listening
Chapter 4: The different ways of conveying empathy to a child or teenager
　　　　　　(and in particular, the section on What is a Big Empathy Drawing?)
Chapter 6: How to say it

This last chapter will hopefully support you in finding the words: sometimes, we feel empathic but get concerned that our words seem clumsy, patronising or don't really convey the compassion we feel.

You might also look at **Chapters 9** and **10**, and in particular, helping children speak about feelings through puppets and through sandplay. This is because having a sandplay with miniatures in the home can really support your child into *showing* you what they are feeling when *telling* you is just too hard. Even the most monosyllabic teenager can be amazingly expressive when offered 'show me' opportunities, and very stuck with a 'tell me' conversation. Similarly, conveying empathy to under-10's through a puppet can work wonders. And then there's **Chapter 11** on using stories. Important conversations can arise out of well chosen stories you read to your child. Pick stories where the characters are having real feelings like loneliness, fear or worry.

Chapter 12: What to do when a child doesn't want to talk - bringing it all together
I think this one is important to support you if you meet a 'don't talk to me about feelings' response.

And finally, have a look at the Appendix II, where you'll find some very particular conversations we may need to have with our children – ones in which we have to give them difficult news of some kind, perhaps about our own separation as parents, about divorce, about illness or even when someone has died. These are the things that children find especially difficult. I've chosen topics that are some of the major reasons why children ring Childline (Childline/NSPCC 2013).

I hope you will find all of these resources of use should you encounter these particular situations when bringing up your child. Because these are the things that parents can find difficult too. I hope you'll find the ideas helpful.

Chapter 1: Why it's good to talk

Why should it make such an enormous difference to communicate something to another person?   Fosha 2000, p.28

Introduction

Some things that happen to children are just too painful or frightening for them to feel and to think about on their own: they need someone to help them. So it's vital that adults who are good at listening can support the child to feel safe in feeling and thinking about their feelings.

And while many children need help to think about their feelings, others need help to *have* their feelings in the first place! For example, children who get angry a lot often need help to feel how hurt they are underneath.

So this chapter will explore the main reasons why it is so beneficial for children and young people to talk about their feelings and to make sense of what has happened in their life with an adult who can help them both feel *and* think. Combined, these reasons evidence the fact that with time and space to reflect with an adult who is good at listening, all areas of a child's life will benefit: their relationships, from now into adulthood: their learning: their emotional and physical health: even their brain development.

1 If we help children to talk about their feelings, we offer them a safe context in which to live their lives

Of course it's far better for a child to feel their painful feelings with an understanding adult, rather than alone in bed at night. Feeling feelings alone may mean the child is plagued by unfounded worries, that Mummy might die for example, or that Daddy will get angry about something the child has done wrong.

In this unsafe context, without a listening adult, the child's often grossly inaccurate thoughts and fantasies can't be corrected (*see* p.32). By speaking about their feelings with a trusted adult, children can feel enormous relief, realising that what they thought to be true is absolutely not true. Unless children have access to thoughtful adult minds through healing conversations, their often unmanageable feelings will remain unmanageable.

2 If we help children to talk, they will learn how to reflect on their feelings rather than 'behave them'

If a child is to develop the capacity to think about his feelings, rather than bottle them up or discharge them in challenging behaviour, then quality conversation time with a listening adult is essential. Without empathic listening, a child is likely to communicate painful feeling through his behaviour. It's only through talking, being heard and discussing together that the child will be able to reflect on, rather than 'behave', the emotional intensity of the painful events in his life.

3 If we help children to talk, it will develop their brains as well as their minds

When a child is able to reflect on what life throws at her, with the help of an understanding adult, positive changes will occur not only in her mind but also in her brain. She will develop new synaptic connections for dealing with stress in the part of her higher brain known as the pre-frontal cortex (*see diagram*). This is the part of the brain responsible for higher human functioning (Steinbeis et al, 2012).

As a result, the child will be more able to control her primitive impulses of 'fight/flight or freeze', the most basic responses we all have to any kind of threat, physical or psychological, real or imagined. Her better capacity for self-control will develop as the new connections form between the higher and the more primitive parts of her brain. These are called *top-down brain pathways* (Cozolino 2002, p.145) which naturally inhibit our primitive impulse to lash out in anger, or run away in fear, or become emotionally numb; so the child will be able to feel and think, rather than act out her feelings.

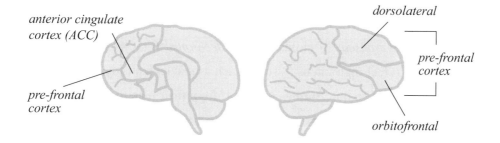

Location of the pre-frontal cortex

When she's under stress, the child will not 'sweat the small stuff', but she'll be able to reflect and react in a way that's appropriate to the situation. She is also far more likely to develop a real capacity for empathy. Research shows more activity in the medial pre-frontal cortex, posterior and anterior cingulate and insula, when people are helped to reflect on and process feelings, and empathise with another person's pain (Mar 2011, Engen & Singer 2013, pp. 275-82). These areas of the brain are key for self-awareness and a 'felt-awareness' of the emotional states of others.

4 If we help children to talk about their feelings, they will be far more able to manage stress well throughout their lives

Having a reflective adult to help you find words for feelings is a 'stress-regulating' activity. This means it can release calming chemicals in the brain. These chemicals dramatically reduce the intensity of a child's sometimes all too urgent feelings of rage, panic, fear or distress (Pennebaker 1993; Panksepp 2002). Studies show that children who regularly receive empathic listening also develop good vagal tone, which means more effective stress regulatory systems in the body. All this leads to better school performance, the enjoyment of more fulfilling relationships, more kindness and better overall ability to use life well (Gottman et al, 1996).

Without a capacity to manage stress, a child can go through life *under-aroused* or *over-aroused*. If children are *under-aroused*, they can often find it very difficult to feel high intensity states such as excitement, joy, delight, awe, passionate love and so on. But by cutting off from their pain in order to protect themselves against further hurt, they also cut off from life. If, on the other hand children are *over-aroused*, they can be agitated, anxious and/or aggressive for much of the time, unable to ever really know inner stillness or calm. Over-arousal means children experience over-the-top reactions to minor stressors.

We would never leave a child unattended if they were in physical pain, so why do we do it so often with emotional pain? Research shows that out of 700,000 children in the UK with problem behaviours, anxiety or depression, three quarters get no treatment (*How Mental Illness Loses Out in the NHS*: report by The Centre for Economic Performance's Mental Health Policy Group, and the London School of Economics & Political Science, 2012). In other words, so many children go unhelped, with awful suffering. Talking with children, in the ways outlined in this book, can do so much to ameliorate this suffering.

5 If we help children to talk about their feelings, they will develop a far more sophisticated language for their emotions

Talking about feelings can enable children to take on board the emotional complexities of a situation. For example, Ben, aged ten, said to me that he hated the boy who had called his mother horrid names. After I'd sat down and talked about it with him, he was able to say, "*I hate him, because he hurt my feelings.*" Later on his thinking became even more sophisticated: "*I guess he must have been really hurt by someone in his life, to call my mother names like that.*" And when a child is helped to find the right words for his feelings, what has been troubling him can lose its power.

6 If we help children to talk about their feelings, they will be able to 'suffer well'

As a therapist, I see so many people who don't know how to 'suffer well'. The 'art' of 'suffering well' means that when you are in emotional pain, you have the capacity to seek out support and comfort from an understanding adult. But when someone doesn't know how to do this, and life deals them some awful blow, they may get depressed, develop a neurosis or turn to some form of self-harming activity such as smoking, drinking or overeating, as a way of self-medicating against the pain. A woman I knew lost her only child in a car accident. Four years later, she too was dead from sclerosis of the liver. She had used alcohol to soothe her pain, as she didn't know how to 'suffer well'. And Matthew, aged 16, became very aggressive when his beloved father died. Before that he had been top of the class and heading for a glowing career. He developed a drug addiction, ending up on the streets despite his family's attempts to help him. There are endless tragic life stories like these, of children, teenagers and adults whose lives are ruined because no-one has helped them to 'suffer well'.

'Suffering well' means knowing that it is impossible to grieve 'without the presence of another', as John Bowlby, the father of Attachment Theory, pointed out.

And when you do find that understanding adult, it means expressing your grief in a deep, embodied way, rather than trying to 'manage it' or endure it. This can be a very rich and transformative experience. Besides the utter relief of accepting solace, a profound personal development can take place. As Hillman (2007) put it so beautifully: 'If there is no time for grief, there is no time for soul'.

No parent can protect a child from every painful life event - a parent who falls ill, a beloved schoolteacher who leaves, the boy next door unexpectedly hits the child, a former 'friend' turns to cyber-bullying, as well as more extreme hurts. Many children don't know what to do with their sad and painful feelings and memories of hurt, so it's vital that children learn the art of 'suffering well'. They need help from a mature reflective adult to be able to do this.

7 Helping children to talk about feelings is about 'opening up their capacity to take in comfort'

This means children will experience first-hand the sheer relief of getting help with their painful feelings, in place of trying to 'manage the unmanageable' all on their own. Margaret Mahler, the psychologist, talks of the child needing to 'merge with the calm and strength of the mother's body' (1968, p.45). This is an apt metaphor for any child who learns the exquisite feelings of letting an adult soothe and comfort them to the point where they feel calm and at peace. For many children, feeling deeply and accurately understood will be an entirely new relational experience.

Arguably the most awful times in life are when we are struggling with something very painful, shocking or overwhelming, all on our own; just as one is always alone in a nightmare! As Judd (2008) says, for many children, help with their feelings means they will start to feel 'more accompanied' in life. Even if the talk-time with the adult is only for one hour a week,

> ...it is something [the child] can carry through the rest of their week, a little torch burning inside of them that reminds them that they are not alone in the world.   Mearns & Cooper 2005, p.48

One should never underestimate the effects on a child of a compassionate interaction with an adult. That person can be called to mind at any time as an encouraging presence. This means that the child will be able to feel the adult's warmth and understanding even when she is not actually there. In short, the adult can become a powerful 'internal presence' (Mitchell 2003, p.290). At the bleakest moments of our lives, such memories can pull us out of ourselves into a warmer, kinder world. For all of us, from time to time, life will be just too hard, overwhelming, shocking or painful. But all this is made far more difficult if you have nowhere to talk about your feelings with someone who can listen and understand.

> Like many other lonely people, Gavin has a deep sense that others do not really know who he is, that others have not really touched down to the depths of his being and witnessed the hidden world that is there.
>
>   Mearns & Cooper 2005, p.20

For many children and young people, a sense of connectedness with just one adult at home or at school is enough to end their deep sense of aloneness, isolation, not belonging, not being understood. They can carry around with them the thought that *"There is one person in this world who really understood/understands me."* And amazingly, research shows that one person can often be enough (Howard & Johnson, 2000: Sroufe et al, 2005).

8 If we help children to talk about their feelings, they develop insight and emotional awareness

> We act, feel and imagine without recognition of the influence of past experience on our present reality.   Siegel 1998, p.29

When we help children/teenagers to talk about their feelings, they develop curiosity about how what has happened to them in the past is colouring their perception of the present. Without help to speak about feelings, many children will never develop this capacity. Instead they go into self-criticism or blame.

 The 'Brain Science' of emotional baggage

Research (Penza et al 2003) shows that when infants and children suffer from emotional stress/distress that is not responded to well, they are vulnerable to developing problems with anxiety, depression or aggression in later life. This is due in part to changes in their brain chemical 'profiles'. The unregulated stress/distress activates unhelpful changes in the neurotransmission of a brain chemical called CRF (cortico-trophin releasing factor) as well as changes in other brain chemical systems involved in the regulation of stress in brain and body.

When high levels of CRF were injected into animals they suffered:

Depression/anxiety/aggression

Increases in heart rate

Decreased appetite

Disruption of sleep

Suppression of exploratory activity

Freezing and fighting behavior

For example, Tim, who has never had any 'talk-time' says, "*I hit him because he is all bad.*" He does not say, "*I think I hit him because I'm feeling rubbish. My Dad moved out yesterday, so any little thing is upsetting me.*" (*and see* p.187)

Some key research by Hauser (2006) found that teenagers who had committed violent crimes (often shooting or stabbing) but who then developed capacity for insight and self-awareness went on to do well in later life. Many of them developed these capacities largely through talking with adults who modelled psychological thinking and the capacity to reflect on painful life events.

> The resilient kids [realise] that their inner world requires as much skill
> as the external environment; they look for the rocks that shipwrecked
> them before ... in that search, they are willing to look inward.
>
> Hauser et al 2006, p.271

From no awareness to self-awareness

Mellor & Sigmund (1975) have tabled four different responses to life problems.

Position 1: *There isn't a problem*

Position 2: *There is a problem but it's nothing to do with me*

Position 3: *There is a problem, it is to do with me but I can't do anything about it*

Position 4: *There is a problem, it is to do with me and I can do something about it*

Mellor & Signmund's Position 1 is of course the most emotionally unhealthy position. It's all about denial. Position 2 is a very common one, adopted by many children and teenagers: "*It's someone else's fault, for example, my parents, my siblings, other people.*" Such children often see themselves as faultless victims. Position 3 shows the capacity for self-awareness but without a sense of appropriate potency to change things and make good things happen. Position 4 is a likely result of effective feelings talk between a child or teenager, and an adult.

9 If we help children to talk about their feelings, they will be far less likely to carry emotional baggage into adulthood

Without help to talk about feelings, all too many children and young people carry painful emotional baggage into adulthood. The thing about emotional baggage is that it can flare up at any time when we least expect it, causing suffering to self and others, particularly those close to us.

By and large, emotional baggage is the result of bottled up feelings which were never validated or empathised with by a compassionate understanding person, at the time the feelings were first stirred up. If only that empathic person had helped the child talk about what was wrong, grieve where necessary and voice their pain and process.

If, on the other hand children can talk about their painful experiences when they are upset, rather than waiting years and sometimes decades or even a lifetime to do so, such feelings can be modified and made manageable by the 'emotionally regulating responses' of the adult.

10 If we help children to talk about their feelings, it can have major and beneficial impact on their self-esteem

To be listened to by a person who is working hard to understand how you experience something, and meets what you say with understanding and compassion, can be such a powerful boost for both self-esteem and self-acceptance.

For many children and young people, as I mentioned above, a sense of connectedness with even just one adult in this way is enough to change their inner world from feeling cold or hostile to feeling warm. The difference between feeling alone and having that one other person who believes in you and understands you, can be immense. Carl Rogers, who created person-centred therapy, called this 'feeling prized'.

When we help a child or young person to speak about feelings (and respond well when they do) they will have repeated relational experiences of:

- Having a voice that is both heard and respected
- Having someone support and encourage them
- Having someone believe in them
- Having someone understand with compassion what it feels like to walk in their shoes
- Having someone meet them in both their joy and their pain
- Having someone relate to them in a way that means they develop a felt knowledge of themselves as of real value and being worthy of compassion and concern
- Having someone help them make the unthinkable thinkable
- Having someone acknowledge that their life has been hard/ too hard
- Having someone not afraid to talk to them about the hurtful things they might have done to others, and help them see that these things are in part a reaction to what has happened to them
- Having someone help them see that relationship can be a source of real pleasure when perhaps it has too often been a source of pain
- Having someone delight in them
- Having someone relate to them in ways that help them realise that relief and solace can be gained from sharing feelings with someone

> If [this adult] thinks it worth the time and effort to try to understand my
> experience, I must be worth the time and effort.   Kahn 1997, p.43

We also know from brain science that when children from birth to six years are given a diet of negative messages, it is as powerful as being under hypnosis (Lipton, 2006). The brainwave patterns of children from birth to six years are often in a state of what are known as low-frequency delta waves and theta waves. This is the very same brain state as in adults under hypnosis! So although it is a very dangerous time for negative messages it is also a potentially powerful time for positive messages.

In addition, the child's sense of self is still forming at this age, so they are in a very receptive state. Hence verbal and non-verbal messages such as "*You are lovely*", "*You have rights*", "*You are worth listening to*" have a profound effect on self-esteem long term. And the great news is that at adolescence, we get a second window of opportunity when the brain is re-wiring: so it's not too late to make a difference through conversations that matter.

FREQUENTLY ASKED QUESTIONS

A *"But won't talking with children about feelings open up a can of worms?"*

> For many adults their own lonely sufferings as children were too
> powerful and painful, so they cut off. This can leave them with a strong
> [apprehension about] 'opening cans of worms'.   Segal 1993, p.179

This question often reveals a fear and unease in the helping adult themselves about the power of painful feelings. The view that "*Some things are best not talked about*" can often be translated into "*Some things are too dangerous for me to talk about because in my own childhood they weren't talked about*." But what do we really think is dangerous about a child feeling deeply understood, met with compassion, warmth and empathy, sometimes for the first time in their lives?

The view that emotions are so worryingly powerful that they must not be talked about doesn't make sense, even if we understand the adult's fears based on their own childhood experiences. This is because the child is living with these painful memories, thoughts and feelings, day in and day out. Moreover for many children the 'can of worms' is already open, when their life experiences have been so painful that they are expressed through aggressive or neurotic behaviour and painful symptoms.

Two of the best-selling children's authors, Jacqueline Wilson and JK Rowling include a huge amount of emotional pain in their narratives. We all know that children can't get enough of these stories. I would argue that this is because the books speak to them about what they feel from time to time. The books stand in direct contrast to the PSHE (Personal Social and Health Education) school curriculum, which tends to offer children exploration of milder, more manageable feelings.

The irrationalities of the 'can of worms' myth

i. "*Talking about it makes it worse.*" This often means that as long as we don't talk, the pain is manageable, when in fact for many children the pain is so unmanageable that it means they are living their lives reeling from unbearable arousal - exploding with aggression or imploding with anxiety, depression blighting their ability to learn, to love, to make friends, to develop emotionally and socially.

ii. "*Talking about something makes it real.*" But the child's trauma *is* real.

iii. "*Talking about it reminds the child about all the painful things that have happened to them.*" This suggests the child has somehow forgotten all the painful things in their lives. Some children will have forgotten or rather repressed their painful memories, but many others are haunted by them every day of their life: seeing their mother fall into an awful depression for example, the day Daddy left home, the day their beloved Gran died in hospital. Children - and young people - do think about these painful things again and again. But without help from an understanding adult, they often think about the painful events in a way that can be far more terrifying and sometimes far more painful than the actual truth of the situation.

B *"What can happen if we keep the can of worms closed?"*

As we have seen above, if we don't talk with children, we risk leaving them with:

i. Incoherent narrative and awful, blighting, shame-based fantasies, and incorrect beliefs about themselves and others

ii. Unmourned grief, brain biochemical imbalance and states of hyper-inhibition and hyper-arousal that can easily trigger aggression, anxiety or depression.

iii. Trauma that can erupt into re-victimisation at any time (*"I do to others what happened to me"*). This isn't the child being bad: re-victimisation is a common response to post-traumatic stress disorder.

And so if we dare not open the 'can of worms', how long do we leave the child with an incoherent narrative, a narrative that so often blights life and learning for the child. A week? A month? A year? Just let them take that narrative with them into adulthood to blight that too? Here are some of the incoherent narratives which children I have worked with have carried around for years:

"Daddy left home because I was boring."

"Daddy left because I was bad."

"Daddy left when I was a baby because I wasn't pretty enough."

"Mum beat me every day because I deserved it."

You blamed yourself to give yourself coherent narrative because nothing else made sense.   Graham Music, 2012, *Why Empathy Heals*
Conference, Centre for Child Mental Health, London

C "Won't we re-traumatise traumatised children by getting them to talk about their trauma?"

Research shows that emotional pain can become trauma when we are left alone with terrifying feelings, rather than someone helping us with them. This is when, as teenagers or adults, the person is in danger of reaching for the bottle, drugs or other forms of self-destructive behaviour (one in five 15-18 year olds self-harmed: Institute of Public Policy Research, 2006). Diana Fosha, an eminent psychologist, has described what she calls 'catastrophic aloneness'. *It is this that can move a child from emotional pain to actual trauma.* In other words, it can be dangerous *not* to talk about feelings. In fact lots of people die from not talking about feelings, because they have turned to alcohol, smoking or drugs instead. Whereas, 'what is shareable is bearable' (Siegel,1999).

But with therapeutic conversations, when the traumatised child talks about what has happened to him, you, as an adult, will be healing his distress by responding with the empathy and compassion that was sadly lacking at the time of the event, which lead to the event becoming a trauma! Freud himself knew about this and so differentiated 're-experiencing' (the healing effect of talking about the trauma with an understanding adult) from re-traumatisation. This is beautifully expressed by Dan Hughes (2012) in the following statement:

I have to go into the event of loss or trauma with the child by being regulated myself - so that the child realises that they don't have to deal with the feelings and thoughts about it by themselves. This is because now someone is there talking about the trauma/loss who is regulated, and they can piggy-back on my regulation. And then together we can make new meaning of the event. I can reflect on the event in a new way so the child has new thoughts and feelings about it, very different from the ones they had before. The new thoughts and feelings are a result of my [being alongside the child with] empathy and reflection.

From a paper presented at the *Why Empathy Heals* Conference,

Centre for Child Mental Health, London, May 2012

D *"Wouldn't it be safer to just wait for the child to bring up painful feelings?"*

No. The last thing many children want to do is to talk about their painful feelings. Their agenda is to play, to have fun with this adult who is giving them their undivided attention. If we wait for the child to initiate the conversation about painful feelings, the danger is that the painful feelings will never be explored so they will never be modified, and the child will be left with their trauma, ungrieved losses and incoherent narrative about major life events.

Of course in the initial period of building up trust between adult and child we need to give the child time to address painful feelings in their own way. But often it will often become clear the child has no intention of doing so! How we address painful feelings sensitively will be explored throughout this book.

2 What to say: how to listen, enquire and comment

> If you do nothing but strive for the deepest possible understanding of the [child's] experience, and if you communicate that understanding, that experience will be life changing.   Kahn 1991, p.103

A healing conversation will naturally address something that is troubling the child, but in a way that the child can hear. The adult will be skilled at putting the child at their ease so that they will want to open up. The conversation will develop, and deepen to an important point of resolution. This might mean the child having a moment of insight or an experience of feeling deeply understood, or a sense of relief at something personal and important being named and talked about. A key component to all this is the adult's capacity for *empathic listening*.

We often think we listen to children, but in the first chapter in this section, I'll be describing the kind of listening that's going to be most effective in terms of helping a child work through what is troubling them. It's a particular kind of listening with our heart and gut as well as our mind. In the subsequent two chapters, I will consider how to convey our empathy to a child, what words to use and how to say it. Put together, these are what I refer to as the *three stages of empathic listening*. Finally, I will cover empathy troubleshooting, for when you feel things aren't progressing well or seem stuck.

Chapter 2: The art of empathic listening

What is empathic listening?

> It is amazing to feel so understood. I knew she understood me deeply.
> It wasn't just that she understood what I was talking about - it was
> that she understood how it feels to be me. Also, I could see that she
> understood how powerful her understanding was for me - that it 'took
> my breath away'.   Mearns & Cooper, 2005, p.45

Empathic listening is having the emotional space in our minds and hearts to feel into, imagine and think about a child's painful feelings. We need to feel as well as think about what the child is saying; otherwise we won't be empathising, we'll be merely observing what the child is saying and feeling, or offering sympathy, not empathy.

Sympathy just doesn't have the incredible healing effects that empathy has. Empathy involves being moved by the child, 'so that the child is touched by your being touched' (Hughes 2007, p.93). Empathy also means being really interested in and curious about the child's life story and important life experiences, and finding appropriate ways to convey that curiosity. In addition, empathy involves being deeply committed to finding the child's meaning about something that's happened to them, or about something they're telling you, and not imposing your meaning.

Can anyone listen empathically?

Some people don't have enough space in their minds to do all this, because they're too preoccupied with their own troubles, and/or because they are emotionally numb because of something painful which has happened in their life, or because they have received too little empathy themselves. That said, I know it's never too late to change things. The very best way of becoming deeply empathic to a child is to be or have been on the receiving end of empathy and compassion yourself.

So if you missed out on this in your own childhood because of how your parents were parented by *their* parents, or because there has been no other person in your life such as an important teacher, relative, friend or mentor who was empathic, the best thing to do is to get some good quality therapy or counselling for yourself. There are contact details and addresses at the back of this book, to help you get started.

Why empathic listening is so important

- Your empathy will make the child's feelings more able to be felt, because it will provide a real connection with the child that makes them feel psychologically safe
- Consistent empathic listening will strengthen and bring about secure attachment between you as an adult and the child
- The child's previously unmanageable feelings will become more manageable
- Feelings will become less frightening for the child because '…you [as listening adult] have felt them and been able to tolerate the experience of these feelings' (Casement 1985, p.82)
- There will be the child's feelings and fantasies about a painful event *before* your empathy and their feelings about it *after* your empathy. The latter will often mean the child will have a whole new perspective on what they've been feeling and thinking, and far less pain

- Your empathy will give the child a feeling of "*Yes that's it, that is exactly how I feel,*" and the sheer relief of being understood and no longer alone with all these powerful feelings that they haven't known what to do with

- If you empathise with the child's anger, it is far less likely that it will be 'discharged' in a non-thinking way (*see below*) - because your empathy has made the anger thinkable. Once the powerful feelings are 'processed' in this way in the child's frontal lobes (the analytical part of the brain - by you thinking about the feelings with the child) their 'reptilian' brain's impulses of fight/flight/freeze, will be naturally inhibited

- The child will develop the essential life skill of being able to reflect on her feelings rather than discharging them or defending against them. Discharging means impulsive actions such as running away, or hitting out. Defending means developing some form of neurosis, phobias, obsessions, panic attacks or bodily-based symptoms such as eating disorders or self-harm

Here are examples of both a lack of empathic listening within parent-child relationships, and empathic listening.

Toddler: Annie (2)

Annie is screaming about not wanting to leave the playgroup.

✗ Unempathic response

    Annie: *Don't want to go home. Stay here.*

    Daddy: *You have to calm down*

Annie: *Don't want to go stay here* (screaming loudly)

Daddy: (shouting) *Just stop this behaviour right now*

Annie screams even louder

✔ Empathic response

Annie: *Don't want to go home. Stay here.*

Daddy: *You love the playgroup. You want to stay here, not go home*

Annie: *Don't want to go, stay here* (screaming loudly)

Daddy: *Daddy knows. Annie wants stay here, not go home, and not go home.*

Annie quietens and lets Daddy picks her up and she cuddles into his lap.

Child: Max (6)

Max's twin brother Ryan accidently knocks over Max's Lego tower. Max has spent ages building it. He screams out in pain and anger.

✘ Unempathic response

Mum: *Now come on Max don't be angry. It was only an accident.*

✔ Empathic response

Mum: *Although Ryan didn't mean to knock over your tower, you feel angry and sad. I can understand that! You had put so much time and care into building it.*

Family in a restaurant: boy (7) and a girl (4)

Mother is clearly tired and irritated.

✗ Unempathic response

Mother: *Look I'm really tired, can you just read something?* (child plays with the sachets of sugar on the table)

Mother: *You are tiresome, stop doing that. Sit up. Stop saying that, it's disrespectful.*

Boy: *Look my tooth has fallen out - the tooth fairy will come, yeah!*

Girl: *My tooth hasn't fallen out!*

Father: *What are you crying about? It's obvious - his tooth has fallen out, he is older than you*

Mother: *How many times have you cried today? Too many times!*

Girl: *I am going to try to get my teeth to fall out.*

Mother: *Don't be silly, put your coat on.*

✔ Empathic response

Mother: *You feel sad because you want the tooth fairy to come to you too - I can understand that - it's really hard waiting for something your brother has and you don't yet, because he is older than you.*

Teenager: Jack (16)

Jack has just run away from home for the third time, since his parents split up. He misses his Dad very much and doesn't have much time with Mum any more since her new partner moved in. Jack agrees to meet his mum late at night in a car park

✗ Unempathic response

> **Mum:** *How could you be so selfish? Just running away and not even telling me where you are?*
>
> **Jack:** *I was safe. I was staying with Amy and her parents*
>
> **Mum:** *Well, why the heck didn't you let me know? Me me me, that's all you think about*

Jack walks away. His Mum does not see him again for three days.

✔ Empathic response

> **Mum:** *I am so sorry that home is not a place you want to be, but a place you want to run from. I would so like to hear how you see things, why they feel so wrong for you. Perhaps we could go and have a cup of coffee somewhere now, as I really want to hear your side of things.*

or

> **Mum:** *I guess for you home is no longer a lovely place but a painful place ... will you help me understand that ... so together we can think of a way of changing things?*

Jack agrees to go to a café with mum to talk things over

Research shows ...

• that children who have been empathised with on a regular basis in childhood have good vagal tone (calm body states), and consequently do better academically, socially and emotionally (Gottman et al 1996)

• that when people are helped to talk about their feelings, rather than trying to make out all is well when it isn't, their body and mind are calmer and far more regulated (stable and relaxed-alert) (Lieberman et al 2011)

• that when people are in pain, someone's empathic presence calms the body (as opposed to no-one being there) (Sambo et al 2010, Derksen et al 2013)

• that empathy in therapeutic relationships leads to better clinical outcomes (Canale et al 2012)

Here are some more examples of both a lack of empathic listening and empathic listening within nursery and school settings.

Toddler: Hiromi (2)

Hiromi screams because Sophie has taken her Peppa Pig toy

✗ Unempathic response:

Teacher: Now come on, you need to learn to share

✔ Empathic response:

Teacher: Sometimes it's hard to share something that really matters to you. Let's put Peppa Pig somewhere safe for the moment and bring out the toys you are OK taking turns with.

Sally (12): Sally's mother had obsessive-compulsive disorder and suffered from phobias and panic attacks. Sally was full of anxiety, which was interfering with her schoolwork. Sally drew a picture of a dream she kept having about rows and rows of toilets full of poo, with handles which didn't work. Each toilet she went to, she couldn't use because it was already full.

✗ Unempathic response

Jacky: *Can you tell me about the picture Sally?*

Sally: *It feels like this sometimes in real life: just far too full of yuk. I just feel so horrible inside sometimes with all Mum's worries*

Jacky: *Never mind. She'll feel better soon and then before you know it you will be drawing lovely pictures like the other girls in your class!*

✔ Empathic response

Jacky: *How painful to feel so full of yucky feelings. Maybe, you feel too full with your mother's feelings as well as your own. When someone you care about is in pain, it is very understandable that you are in pain because of their pain.*

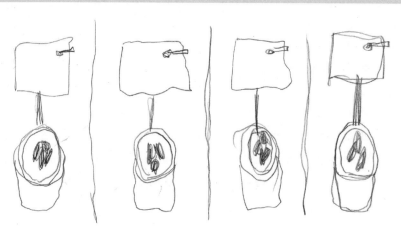

Sally's dream

The Science of Empathy

The attachment research is very clear. If you've been empathised with as a child and you're touched by that empathy, you let it in; you learn to empathise (Gottman et al 1996). In the brain, this means that when you see another person hurting there is an 'opioid withdrawal' in parts of your brain called the anterior cingulate and anterior insula with a mass of connections into the pre-frontal cortex, the cerebellum, and the brainstem. *In effect, this means that you are in pain because of the other person's pain* (Eisenberger et al 2003, Zubieta 2003, Decety & Jackson 2004, Singer 2004). It's called being *distress averse*. You grow up wanting to help the weak or defenceless.

A fascinating study recently showed how a distress-averse rat was given the choice to eat a piece of chocolate or help an entrapped rat. Amazingly the rat first helped the entrapped rat and then shared the chocolate with him! (Ben-Ami Bartel et al 2011). If, on the other hand, a child is *insecurely attached*, meaning that all too often his own feelings have not been met with empathy, the child may suffer from an *empathy deficit*, a reduced ability to feel other people's emotional state. Moreover, if your feelings have repeatedly been met with anger, indifference, ignoring or even abuse, you can become *distress excited*, not distress averse (Armstrong-Pearlman 2012, Steele et al 2002). This means that when you see a person in pain, the reward centres in the brain light up, not the empathy centres. You want to hurt the weak and defenceless because it gives you a kick.

> Aggressive adolescents showed a specific and very strong activation of the ventral striatum (an area that responds to feeling rewarded) when watching pain inflicted on others, which suggested that they enjoyed watching pain.   Decety et al, 2009

So because of distress aversion and distress excitement, the world is witness to outstanding acts of kindness and outstanding acts of cruelty!

The prevalence of bullying in schools is such a stark reminder of the empathy deficit in so many children (Gini et al 2007). Almost half (46%) of children and young people say they have been bullied at school at some point in their lives (Chamberlain et al 2010). In 2011 for example, 30,000 children called ChildLine about bullying. Research shows that bullying can damage the child's developing brain, particularly areas to do with short-term memory (hippocampus) and emotional processing (corpus callosum) (Teicher et al 2010). There is concern whether or not this damage can be repaired. Bullying can also result in depression and anxiety and poorer school performance (Gladstone et al 2006, Vaillancourt et al 2011, Thomas et al 2007).

Hence our work is so vital in ensuring all children receive empathy, if not at home, then in a school or other settings and as early in their lives as possible. And the bullies? Over time, the distress excited child will feel the practitioner's compassion for the hurt inside then, for the infant they once were, whose painful experiences did not meet with sufficient compassion, understanding or apology. As Camila Batmanghelidjh (2010) says of her most hardened teenagers, 'What they need is not more and more punishment, but to be helped to feel again'.

Notice how Jackie didn't try to persuade Sally not to feel what she was feeling. Instead, Jackie empathised with and 'contained' Sally's pain, talking about all the different parts of it: Sally's bad dreams stopped.

When your empathic listening is effective, it can deeply touch a child. Sometimes the child will take up what you've said and develop it. At other times, they will do something else, or the feeling of relief and calm in the room, created through the connectedness between you, will be tangible.

Oscar (13): His parents split up. It shocked Oscar to the core.

> **Oscar:** *My sandplay picture is called 'Boy in Bits' because I was broken when Dad left.*
>
> **Adult:** *So so painful Oscar, and worse with the shock of never imagining such a thing could ever happen to you.*
>
> **Oscar:** (bangs a drum in the room) *Like that,* (bang) *the shock* (bang) *shocking me and shocking me* (bang bang) *and shocking me again* (bang, bang, bang)
>
> **Adult:** (punctuating her words with pauses) *So much shock - so much pain - again - again - and again*

> **Amy (6):** Amy lost her Mummy for about an hour in a department store and remembers it bitterly.
>
> **Amy:** *I cried for my mum for a long, long time.*
>
> **Adult:** *So when you reached for her, she wasn't there*

Amy starts drawing. She says she is drawing a star falling out of the sky with no-one to catch it.

When a child is touched by your empathy, over time, he is likely to feel more empathic towards himself and towards others.

Tony (7) wanted more alone time with his Mum. So he got his little brother into trouble for something he hadn't done. This meant the little brother was sent to his room. As a result, Tony got his mother to himself. The problem was he felt very guilty about it. When Mum found out, Tony was given chores as a consequence.

But Mum was smart. She also did a 'time-in' with Tony. She said, "*What you did, getting your brother into trouble, was not OK, but I do understand you wanted more alone time with me, and I think I haven't been good enough recently in letting you know how much I love you, and giving you enough special you and me time*". Because of this empathy, Tony started to feel kinder towards himself, and the feeling that he was very bad for doing what he had done went away. His mother's understanding resulted in Tony saying sorry to his Mum too. He also started to play in a more thoughtful way with his brother.

So many children don't yet have a capacity for empathy. If they are to develop one, they need to have been *repeatedly empathised with*.

We really cannot go on ignoring the fact that children's incapacity to acknowledge distress in others at age eleven has been linked to parents not acknowledging their distress when they were infants (Steele et al 2002).

Chapter 3: The three key stages of empathic listening

Stage 1: Think, feel and imagine into the child's emotional pain

Stage 2: Enquiry: when the meaning of a child's life experiences is unclear

Stage 3: Finding the right words and right tone of voice to convey your empathy

Stage 1: Think, feel and imagine into the child's emotional pain

> Let the child impress you, excite you, impact you, evoke your curiosity.
> They need to know that they have the power to affect you. They need to
> 'feel felt' by you.
>
> Siegel 1999, p.143

Thinking, feeling and imagining yourself into how life has been for a child, demands effort, concentration and emotional engagement with the task. As I mentioned in the previous chapter, thinking without feeling is not empathy.

In order to get a sense of how the child's past is impacting on their present, it's important to get as much information about what life has been like for this child, and, in particular, who their major attachment figures have been, and then, any information about losses, separations, shocks and traumas the child has experienced.

Sometimes people say to me, "*I would rather not read the notes*". I always reply, "*Read the notes*". There is no virtue in grappling about in the dark, so to speak, when knowing, for example, the fact that a six year old has already had four major losses in his life, or that he pushed his little brother down the stairs out of jealousy and as a result his brother had to go to hospital, can make so much sense in terms of how he is behaving now. Images of pushing a brother down the stairs or describing himself as evil for 'injuring the little ones' may come up in the play of a child with such a history. You do him no service if, at such a time, you fail to read the connections between 'life story' and 'play story', or just expect the child to tell you what is going on. So many children will never tell you directly!

So knowledge about the child's history is vital to deeply inform your empathy. And for some children, in addition, whilst they don't mind us knowing what has happened, they don't want to have to tell us themselves. It can feel like climbing Everest.

How to approach Stage I

> The [child] depends on the [adult's] courage to experience what
> he cannot experience, so it's safe [for the child] to experience it.
>
> Grotstein 2005

As the quotation above suggests, it is important to know that it will take courage, to think, feel and imagine into what you know about this child and his life experiences. What, for example, must it be like to be smacked for the first time by a loving parent, when you are just four years old, or to be told at six, that your parents are splitting up, or to see, at age eight, your father fall into an incapacitating depression at losing his job, or to be moved on to your seventh school by the age of ten? That said: you do need to feel pain about the child's pain, but not so much so that you get lost in it and lose your thinking.

Take the time to do the thinking, feeling, imagining, and letting what you know about the child's life, and what the child is saying and/or doing, impact you. This is the opposite of responding impulsively. Be aware of how you are reacting physically and what is happening in your gut. Do you feel moved or overwhelmed, cut off or flooded? Might what you are feeling be similar or different to what the child is feeling? If the feelings the child is having are very painful and/or intense, can you bear this level of pain? Or are you trying to cut off from them (because of painful feelings in your own childhood)? Do you have an impulse to stop the child having the feelings they are having, because they are painful to you?

The 'capacity to contain' (a well-used term in psychology) means that we can bear the child's painful feelings without cutting off from them, dismissing them in some way, giving the child a lecture, offering quick fixes or moving them into 'happier' feelings. When you are able to do this, you can help transform their painful experiences into something that can be thought about, thus modifying or alleviating the pain. In turn, the child will experience you as someone with whom they don't need to censor anything or give a smaller version of their big feelings. They will see you as someone who is not threatened or overwhelmed by the intensity of their feelings: for example, shock, hate, or despair.

When a child does not have access to an adult who can 'contain' in this way, they are deprived of a chance of working through their troubled feelings and modifying them. The child is then left with their painful feelings, but sometimes in a more disturbing version because of the adult's failed response to them. The child can become afraid of their feelings, seeing them as something dangerous, something to be avoided, something to be forgotten, denied, hidden or defended against.

Thinking, feeling and imagining into the child's experience

Emily, my three-year-old niece, came to the train station to meet me. She really wanted to come in her new pretty party dress, but there wasn't time, so she had to come in her old painting trousers. Usually delighted to see me, she was so full of fury she didn't even look at me. She was entirely silent on the journey back home. Once in the garden, she started to throw the plant pots in the pond. On seeing her little girl become so aggressive, my sister said, *"Emily is committing acts of petty vandalism in the garden"* (my sister is a linguist!).

I took the time to imagine into what it must have been like to be a three-year-old with a lovely new party dress, to be full of excitement at the prospect of wearing it to meet her aunt at the station and receiving her aunt's delight. But then comes the crash of disappointment when all this doesn't happen. As a result of this 'thinking, feeling and imagining in' I said, *"You know Emily, I think you are not just a bit cross about not being able to come to the station in your party dress, you are very, very cross and really hurting. You so wanted to meet me with your new party dress".* Emily gave a big sigh and said *"Shall we play on the swing now?"* She could move on from all that pain, probably because she had felt 'met' in her pain by my empathic concern.

To be understood is what we all want and need as human beings. It heals so much. Sometimes reading poetry can help the process of thinking, feeling and imagining into a child's pain. Take, for example, the desperation conveyed in the poem opposite when a child feels his depressed mother does not hold him in mind. Instead, he feels 'abandoned in thought' by her. This is why it's so important for a parent who has to be away from a child for any length of time to send loving texts, notes, emails or video messages. The child will then know that she is being 'held in mind'. Bowlby (founder of Attachment Theory) knew this when he wrote that if a child is secure, it means that he knows his parent is 'readily accessible to him, rather than [an] actual or immediate presence' (Bowlby 1973, p.202).

Picture of a child who fell out of his mummy's mind

Today he fell out of her mind
Her arms became too limp and long
He fell right down the front of her,
Got all-torn-up and paper-binned.

Now searching for his littered self,
He walks among his dreadful grief
And finds a lethal world of just-himself,
There is no lovely here.

He longs
That she might read the calling of his eyes
remember me, remember me,
That she might see
just once,
And feel his falling from her mind
Yet has no words to speak of how he'd tried to cling
But helpless, lost his grip
And blown away like little dust.

He only wanted life,
He could not find it without her.

(The Author)

Holding in mind all the emotional themes in the child's life

As part of this Stage 1: *Think, feel and imagine into the child's pain*, it is vital to ensure that you are not being emotionally blocked on any of the child's issues. For example you might be feeling into the child's anger very well but perhaps not fully holding in mind the depth of a child's yearning for her absent father or her anxiety about being shamed at school. The chart on p.382, entitled *Common Themes for Painful Childhood Experiences* (Appendix III), is a check-list to help you feel and think into the complexity of what the child may be experiencing. It can also be a useful aid to help reflection on contradictory feelings the child may have, such as a hate for a parent but a longing to be cuddled by him.

Hold in mind the emotional themes common to the child's play story and life story

When a child is playing out their feelings rather than talking directly about them, it is even more important to consider all the potential emotional themes. Think of the emotional themes that are common to both the child's *play story* and their *life story*. It is these that will, in part, inform your empathic response. I will give several examples of this in the chapter, *Different ways of conveying empathy*.

Here is an adult who is thinking about a child's pain but not doing the work of feeling and imagining in, or that of holding in mind the key emotional themes relevant to what she is going through. On reading this, you will probably feel the pain of the misconnection in the dialogue.

Megan (14) is living in a residential care home, because neither parent (divorced) wants her to live with them. Both said that Megan was too angry and too difficult. Megan has just found out that her mother is going to live with her new boyfriend.

Megan: *My Mum is going to live with Lee (new boyfriend)*

Adult: *When did you find out about it?*

Megan: *Last week*

Adult: *Did you tell your mother what you felt?*

Megan: (silence)

Adult: *When will you next see your mother?*

Megan: (silence)

Adult: *If your feelings about it were a colour, what would the colour be?*

Megan: *Red, I guess*

Adult: *Ah, angry. But that is often what you feel, isn't it Megan? And that is partly why your Mum didn't want to live with you? It will be good when you learn to control your anger. I can help you.*

Megan: (silence)

Adult: *If your Mum was here now, what would you say to her?*

Megan: *I love you Mum and I'm so angry at you for not wanting me*

Adult: *And that's what you have been thinking, is it Megan?*

Megan: (silence)

Adult: *OK, it's time for us to finish today*

This is not a healing conversation. In fact for Megan it may have been the opposite, the adult opening up the wound by talking about it, but offering no empathy based on having really taken the trouble to think, feel and imagine into the child's pain. If you refer to the table *Common Themes for Painful Childhood Experiences*, you will see how the adult has failed to address, and so failed to empathise with, all the themes relevant to what Megan is going through now: for example, grief, loss, low self-esteem, not belonging, (*'pushed out in the cold'* in particular) *shock* (at hearing the news) and *jealousy* (in particular *'watching her love go to him not me'*).

If the adult *had* felt about and imagined into Megan's pain, she might have said something like this:

Response 1 (validating empathy with psycho-education)

> **Adult:** *No wonder you are angry with your Mum for choosing to live with Lee and not you (emotional theme, the 'unchosen'). So painful that your Mum can't love you in the way you want her to.*

And if it was appropriate, depending on the adult's relationship with Megan, how long she'd been talking with her and so on, she might add some psycho-education (*see* p.97):

> **Adult:** *When parents don't love kids well, the kids often think it's because they are unlovable or it's their fault, or they've done something wrong. But you are very lovable. Many times the real reason is that some parents can't love their children in the way the child longs for, because no-one loved or cared for them well enough when they were children.*

Response 2 (empathy delivered by the adult talking as the child, offering a 'wondering' enquiry)

> **Adult:** *Megan, can I see if I can understand what you are feeling by speaking as you for a minute and talking to your Mum using the puppets?*
>
> **Megan:** (nods)
>
> **Adult:** *OK, could you choose one of these puppets to be your Mum?* (Megan does so). *Can you let me know if I am right or wrong by banging this drum after each sentence if I am wrong and this triangle if it is what you are feeling?*
>
> **Megan:** (nods again; the adult turns to the chair where she has placed the 'Mum' puppet)
>
> **Adult:** *OK here's goes … Maybe a part of you might like to say to your Mum something like this …*
> *Mum, why can't you love me like you love him?*
> *Mum, I so want you to love me like you love him*
> *Mum, I am so angry that you want to live with him and not me*
> *Mum, it felt like you got rid of me, like a piece of rubbish*

Megan does four tings on the triangle and one bang on the drum. The room is full of sadness. After a long silence, the adult allowing Megan's feelings space to breathe, the two of them resume their conversation. (*For more on the drum/ triangle technique, please see* p.97)

Response 3 (empathy delivered straight)

> **Adult:** *If your Mum were here now what would you say to her?*
>
> **Megan:** *I love you Mummy, I miss you so much.*
>
> **Adult:** *And I guess that what you would long to hear Megan, is for your Mum to say she loves you and misses you too.*

Stage 2: When the meaning of a child's life experiences is unclear: the importance of enquiry

> The adult may know the child's diagnosis, symptoms, history, and current relationships. The adult may know how other children have experienced similar events. But the adult does not know this [child's] experience of the event until the child gives expression to the experience.
>
> Hughes 2006, p.82

Sometimes, despite imagining into the child's life, you are unclear how the child is experiencing a key person or key event in their life, unlike with Megan in the example above, who clearly expressed what she felt.

i. The child talks about a painful life event without in any way indicating or saying what they feel about it

ii. There is no clear parallel theme between their life story and what they play out

iii. The child has painted a picture, or made a sandplay, but not really expressed any feelings about it

When this happens, before offering an empathic response, it is important to be sure how the child is seeing things, the meaning they have given to that life event.

Adults sometimes fail the child here, by *assuming* a child's meaning rather than enquiring about it. This is often known as making 'wild interpretations' or using 'closed' meanings. Closed meanings are often born out of a belief (in or out of our conscious awareness) that we really know what is in the child's mind. We think we know the meaning of a particular thing or event in the child's life and play, drawing or dream, and that these things tend to have the same meaning for everyone. For example, with the influence of Freud in the psychological treatment of children, historically when the child drew a snake some practitioners would always see it as representing a penis: a sand mound as representing a breast: a child between a man and a woman meaning the child wants to split up Mummy and Daddy. These are closed meanings. But as Fonagy et al say (1997, p.11), 'We can never know for sure what is in someone else's mind'.

It is also of course very psychologically damaging to tell someone what they are feeling without asking for their meaning. According to the child's backdrop of life experiences, a snake for one child may mean a creature that is slowly plotting a sinister death. To another, it may be like a large, colourful worm and have no such frightening meaning whatsoever; to another, something entirely different. So let's never assume what the child is feeling about something in their life. Always ask them.

Out of our conscious awareness, even if we don't use closed meanings as described above, we may inadvertently project our own meanings onto what the child is telling us or doing in their play. Even those of us with experience still have to keep making sure we're not doing this. Because, as I mentioned above, being told what you are thinking or feeling can be experienced as a psychological assault, a maddening experience, a crashing into the child's particular reality of their situation.

When told they are feeling something they are not, the emotionally healthy child might say something like: *"You are wrong,"* or *"No, that's not right,"* or more likely, *"Can I go to the toilet now please?"* or *"Can we just play chess today?"* knowing they will not wish to speak about their feelings with this person again. The trust is broken and the adult is unlikely to win it back easily, if at all.

But the awful thing is that some children won't or can't protect themselves in these ways, but instead, just put up with being told what they are feeling. They can lose a sense of who they are and instead see themselves in terms of how the adult sees them. It's not good for any of us to be told how we're feeling, but it is particularly damaging for children to be told they are feeling something they are not, because they are still forming a sense of self. Here's an example of an adult assuming the child's meaning, rather than checking it out with the child.

Josh (9) tells a trusted teacher at school about the domestic violence he has witnessed that morning. But he does not talk about what it made him feel. The teacher assumes that Josh is in shock, grieving. An understandable mistake. So she moves straight to empathy, without asking Josh what he is feeling about what he saw: *"How dreadful for you, Josh"*. Josh mumbles and says sorry but he had forgotten he needs to be somewhere else and leaves very abruptly. Inside he is reeling because he trusted this teacher, but right now he feels very let down by her, because she has assumed what he was feeling and did not ask him what seeing his Dad hit Mum felt like.

How to approach Stage 2

The teacher's empathic response may be absolutely right for many children in these circumstances, but for a few children she will be totally wrong. When I asked one child I worked with what he felt about his Dad hitting his Mum, he told me it made him proud of his Daddy: *"Go for it Daddy"* he said, *"My dad's so strong"*. With the *"Go for it Daddy"* response, whatever you might feel, you can only be curious in an accepting way about how the child got to this in his mind. So go ahead and ask Josh. You can say things like,

> **Adult:** *What was that like for you Josh, when your Dad hit your Mum?*
>
> or
>
> **Adult:** *What did it make you feel?*
>
> or
>
> **Adult:** *Will you help me understand how that was/what sense you have made of what happened?*
>
> or you can ask the child to draw how they experienced what happened to them
>
> **Adult:** *Will you show me in a drawing, what watching your parents fighting made you feel?*

The child's drawing will often help you to really refine your empathic response and the words you use *(for much more on this, see Section 4, p.211)*.

What to do when the child doesn't want to respond

How do we enquire about the child's meaning when significant things seem to be happening in his play or through a drawing but he doesn't say what something means or feels like? When a child plays, or makes an art image, one thing you can do is to simply interview one or more of the child's images *(see p.236) for detail on this kind of work)*. Instead of inferring the child's meaning, we can be curious about what the child wants the images to communicate. Here is an example.

> **Abigail (7):**
>
> Has a Mum who sometimes drinks too much. Abigail told a teacher about coming home to find her mother in a drunken stupor. Abigail relates the story with little indication of what she was feeling about what happened.

In her play with toys, Abigail puts a baby behind a little grey door .

✗ Inferring meaning response

Adult A: (thinks) *This means Abigail feels shut off from her mother because of the drinking problem.*

Adult B: (thinks) *Burying: this means that Abigail wants to hide from her mother's problem.*

Such thoughts maybe totally wrong. Maybe adult A feels shut out from someone in her life, and adult B may want to hide from something in her life!

Abigail's hidden baby

✔ Asking the child for their meaning

Jess: *Hello baby behind the little grey door, what's it like for you down there?*

or

Jess: *Baby behind a little grey door, I wonder what it feels like for you down there. I wonder if it feels good or bad?*

Abigail: *It's good because when I close my bedroom door, I have a special secret safe world with just me and my teddies.*

Jess: *So I'm wondering if you're saying that sometimes you feel it's best when you are not with people - just alone with your teddies - it feels safer that way.*

Abigail: (grins and nods)

Luis (9):

His real Dad left and mother has re-married. Luis draws the picture on the next page. We don't know how he feels about this.

> **Luis:** *When I am with my step-Dad I become a bit like a snowman.*
> (Luis has given no indication of what that feels like)

X Inferring meaning response

> **Adult:** *It must feel hard to be so frozen and voiceless with him* (this is the adult's assumption. She needs to get more information from the child about his own meaning)

✔ Asking the child for their meaning

> **Adult:** (being curious) *I'm wondering what that's like for you, being that snowman?*

or

> **Adult:** *If the snowman could talk, what might it say?*
>
> **Luis:** (being the snowman) *Never ever will I let you know the real me! I have layers of padding and a stick-closed mouth that will never ever open for you.*
>
> **Adult:** (now has the child's meaning, so can empathise) *So snowman, you really want to keep your Step-dad from ever getting to know you, getting close to you. That really matters to you so much.*
>
> **Luis:** *Yeah, it does. My Dad is my Dad, not THAT man.*

What a gift for children! When we make the effort to find out how *they* experienced something that happened to them in their lives, rather than imposing our own meaning.

Luis' drawing (see previous page)

What to do when you are curious about a child's meaning and they remain silent

It is important to be totally non-pushy if there is no answer to your gentle enquiry for their meaning. The best we can do if this happens is to return to Stage 1, thinking, feeling and imagining into the child's emotional pain, and reflect on whatever emotional themes common to their life story and play story that emerge. If you really don't have a clue of the child's meaning, as there are no parallels between play story and life story and the child is not telling you about the meaning, you just have to wait! And simply accept and notice what the child is doing. Just stay silent until things evolve more clearly. Wild guesses are out!

Stage 3: Finding the right words and right tone of voice to convey your empathy

This stage involves taking the time, informed by Stage 1 and Stage 2, to find the right words and the right way to convey your empathy. This stage also means being able to hold in mind the complexity and range of human feelings.

Basically, we need to find words that will enable the child to feel we understand what is actually happening to them. That we get it! And in conveying empathy, we won't just use words; we use body language, tone of voice, facial expression as well.

This is what a caring mother does when her baby is cold or wet or in pain - she uses her face, her body and her voice tone to convey that she really understands how uncomfortable her baby is feeling. The child who has rich verbal and non-verbal language used for him in this way will no longer feel alone with the painful or troubling feelings with which he is grappling.

Like babies, the research shows that children usually need more colour (melody and rhythm) in a voice (in comparison to adults) in order to fully engage them (Trevarthan 2008). They often play with their own voices. Also, remember to punctuate what you say with appropriate pauses and variations in speed. Think of your voice as having a:

> ... soothing, almost sing-song quality, punctuated with sudden expressions
> of surprise or delight. This is likely to reduce the child's defensive
> behaviours and assist her in feeling safe.
>
> Hughes 2011, p.174

Your healing may at times be just as much in *how* your words are said, as in the words themselves. Many children can't hear words (however brilliant) when there is insufficient warmth and animation in the adult's voice. In light of this, Kahr (2006) made the point admirably:

> The musicianship of the [practitioner] may well prove to be one of the
> most transformational ingredients in the encounter. The [child] will
> be deeply affected by our tone of voice, our accent, the volume of our
> voice, the pitch of our voice, its cadence, its flow, its pressure. The
> human voice can pierce the eardrums of the vulnerable [child] with a

cruel intensity, and I do know of many [people] who have dropped out of [sessions] or who have felt injured by [the practitioner] who speak in a particularly strident voice … Many [practitioners] with whom I have conversed over the years speak in a markedly biting tone, devoid of warmth and musicality.

From a lecture at the Centre for Child Mental Health, London

So voice tones can hurt but they can also be so healing. Seltzer et al (2010) found that a soothing voice used to comfort distress was nearly as effective at releasing optimal levels of the calming chemical oxytocin as a hug! In light of this, your voice will be an asset to a healing conversation with a child.

So how our words are delivered at Stage 3 is key. They need to be offered to the child in a gentle 'wondering way', the opposite of saying, *"I think you feel like this"*. Spoken in this way, empathic understanding will be co-created. The child knows that they can correct the adult if the adult has got things wrong, and that his correction will be respected and accepted.

How to approach Stage 3

The most important thing to keep in mind is that just because children are very young doesn't mean that they don't feel some of the complex feelings we do as adults. Some adults think that when talking to children about feelings they should only use a few primary emotion words, such as sad, angry, scared, happy. This is patronising, because children feel the whole range of feelings. The difference is that they often have the *sensation*, without having the words, which would enable them to properly think about and process that feeling. Hence they are often in a state of 'unthought known' (Christopher Bollas 1987). In other words, *"I know it but I have not yet had a thought about it"*.

So it is up to us to help children to move from the unthought known to the thought known by supporting them with appropriate words resulting from our reflection during Stages 1 and 2 of empathic listening. In a state of unthought known, the child is vulnerable to communicating his feelings through actions not words, as I described in Section I. Some of these actions of course can be destructive for the child themselves and those around them.

Here are examples of conversations with children that are not healing because, in each case, the adult's response to the child is 'word impoverished', and also, in some cases, infers meaning.

Beth (8) drew a picture of how she felt (*see below*) when she had lost her mother to her drug addiction (cocaine), and how her mother never really played with her or talked with her anymore. As the listening adult, we can't just say, "*How sad*". This small everyday word is not big enough for the child's pain.

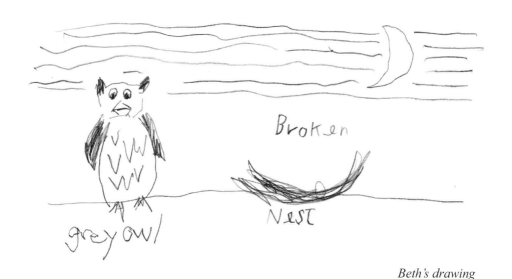

Beth's drawing

> **Beth:** *In this story, the baby owl waits and waits for his mother to return He waits for food, for cuddles, for anything. He is so cold, the nest is broken, the dark nights go on and on. One day he's knows his mother is gone … forever*
>
> ✗ Impoverished response:
>
> **Adult:** *Very sad*
>
> ✔ Empathic response:
>
> **Adult:** *The little baby owl, he's known a terrible aloneness …*
>
> *or*
>
> **Adult:** *Wanting his mother so badly and the awful knowing that she's gone.*

Petra (9) used to have a happy Mum, until one day her father unexpectedly walked out on the family to live with another woman. Now Petra's Mum is riddled with bitterness and thoughts of revenge. She tries to turn Petra against her father. Previously a playful and empathic mother, nowadays after school, Mum tells Petra she has to work and suggests that Petra 'just does something fun on her computer' or watches TV. The adult working with Petra knows all this information about Petra's life, as conveyed by social workers and verified by Petra herself.

In the 'talking about feelings' session, Petra draws a barren desert (*see next page*). She says once it was a beautiful place but then the water ran out. She says the wilderbeest are trying to get to the water hole but it's just an illusion because they are so thirsty. There is no water. Even the cacti have started to wither and die, she says. In this case, the listening adult has clearly not carried out Stage 1 or Stage 2 of empathic processing as outlined above. In addition, her response lacks a rich vocabulary for the child's complex feeling states.

Petra's drawing

❝

✗ Impoverished response to Petra:

Adult: *Wow, a story of angry feelings today.*

Adult: *Those cacti look really spikey.*

Adult: *The wilderbeest look so cross for not finding water.*

Adult: *You must be so cross with your Dad for leaving you all.*

Petra: (listening) *Oh I forgot I have to leave early today, because of the school play rehearsal* (and she gets up to go)

❞

The adult clearly thought that Petra must be angry, failing to take on board, and imagine into, the terrible loss that Petra has suffered, first her father and now her mother. The latter is physically present but emotionally absent. The adult is not thinking, feeling and imagining into the possible desolation, the emptiness, the longing for how things used to be, living in a world which has lost all its loveliness as shown in the clear tie-up between the emotional bleakness of Petra's life story and her play story. As the adult is so invested in the emotion of anger above all other emotions, we can only wonder if it is she herself who is so angry, and that this is being projected onto the child.

So how could an adult have responded to Petra using a rich emotional language? Here is a suggestion:

> **Adult:** (response informed by holding in mind the themes common to both the child's life story and her play story) *So you are showing me a world that has lost all its loveliness, where the animals are so desperate for water* (possible metaphor for love) *and yet there is none, and no-one to help them find it, just all alone in this barren place.*

Putting it all together

By way of bringing together the main points above, I will conclude this chapter with two examples. One is of an adult who is not going through all three stages of empathy and so the conversation with the child is not therapeutic. The second is of a practitioner who goes through all the three stages of empathy, and whom I would say shows the ability to make a profound connection with the child. I hope you will now feel more able to do the same.

Connor (8) has been bullied a lot by his older brother. His mum has found the brother hitting Connor on several occasions. Sometimes the brother is verbally abusive. Connor's mum dismisses it by saying *"Boys will be boys"*. At other times, Connor's brother is very nice to Connor. One day Connor behaves badly in class, tears up the work of another child, and scribbles on it. He is sent to detention. Two teachers witnessed the event.

The first teacher tries to influence Connor through fear, anger and shame. She shows no enquiry or curiosity for what Connor may be communicating about his inner world and/or actual painful life events through his troubled behaviour. After detention, she makes the following comment:

> **Teacher 1:** *Connor, how could you be so cruel to Kieran? Now just grow up, and stop being so stupid.*

The second teacher follows all three stages of empathy.

STAGE 1: Think, feel and imagine into the child's emotional pain

Whilst Connor is in detention, the teacher lets herself be impacted by thinking and feeling about the violent outburst. She feels a sense of hurt, shock and pain. She thinks about what she knows of Connor's home life. He has mentioned a few things about his big brother before. She wonders if Connor feels hurt, shock and pain when his brother attacks him. The shock of being hit, all the more so, because she knows that Connor's brother is lovely to him at other times. In reflecting on Connor and considering if perhaps his behaviour was a communication, she has an image of Connor as a little animal fighting for its life. She thinks whether this might be how Connor feels, when his brother (ten years older than he is) attacks him in such a shocking way, and no-one seems to take notice.

STAGE 2: Enquiry: checking out the child's meaning

After detention the teacher sees Connor. In a very soothing tone, to ensure no shaming or anger in her voice, but rather a tone of open and accepting enquiry, she asks him to help her understand the meaning of his behaviour.

> **Teacher 2:** *Hello Connor, I know that something happened in class today. I imagine something was triggered in you when you went for Kieran's work. Would you help me understand what was happening for you?*

Connor just shrugs his shoulders. So the teacher moves on to Stage 2. Connor knows the teacher is aware of what is happening for him at home, but hates anyone talking directly to him about it. This may be because of his ambivalent feelings towards his brother - he loves him and he hates his attacks.

STAGE 3: Finding the right words and the right way to convey your empathy (and allowing co-created understanding)

The teacher is still enquiring in this stage, whilst at the same time moving towards empathising:

Teacher 2: *I wonder if sometimes the world feels a bit like this for you (draws a simple picture of a cold harsh attacking place). I wonder if it feels like a cold hard place, and so you feel very unsafe sometimes. And maybe by lashing out at Kieran's work, you were letting us know how you feel lashed out at from time to time. But grown-ups sometimes get things wrong, so will you change the picture to be right for you?*

Teacher's drawing

The teacher hands Connor the pack of marker pens. Connor says the picture is right as it is, but also draws in lots more spikes and some horrid looking dark clouds.

Connor's response

> **Connor:** *Sometimes it makes me not want to go home anymore Maybe I could just find a place under a bridge or a hole to live in instead.*
>
> **Teacher 2:** *So I didn't really appreciate until now just how unsafe, spikey and harsh things can be for you. And how it's so awful for you sometimes that you would rather live in a lonely place than have to suffer anymore. Thank you for letting me know.*

Through this co-created understanding, the teacher realises that things have to change at home. Either the mother will have to change things or, if not, it would be time for other professionals to get involved and address the sibling abuse. The Head and the teacher meet with Mum, and explain the situation.

67

Fortunately Mum takes things very seriously and agrees for the older brother to be offered therapy. Mum is far more vigilant at home, and gains advice from a parenting counsellor on how to hold firmer boundaries. Connor is no longer hit by his brother.

Chapter 4: Different ways of conveying empathy

Of course, children can only experience empathy if it is conveyed in a way that they can hear. So it is vital to have more than one way of conveying empathy, as many children will not let you go ahead and empathise in the way you want to. Some will spit out what you say, so to speak, blocking their ears and complaining "*Don't talk to me about feelings*!" So when we're wanting to convey our empathy with children and teenagers, we've got to be richly resourced. In this chapter, I'll look in detail at three key ways of conveying empathy.

3 key ways of conveying empathy to a child/teenager

1: Speaking directly or indirectly

2: By doing a drawing, or using some other art form

3: By asking to speak as the child

1   Conveying empathy to a child/teenager: speaking directly or indirectly

Often the big question when talking to the child and conveying empathy is whether to refer directly to actual issues in the child's life (*speaking directly*) or to do it all through play, image, metaphor or storytelling (*speaking indirectly*).

In other words, we always have to consider whether this child, at this particular time, will find direct discussion about what is happening in their life threatening, painful, even a breach of trust; or, will he or she find it, as we hope, to be really valuable and a real relief? The relief is a sense that *"At last what has been troubling me for so long is finally being spoken about."*

When a child communicates to you entirely through play and does not want to talk about their life: how to respond

It is possible for a child to move from being troubled into a state of emotional wellness, just by both of you communicating through metaphor, play or story, and never referring to actual events in the child's real life. In other words, as long as you empathise *within the metaphor of the child's play or storytelling*, talking about 'real life' is certainly not necessary for resolution and change.

Children often choose 'indirect expression' in this way and don't refer to events in their life because it offers them protection: *"It's not me who is feeling sad, it's the sad pig in the story"*. Talking about their life (direct expression) for these children may feel just too frightening, shaming, intrusive, and painful. Many fear judgement or criticism. Usually this is because they have had little or no experience of empathic response. If you do talk directly with these children about their lives, some will remain silent, others decide not to see you anymore, and others will tell you to stop it in no uncertain terms. That said, after a while some of these children might move into being able to both tolerate and even appreciate you talking directly about events and people in their life. This is particularly the case when you have built up a really trusting relationship together, and you've 'earned the right' to be direct.

Some of the common signs that tell you that a child needs you to work indirectly

a. *When you asked in your first talk-time together, "Do you want to know what I know about you?" the child said "No".*

b. *When you asked in your first talk-time together "Do you want to know what I know about you?" and the child said yes: he listened, but even with your empathy, he seemed to find it difficult to hear you and did not add to or develop what you said.*

c. *You may have tried a gentle wondering, for example: "I am wondering if you ever feel sad like the elephant in your story?" and the child responded in a way that showed you that she found this threatening, intrusive, or emotionally dysregulating.*

d. *Sometimes when you know the child well, you will just 'pick up' small facial and bodily cues and know that direct speaking is too much for him or her at this moment.*

So how can we progress from here? Here are some options.

Speaking indirectly

Option 1: *Empathise with the events/characters in the child's play*

Poppy's (6) Mum has real financial worries and no helping members of the family or friends. So Mum often shouts - particularly when Polly has a distress tantrum. Mum has said she feels guilty about this but sometimes just snaps. Polly is now reported by school to be a very angry child with a short temper. Poppy has been playing for about half an hour with some 'moon men' she made out of clay. Poppy has said that sometimes she feels like she is a moon man and would like to live on the moon away from everybody on earth.

> **Poppy:** *Moon men don't have hearts and they are angry all the time.*
>
> **Adult:** (using indirect expression to refer to Polly's anger at school and her probable hurt when her mother snaps at her): *Maybe it's not safe for them to have hearts and feelings, when they feel that big people don't see how much they are hurting inside.*

Option 2: *Talking about another child (real or fictitious)*

Talking about another child, who had a similar dilemma or troubled feeling, and how they resolved it, can be very therapeutic for a child or teenager. It's very reassuring for the individual to hear that other children have felt how they have, got through it and resolved the issue successfully. If you don't know of such a child/teenager with a similar dilemma, create a story! When you make up a story of a child/teenager who has a similar issue, make sure the context is sufficiently different, so the child/teenager you are talking to doesn't smell a rat!

Hailee (10) kept getting angry with her Mum who had to go abroad a lot to work. When her Mum returned Hailee was so cross that her angry feelings blocked her sad feelings. Hailee would not have tolerated her school counsellor talking to her about this directly

> **Adult:** *I heard about a girl once. Her name was Ruby. She felt very wobbly inside when she hadn't seen her Dad for a while because Dad had moved out after Mum and him split up. But Ruby's wobbly feelings came out in cross feelings* (indirect reference to Hailee's maladaptive feelings). *So when she saw her Dad, she shouted at him and got very cross with him because she couldn't find the words to say she felt wobbly inside ... So then Dad put*

> *Ruby in time out so she felt even more horrid and alone* (indirect reference to how Hailee's maladaptive feelings bring her further and further away from getting her emotional needs met by her mum). *Until one day someone helped Ruby to find the words to say, "Dad, sometimes when I don't see you for a long time, I feel I'm losing you." Her Dad gave her a great big cuddle and told her how brilliant she was for being able to tell him. Ruby felt a deep sense of relief at having found a way of saying what she truly felt. She felt stronger and calmer inside.*

Speaking directly: How to refer directly to some painful feeling or actual event in the child's life

Direct expression is appropriate when children are open to or actively invite reference to their life. When you speak directly, they are clearly listening to what you say and taking it in, even if they say nothing in response. Take the child's lead on this. Here are key signs that the child will find this form of intervention of real value.

a. *The child already moves in and out of play to talk about something in their life, and/or speaks about herself or her family: for example, "I hate my little brother, you know", or, "I'm worried my Mum might die." Such a child may get really annoyed and feel you are mis-attuning if you suggest they listen to a therapeutic story you made up (a form of speaking indirectly). They may need you to talk straight about what is happening in their life.*

b. *The first time you saw the child and said, "Do you want to know what I know about you?" they were really interested and engaged and added to and developed what you said.*

c. *Other adults in the school or other setting have said they have talked freely about events or people in the child's life with the child.*

d. *Over time you have established a trusting relationship with the child so you sense that through this, and through the child's growing interest in psychological thinking, you've 'earned the right' to be direct. You tentatively try it out and it works.*

e. *The parallels between the emotional themes in the child's play, and those in her life are very strong, so you tried a gentle wondering into the air and she has responded well.*

When you venture for the first time into the realm of referring directly to events in the child's life, tread softly, demanding nothing in return. In other words, do it tentatively, and in a way that does not require an answer if the child does not want to give you one, and if they want to, they can ignore you. If you get a 'keep out' response or a resounding silence, respect it, and return to the safe realm of indirect expression. Stay there, until something shifts in your relationship so as to make you think that the child now seems that much more ready to move out of metaphor, and into reality. Then you can have another gentle try.

Speaking directly
Option 1: "I'm wondering if ..."

It's always a good idea to pose a question in a way that is like musing, like blowing a feather into the air, as opposed to slamming a door. So starting a sentence with *"I'm wondering ..."* is a good way of doing this:

> ✔ **Adult:** *I'm wondering if you ever feel like the sad cat in your picture?*
>
> *or*
>
> ✔ **Adult:** *I'm thinking about whether you ever feel like the volcano in your drawing?*
>
> *instead of -*
>
> ✘ **Adult:** *Do you feel like x in your picture?*
>
> *or*
>
> ✘ **Adult:** *Which figure in your story/sandplay picture is most like you?*

These last two questions have a far more demanding tone about them, and so could feel invasive to the child and cause them to close off from you and the conversation.

If the child does respond to your 'wonderings', remember to empathise. It is never OK to get a child to feel something and then abandon him there by empathic failure.

Lamis (7), a very gentle girl, was being bullied at school, but the school were not taking it seriously, telling Lamis' mother that she was just putting herself in victim role and should learn to stand up for herself (an all too common emotionally blind response to school bullying).

Lamis' drawing

> **Lamis:** *This is a sad gnome who is too scared to live above ground. So he lives under a toadstool. He feels safer that way.*
>
> **Adult:** (decision to come out of metaphor based on Lamis having often spoken about events in this life) *And I'm wondering if you ever feel sad and scared like the gnome in your story?* (said in such a way that the child can simply not answer if you are wrong, or if they don't want to answer).
>
> **Lamis:** *Yes, I do when the bullies make me feel so frightened all the time.*
>
> **Adult:** *How dreadful, and perhaps even more so because none of the grown-ups at school seem to realise how bad it is for you and haven't helped you yet. And how brave of you to tell me so clearly how you feel. Now we can think together how to get this to stop.*

Option 2: *Responses that help the child to make connections between their play and their life*

Carla (7) talked about her depressed father in the first talk-time session with the adult. Carla's father had became depressed after his mother died. Carla has now made up a story about a lonely rabbit who falls into a swamp of sadness and gives up.

> **Adult:** (using direct expression) *Your story reminds me of what you said last week about your Dad. Perhaps sometimes you feel a bit like that lonely rabbit falling into the swamp of your Daddy's sadness and feeling dreadful?*

Debs (7) told her residential social worker all about her home being noisy and messy, with too many strange people coming and going (reference to drug dealers). Then one day Debs made up a story in play about a little frightened worm who lived in an upside-down world in an upside-down sky where everything fell out of everything because it was all so upside-down.

> **Social worker:** *I'm thinking about your story and it reminds me of what you said about your home with all that noise and mess and strangers coming in and out, and I'm wondering if that felt so unsafe and even mad-making for you at times, just like for the worm in your story.*
>
> **Debs:** *Yes worms just need a nice quiet life and to live the right way up.*
>
> **Social worker:** *And perhaps just like the worms you long for that when you've known the opposite.*

Option 3: *Does this remind you of anything?*

> **Ted (6):** is described by teachers as angry, but then they also describe Ted's father in the same way
>
> **Ted:** *The big fish is biting all the little fish. He is that cross you see.*
>
> **Adult:** (using direct expression) *Everyone feels very angry from time to time. Does your story/picture remind you of anything or anyone in your life?*

Using tentative enquiry

Always be open to the child correcting you or showing very clearly by their non-response (or actual withdrawal) that a comment you've made about their life or their play is wrong. You may say something like *"Please tell me if I am wrong, or may not have got things quite right."* So this will lead to a co-created empathic understanding. The Mentalisation programme (AMBIT Adolescent Mentalisation Based Integrative Treatment) at the Anna Freud Centre London refers to this as 'sharing your first effort':

> The important point is to get to the sharing of your 'first effort' - and to invite the young person to help you improve it … this marking helps 'wake us up' to the fact that somebody is trying to offer a *"best guess at how I see what is happening right now"*. The marking invites the [child] to mentalise!
>
> Dickon Bevington, Lecture on Mentalisation, The Association of Child and Adolescent Mental Health, Anna Freud Centre March 13, 2013

The capacity to 'mentalise' means the ability to reflect on our experiences and take interest in thinking about our own mental states and that of others. Or as David Mallan (2009) puts it simply, the capacity to 'think about thinking'. Once children and teenagers develop this capacity, it enables them to think about feelings under stress rather than just discharge them in troubled behaviour or defend against them, leading to neurotic symptoms.

So to summarise: before responding to a child empathically, always ask yourself, which is the best way of delivering my empathy? Will the child be able to take in what I'm saying if I speak to him directly about a particular life event, or painful feeling, or does he need the protection of an indirect response, perhaps through metaphor?

Now onto the second way of conveying empathy.

2   Conveying empathy to a child or teenager: by doing a drawing or using some other art form

For some children, conveying your empathy with a drawing or puppet play or a few miniature dolls can be far more powerful than just using everyday words. It can capture the child's attention far more effectively. All too often, 'just words' fall on deaf ears: this is because the child is not paying attention, or they are experiencing what you say as just 'another adult lecture' or 'irrelevant adult words'. Here are some key techniques. I will start with the *Big Empathy Drawing* technique.

What is a Big Empathy Drawing?

This is a way of communicating your empathy to a child or teenager through a quick sketchy drawing that you do in front of them (executed in about a minute) or that you have done in your own time and brought into your talk-time together.

It can help you connect with a child or young person, often when other ways of connecting are not working. It is an interactive technique, where you and the child work together to find the most accurate empathy for what they are experiencing.

The Big Empathy Drawing enables you to help the child reflect on key emotional themes in their life and to correct any negative self-referencing (for example, *"I was the one to blame for Daddy divorcing Mummy"*). As a result, raw primitive feelings can be properly processed, and thought about. This creative strategy is a form of communication that brings relational depth to dialogue between adult and child.

The Big Empathy Drawing also takes the pressure off the child to always be the one who has to speak about his feelings. As child psychotherapist Valerie Sinason says (2008), *"So the child isn't having to be the one that everything is coming from."*

How to work with a Big Empathy Drawing (I)

Present your drawing to the child you are working with when there is enough of a working alliance between you. In other words, the child values coming to see you, and trusts you.

- *What you will need*

  » You will need a very big piece of paper (A1 (flip-chart size) or A2 are best) and some big thick felt pens (various colours).

- *What should be in your drawing*

  » The child's presenting feelings, behaviour, defences, experience.

  » Key emotional themes in the child's life that you know to be the case. These will include the more vulnerable core feelings that the child is aware of or defending against, for example shock, hurt, fear of loss (where there is defence, these feelings may need to be presented within the protection of metaphor). It can be useful to refer to the list of *Common Themes for Painful Childhood Experiences* (see Appendix III). Reference to the list goes some way to ensure against just considering emotional themes that have been significant in our own lives, rather than the child's.

  » You can draw things, but also feel free to use key words or short phrases as well, for example, *go away, too lost*, or *help*.

- *What should NOT be in your drawing*

  » Lots of detail about the child's life.

  » Too many emotional themes - picture is over-full and confusing.

  » Too much detail of anything - don't clutter it.

You'll need to decide whether you are going to speak directly or indirectly through the Big Empathy Drawing. Before doing your drawing, think about whether the child needs your drawing to be indirect expression (communicating through metaphor or story) or speaking directly if they have already shown you that they need you to talk openly about events in their life! If you don't, and offer metaphorical disguise, they might get frustrated as I've mentioned. This decision will dictate what you do and don't include.

If you are using indirect expression, you can still include the emotional themes key to the child's life but they will be set in a metaphorical context with no direct reference to the child or any people in their world. With indirect expression you would start by saying something like this: *"Sophie, I wonder if things sometimes feel a bit like this. There is a little fish and one day he got caught in a big blob of smelly seaweed, and then ..."* So the only statement is *"I wonder if things sometimes feel a bit like this ..."* but then you are off into metaphor! Here are three examples of actual Big Empathy Drawings used in talk-time with children, and there are many more examples in the following chapters.

Using the Big Empathy Drawing with a child as a response to a stuck and painful situation in his life

Ethan's (6) behaviour had gone downhill since his baby step-sister was born. He was now angry with his mother a lot of the time. She felt angry with him as a response. Their relationship had been strained in this way for over two years.

We know that so many children feel that a new baby threatens their loving connection with their mother and that this can result in both challenging behaviour and an accompanying adverse biochemical reaction in their brain. There is a withdrawal of the anti-aggression, anti-anxiety 'well-being' chemicals known as opioids, and a high activation of the stress chemical called acetylcholine (Panksepp 1988). When this happens with other mammals, it makes them very aggressive to each other.

How to work with a Big Empathy Drawing (II)

• Introduce the task to the child

Say to the child, "*I wonder if this is what you are feeling?*" or, "*As I think about what you are saying, I'm wondering if it feels something like this ... ?*" Now draw your Big Empathy Drawing. If you have drawn the picture before meeting the child, perhaps in response to something he has done or said in previous talk-time, you can do similarly: "*I've been thinking about what we were talking about last week, I wonder if I've properly understood things?*" or, "*I've been thinking about the story you told last week, I wonder if I have understood it correctly?*"

• Start drawing

Although to the child your Big Empathy Drawing will appear very spontaneous (it needs to be finished in around a minute), you may well have thought previously about what you might draw, so that it is a real 'fit' for the child as comment on the emotional themes they are dealing with.

You don't have to be good at drawing: in fact, the simpler the better. Stick figures will do. Splodges and circles and arrows will do. Think of it as a collage, add words and phrases if you like as well. Whether you are drawing in the child's presence or showing them a picture you have drawn before the talk-time, when you start explaining the drawing offer empathy verbally as you go.

• Pass the pen to the child for correction

Once you have finished your drawing, say to the child, "*Here's the pen. I may have got something wrong,*" or "*But grown-ups sometimes get things wrong, so will you change the picture to be right for you?*" Hand the pen to the child who can then change your drawing to make it more closely fit what he is feeling or trying to communicate. Remember that the picture is now the child's property, not yours. So he can do to it what he likes. To date, I've never had a child tear up a Big Empathy Drawing!

> ### • Acknowledge and empathise with the changes the child makes to your picture
>
> The child might say something like *"Nope, that's about it really"*. In other words, he is confirming that what you have drawn is indeed a clear grasp of the situation or of his painful set of emotions. So then you might empathise again with the child, once he has verified the 'specific pain' in your picture.
>
> Other children will change quite a bit in the drawing, speaking or not saying anything as they do. Whatever the child changes, acknowledge the change. For example, *"Ah ,so you've drawn the angry people in your world as far more attacking than I did. Thank you for letting me know that, I hadn't fully understood just how big the attacks were. How awful for you."*

Ethan's aggression is thus understandable. A chemical balance and calmer happier feelings can be re-established if a child is soothed and comforted with an adult who acknowledges and helps him feel his underlying feelings of hurt and loss, and enables him to feel understood.

We can't just say to Ethan, *"How sad."* And we can't use words like agony, despair or yearning, because these words are not the right ones for very young children. But we can respond to Ethan by conveying our empathy in a drawing. This is what I did.

In reference to the table *Common Themes for Painful Childhood Experiences* (Appendix III), the theme of course that jumped out at me when thinking about Ethan was *Jealousy/Sibling agony* and in particular *Using my eyes to drink in someone else's Garden of Eden*. There might also be a theme of *Not belonging*, and in particular, *Left out* and *On the outside*.

Sibling agony triggering anger is not mere opinion on my part, but a neuroscientifically evidenced aspect of the human condition. We know from neuroscience how the pain centres are activated in the brain even with the mildest experiences of feeling not included (Eisenberger, Lieberman & Williams 2003). It was this that informed my response to Ethan. Here it is:

> **Margot:** *Your mum says that since your baby sister was born, you have got very angry and she gets angry with you and then it's horrid between the two of you. But my guess is that anger is not the only feeling you have. I'm wondering if it's a bit like this. (I start drawing - see below) Here's angry Ethan, but then there's hurt Ethan. Hurt Ethan used to be the one in mummy's arms, but now it's the new baby. Ethan has to watch what he used to get, now going to someone else. I expect that must be really painful at times. (Ethan is nodding) But grown-ups sometimes get things wrong, so would you use the pen to make the picture more right for you?*

Margot's Big Empathy Drawing   *Ethan's response*

> **Ethan:** (eagerly taking the pen, draws some blue blobs)
> **Margot:** *What are they?*
> **Ethan:** *Oh they are my heart tears.*

After this important conversation, with Ethan's permission, I met with Mum and Ethan, and I told Mum what he was feeling. Mum felt both shock and compassion. She apologised to Ethan. She was careful to ensure that she gave Ethan special one-to-one time at some point every day. Ethan was no longer an angry little boy and they resumed a physically affectionate relationship, which had tragically been lost for over two years.

Using the Big Empathy Drawing with a child as a response to their play story

Declan (9) was offered counselling in school as he was unable to learn most of the time. His mother gave birth to Declan when she was just sixteen. She had been brought up in the care system herself, as her own teenage mother had not coped with looking after her.

Declan was clearly terrified of his mother. His teachers said they often felt terrified of her as well as she seemed to be angry all the time. Some days she would drop Declan of at school shouting "*And you better behave today at school otherwise you will know about it when I see you tonight.*" On those days, Declan would lie on the classroom floor humming and staring blankly at the ceiling. On other days, she would drop him off without saying goodbye, as she was either on her mobile phone or listening to music with headphones. Declan's father left when Declan was four. Declan loved his Dad very much and seemingly Dad had been loving and playful. Declan saw Dad only once or twice a year as Dad now lived in Africa. Declan missed his Dad very much.

Declan made a story, firstly played out with little figures in a sand box. The he draw bits of the story on a large piece of paper. *"Just as the mouse falls asleep, the dogs bark at the moon, so the mouse wakes up screaming. He ends up at his favourite ice cream shop - but the shopkeeper says no ice cream today. He is just selling spiders and locusts instead. So the mouse leaves, but a dog bites him because he says he's rubbish and so he falls down a toilet and ends up in a soup kitchen where people give him yucky dog biscuits with nails in them and it's so awful he's sick. There's so much sick that the world comes to an end with all the sadness floods. So the mouse ends up on a cloud looking at the moon. It's such a lovely lovely moon but then suddenly the mouse falls off the cloud and dies. The end."*

Declan's drawing

My reflective process when thinking of a Big Empathy Drawing for Declan

I considered whether to use indirect or direct expression with Declan. I decided I needed the protection of indirect expression, so my drawing was going to communicate empathy through metaphor rather than referring to actual events in Declan's life.

In my mind, I referred to the table *Common Themes for Painful Childhood Experiences*, and particularly thought of the following themes that were present in both Declan's life story and his play story.

Firstly, *Feeling powerless*. In Declan's play story, the mouse in the story was powerless to stop the awful events around him. In real life, Declan's only response to his frightening mother was to lie on the floor and hum. He clearly felt powerless to do anything else. Secondly, the themes of *Alone/lost/lonely*. In Declan's play story, there was no-one helping the mouse in a frightening world. He was so alone, and there is no-one to catch him when he falls. I knew that Declan lived alone with his mother who was not a 'place' of safety for him, but a place of alarm.

A third theme was *Life as a struggle*: yes, life for the mouse in the story and for Declan was indeed 'full of crazy muddle'. Fourthly, the *World as cruel and harsh*. The world in Declan's play story was without kindness, it was a nightmare world where a shopkeeper who was supposed to be selling ice-cream sold spiders and locusts, dogs bit and barked, and the soup kitchen gave no soup, just yucky dog biscuits with nails in them. And mothers are supposed to be loving and kind, not harsh and frightening as Declan's was.

Two final themes may reflect more of Declan's feelings. The mouse was 'rubbish' in the play story, and Declan clearly did not feel valued by his mother: so we had the theme of *Low self-esteem*. And finally there was blatant reference to 'the sadness floods' in Declan's story, and we know that Declan missed his beloved father so much, probably all the more poignantly in contrast to his frightening mother. So the theme of *Grief and loss* is powerfully present.

The above are indisputable. I also allowed myself other musings, but chose not to put these in the Big Empathy Drawing as I might have been wrong. I had not at this point carried out Stage 2 of Empathic Listening with these thoughts (*asked the child for their meaning, see* p.52). These are some of my 'musings:

• •

Play story: There was a brief moment of respite and a glimpse of a more benign world where the mouse enjoyed the moon but that moment was soon lost when he fell off the cloud.

Life story: *Perhaps a reference to the little contact Declan had with his beloved father?*

Play story: The mouse dies, the world ends.

Life story: *Perhaps this is what Declan felt, that his world ended when his beloved Dad left and/or with the attachment rupture when his mother leaves him at school with a frightening angry exchange as their only parting?*

• •

Here is a replica of the Big Empathy Drawing I drew for Declan and my accompanying words. The drawing and words convey my empathy. Keeping it simple is the way to go. No more than four or five images. As I've mentioned, it's important not to over-crowd your drawing, otherwise the child will switch off. Just stick to the few essential themes, to show you have understand what is specific to their emotional pain.

Margot's Big Empathy Drawing   *Delcan's response*

Margot: (showing Declan my drawing) *So Declan, can I see if I have understood your story? The mouse has no power in this cruel attacking muddled world. So alone, no-one helping him, no-one there to catch him when he falls. There are good things in his life - yummy ice cream and the moon, but these too are lost to him ... perhaps like the death of everything good in his world and so the sadness floods. I'm so sorry mousey has known so much pain and so little kindness* (empathy based on indisputable facts about Declan's life and that of mousey in his story). *But grown-ups sometimes get things wrong - is there anything you would like to change in my picture to be right for you?*

Incidentally, I could have also talked directly to the mouse in Declan's first sandplay, like this:

> **Margot:** *Hey mouse I am so so sorry that life has been so hard for you and that you've been left too alone with all that hurt.*

Declan took the pen and made the crazy attacking muddle far messier and put a 'protective red heart shaped shield' (his words) around the moon and the ice-cream. He grinned and said *"Oh yes they are safe in my heart you know."* So as often happens with the protective safety of the metaphor, the child comes out of metaphor and personalises the story at the end.

> **Margot:** *Thanks Declan for showing me that actually the crazy attacking muddle was more messy than I have drawn it. But I am so glad the mouse has known lovely things as well as all those painful things, how smart of you to keep them safe in your heart!*

This of course is an indirect reference to the fact that Declan had known a good warm loving world in the form of his Daddy; how healthy of him that he wished to protect the memory of his Daddy.

With a child more able than Declan to reflect on his life, more emotionally aware and articulate, you might use questions (Stage 2, Empathic Listening, Chapter 2, p.52) before coming in with empathic response, or ask him where the main emotional charge is for him in his story.

> **Adult:** Phew, what a moving story. If you were someone who lived in the mouse's story world what would you be feeling about all this going on around you?
>
> or
>
> **Adult:** Out of all the things that happened in your story, which is the most important, do you think?

Using the Big Empathy Drawing as enquiry as to what specific aspects of their life are particularly difficult or painful

When a child is not saying what is bothering her, but her behaviour is clearly showing that something is very wrong - you can also use the Big Empathy Drawing as enquiry. As you will see, this example also illustrates how to use indirect expression (story) to convey empathy rather than referring directly to events in the child's life.

Sophie (7) was referred to a SENCO called Karen because her schoolwork and behaviour had suddenly deteriorated. She was becoming aggressive and defiant. There was also some jokey sexualised behaviour, which involved goading other girls. Sophie was an only child. For a long time now, there had been just her and her Mum. Social services had become involved at one time, when Mum became depressed after being rejected by a boyfriend. The social worker was concerned that Sophie had became her mum's confidante. Apparently Mum often told Sophie about things not appropriate for seven years olds to know. She told her about her miscarriage for example, what sex feels like, her father's impotence problem, and the divorce proceedings. The social worker had asked Mum not to relate to Sophie in this way, but Karen was concerned it might still be going on.

Then one day Sophie's life, as she had known it, changed. Mum asked George her new boyfriend to move in with them, and there were other problems.

Mum very guiltily informed the teacher that on three occasions, Sophie had come home from school and burst in on her Mum and George having sex. Sophie would not talk directly to anyone about her life; people had tried, but she just hid under the table with her hands over her ears. So the SENCO used the Big Empathy Drawing, choosing emotional themes she thought might be underpinning Sophie's troubled behavior.

Karen's reflective process when thinking of a Big Empathy Drawing for Sophie

Before meeting Sophie, Karen entered into the Stage 1 of empathic listening: thinking, feeling and imagining into the child's emotional pain (*see above* p.43). She was unclear as to why Sophie's behaviour and school work had gone downhill, but in terms of events in Sophie's life she considered the following themes might cover some of what Sophie was going through (*See Common Themes for Painful Childhood Experiences*).

• •

Theme 1: *Life as a struggle, overwhelming, chaotic, all too much,* and in particular, *Seen too much, heard too much and thought too much*

Theme 2: *Helpless/powerless to change things*
Possibly feeling disturbed and over-burdened by everything her mother had told her. Possibly feeling disturbed having found Mum and boyfriend having sex

Theme 3: *Not belonging/left out*
Possibly feeling pain at there having been just been her and her Mum at home, and now a third person who was sleeping with Mum

• •

As a result of this process of imagining in, the task for Karen was to try to come up with a Big Empathy Drawing that covered all these emotional themes and then see if Sophie connected with any of them. She actually did two Big Empathy Drawings as we will see, all using indirect expression.

Picture 1: Karen's drawing

Picture I (indirect reference to what it feels like to be told all this inappropriate adult stuff by Mum)

> **Karen:** *Sophie I wonder if things sometimes feel a bit like this. There's a little fish, and she's swimming along and suddenly she finds herself all muddled up in grown-up stuff. And the stuff sometimes feels exciting and sometimes confusing and sometimes awful. And sometimes it's like just too much and the fish wants to be swimming in the clear blue sea again, free of all the grown-up stuff.*

Picture 2 Reference to George having moved in, and to Sophie finding Mum and George having sex

> **Karen:** *And then sometimes in the deep, deep sea there are two whales and the little fish sometimes feels so different from them, not part of what they have got, like on the outside looking in.*

Picture 2: Karen's second drawing   *Picture 3: Sophie's response*

Picture 3 Moving to Stage 2 of Empathic Listening: Check out the child's meaning of what she is experiencing (if unstated)

> **Karen:** *Will you change the pictures to make them right for you?*
> *(Sophie took the pen. She paused very thoughtfully. Then she put party hats on the whales)*
> **Sophie:** *Like a party, but the little fish, it's not invited.*

> **Karen:** *So if the little fish could talk to one of the whales what might he say?*
>
> **Sophie:** *Dunno.*
>
> **Karen:** *Can I be the little fish and you tell me if I have got it right?*
>
> **Sophie:** (nods)
>
> **Karen:** *Hi big whale, it used to be just you and me, and now it's you and the other whale, and you seem to be having special kind of parties and I don't think you know that I am hurting so much about feeling on the outside.*
>
> **Sophie:** (clings tightly to her favourite little bear puppet and nods) *My heart, it's not well you know.*
>
> **Karen:** *How did it get to be not well?*
>
> **Sophie:** *When Mummy asked George to live with us.*
>
> **Karen:** *Oh wow, so hard, I can see that. For so long it's been just you and your Mum and now there's George. No wonder your heart is hurting when you feel on the outside and maybe in other ways too.*

How to help your creative juices flow when you offer a child a Big Empathy Drawing

When you are doing a Big Empathy Drawing, you are 'in movement'. This means that the big cauliflower part at the back of your brain, called the cerebellum, is being activated. Scientists have found that activation of this part of the brain is not only responsible for physical coordination, but also better co-ordinated thinking processes. In short, if you are 'in movement', your thinking is often far better than if you were just offering the child empathy from a 'sitting still' position.

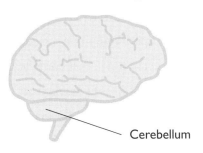

Cerebellum

3 Conveying empathy to a child/teenager: by asking to speak as the child

Now let's look at a third way to convey empathy. When a child has suffered some trauma or loss but isn't talking about it, some adults think that if we wait patiently, give the child time, they will at some point just tell us what they feel. For many children, this waiting will yield absolutely nothing. As I've said above, many children and teenagers are not yet able to think psychologically, so emotions remain at a level of sensation and arousal: remember Bollas' telling phrase? - 'the unthought known' - '*I know it, but I have not yet had a thought about it.*'

In other words the child's feelings have never been formed into coherent thoughts. Such unprocessed feelings all too easily present as challenging behaviour or bodily symptoms (for example, bedwetting, soiling, headaches, some forms of asthma and so on), as I discussed earlier. If we want the child to change, and to be able to think psychologically, we'll need to model it.

That means using words and concepts relevant to their lives. One way of doing this is the Big Empathy Drawing, as we've seen. Another way is speaking *as the child*. This is when we are totally sure we know what the child is feeling (we have indisputable facts about the human condition and we know the child's meaning). Or, alternatively, you can use this technique when you have a pretty good idea of what the child is feeling but you can check out your thoughts with the child.

It can really help the child such a lot to hear you putting feelings into coherent thoughts; the unthought known can become the thought known. When you present your words tentatively, asking for the child's feedback and correction, the child has opportunity to consider the validity of what you say. Many people worry that the child will just comply. But how you present the words will never be as clichéd as "*You are feeling sad*", or "*You seem angry about that.*" Instead you'll be constantly asking for her feedback on your '*best first effort*' (*see* p.78) - so the processing - and the meaning - will be co-created. Here is one creative way of doing this.

You will need two musical instruments (a triangle, a tambourine, a drum) or equivalent (for example, a spoon on a pan) that makes a noise. Ask the child if you can speak as her for a bit. If you say something that she feels is true for her, she can ting the triangle. If you say something that feels wrong for her, as it's not something she's feeling, she can bang the pan with the spoon. You'll find a couple of examples of this way of working on p.51, p.105 and p.201.

When empathy isn't enough: situations where the child needs psycho-education as well as empathy

There are situations when empathy is not enough to help a child or young person with what is deeply troubling for them. What is needed in addition is psycho-education. Psycho-education means giving the child indisputable facts about the human condition, when, without such information, he continues with irrational and often very negative fantasies about himself that are blighting his quality of life (negative self-referencing: an example might be, *"I was to blame for Mum smacking me."*)

Here are examples where it was vital that empathy was coupled with psycho-education (Chapter 11 *on therapeutic storytelling covers the use and necessity of psycho-education for some children in a lot more depth*).

Where psycho-education was needed alongside empathy

When **Kirsty (8)** was three, she burnt the house down by accident. On one level, her Mum knew Kirsty could not be held responsible, but on another level she hated her for bringing such trauma and misery into her life. It was as if she saw her as a malevolent arsonist, and as if Kirsty had an adult's capacity for intention and planning. As a result, she took Kirsty to live with an Aunt she barely knew: it was more than three months before Kirsty's Mum could face her again. The accident had effectively burned up her feelings for her daughter.

The 'meaning' Kirsty gave to these tragic events was that she was very, very bad. She behaved in a way that matched her view of herself. At one time, she was found by a teacher looking into the mirror at school and saying *"I am Satan's child."*

Emma, the adult working with Kirsty, knew that Kirsty was very confused, and that under all her presenting anger were probably deep feelings of guilt, shame and grief at losing her mother's love. Emma also knew that Kirsty needed help to realise that three-year-olds can never be held responsible for such an act. Kirsty knew that Emma knew about the house burning down. So Emma did this Big Empathy Drawing:

Emma's Big Empathy Drawing

> **Emma:** *Kirsty, will you help me understand more about what it feels like to be you? Because I know from time to time you are very unhappy and I think we can work together to change this. So I'm going to do a drawing. Will you tell me what I have got right and wrong, after I have finished the drawing?*
>
> **Kirsty:** (nods)

Emma: *(As she talks, she draws Big Empathy Drawing 1) Well, my guess is that because of the house burning down when you were three, you sometimes feel really bad. And maybe little Kirsty felt she should have been put in prison. And your Mum said that before that time, you were happy and lovely. But I wonder if all that got lost somehow in all the pain and hurt. But I've seen glimpses of lovely happy Kirsty and she's just delightful*

Emma: *But I think you have also got something wrong here. It wasn't your fault that the house burned down. With such little children grown-ups are always in charge. That is why no-one ever, ever puts three-year-olds in prison. OK I've said enough for now. Here's the pen. Will you change the picture to show how things really are for you? Just go ahead and change the pictures.* (Kirsty makes one change to the drawing. She writes "I am bad" over the girl's face)

Kirsty: *The only wrong thing is that you didn't say that the badness got into my brain.*

Emma: *Wow, I see now. How painful and horrible for you to have lived with feeling you were all bad, for all these years and that it went in so deep, even right into your brain.*

Kirsty's response

The drawing meant that Emma has gained Kirsty's attention. So, as they both go on to play with clay, Emma manages to give Kirsty more psycho-education. These things are said, not all at the same time but interspersed into their conversation about other things over time, and their model making.

Emma's psycho-education

i. Kids often think that when bad things happen, it's their fault.

ii. Kids don't know the difference between a box of toys and a box of matches, and no-one helped you to know the difference.

iii. You didn't know how dangerous matches can be. You didn't know that matches can cause so much harm.

iv. It was an accident.

v. By law, grown-ups must always be in charge of three-year-olds and so three-year-olds are never seen to be at fault in terms of what they do.

vi. So you think you failed the grown-ups, but actually the grown-ups failed you.

vii. Mummy sent you away because she was angry, and maybe you are so angry now because Mummy sent you away.

Emma continued with play interspersed with psycho-education and empathy for several sessions. In a later session Kirsty, who had clearly been thinking, said: *"You mean it wasn't because I was evil, it was because I was three."*

The shift in Kirsty was very tangible, as was her relief. It was as if she was becoming ready to surrender her defences held so firmly for five years. This was because it was the first time someone had bothered to explain what really happened on that dreadful day. As a result of the combination of psycho-education and empathy, she had new thoughts and feelings about the event, rather than just *"I am evil."*

With Kirsty's permission, Emma brought in Mum to the next session. Mum apologised, agreed that three-year-olds need constant supervision and that she was not in the room at the time. She also said she should never have sent her away and regretted it deeply. Kirsty was visibly moved. Perhaps because the conversations with Emma and then with her mother had changed the entire basis of who she felt she was, Kirsty became withdrawn at school for a while and no longer aggressive.

It was as if it took her some time to build an entirely different sense of self, one she herself didn't quite know yet. After a while she began to function well, emotionally, cognitively and in her relationships.

Xavier (7) adored his grandfather. However one day he shouted at his grandfather because he hadn't been allowed to take his large truck to the cinema. His Mum had told him how wrong he was for shouting like that. The next day his grandfather died from a sudden heart attack.

Xavier concluded that he must have caused his grandfather's heart attack. He told his mum, but very upset herself at the loss of her father, his mum just said *"Don't be silly, of course you didn't."* Not at all reassured, Xavier had great difficulties sleeping each night. His mother would often find him walking around in a half-dazed state saying, *"Hurt me, kill me, hurt me"* over and over. So Mum found a counsellor, Mike, to help. Mike did this Big Empathy Drawing for Xavier.

Mike's Big Empathy Drawing

Mike: *Your mum has told me about your nightmares and your sleepwalking, and your grandpa dying. Will you help me to understand what it's like for you?*

Xavier: (nods: Mike begins to draw)

Mike: (as he draws) *I guess you feel so sad and hurting after your lovely Grandpa died. Mum told me what great mates you were together. But perhaps you have other feelings too - maybe there's a part of you that is very cross that your grandpa left you, a part of you that wants to say "Why did you leave me?". Then maybe guilt that somehow you are to blame for him leaving you. Would you change the picture to make it right for you?*

Xavier: (Xavier said the drawing was right as it was) *But I am drawing barbed wire round the lump of guilt because it's been spoiling my life.*

Mike: *Wow, that sounds so hard and so painful. I'm wondering if you are thinking that your shouting the day before your Grandpa died, hurt your Grandpa's heart in some way?*

Xavier: *Yes I do think that.*

Mike: (moving into psycho-education) *But hearts don't get hurt because someone shouts. They wear out over time, because when someone gets old, their heart can get tired and then their body stops working. So it absolutely wasn't your fault that your Grandpa died.*

Xavier: (goes very quiet) *I didn't know he was old 'cos he always played football with me. I didn't think that old people could still play football.*

Mike: *Oh Xavier, I'm sorry you didn't know that until now, and that all this time you were thinking you made your Grandpa die. What a terrifying thing to carry around in your mind. No wonder you have been having nightmares.*

Xavier's response

Let's end this chapter with an example which illustrates how empathy can be used together with different creative techniques when a child or young person is struggling with a deep-seated issue.

When working with **Simon (13)**, what often came to mind were the words of the trauma specialist Bessel Van der Kolk: 'Trauma makes you fight the last battle over and over again' (1999, p.17). Simon had been fighting 'the last battle' on a daily basis for eight years. An only child, he had watched domestic violence for the first five years of his life. He remembers hiding under the table whilst hard objects were being thrown at his mother by his father.

When Simon was five his parents split up. For many reasons he was taken into care. He was labelled as being on the autistic spectrum, because of his strange fighting movements and the fact that he seemed to be locked in his own little world. He had no friends. But it would have been hard for anyone to be his friend because of his perpetual kung fu actions, and make-believe attacks. He was threatening, but would never actually attack anyone in reality.

Simon was also obsessed with the army and was often found wearing bits of army uniform. He would be escorted back to the children's home by the local policeman because he had been found hiding up a tree in his army uniform and frightening elderly passers-by with his 'on guard' movements.

Simon had talking time with me once a week, over an eighteen month period. He knew I knew about the too-hard start in his life. At first, empathising with the little boy, who had hidden under the table in such awful circumstances, by referring to the 'unhelped' catastrophically alone wounded soldiers in his play, just didn't touch him. It was only after he did loud bombing noises from a fighter plane and I said *"Wow, what an amazing bomber pilot"*, that he came to life and said, *"Yes you're right."* In other words, I was acknowledging his defence of omnipotence. Soon I realised that this was a defence against core feelings of having known unbearable helplessness, and so a determination never to feel like that again.

However after many sandplay sessions where we got nowhere, Simon switched to playing on the electric keyboard (I always have one in my room. They are easy for children to make very pleasing professional sounding music). Somehow the music took Simon into his core affect states. In those 'music sessions' there was no killing. The music became sadder and sadder and more and more laboured. Sometimes he found sound effects, which simulated screaming.

After a while Simon returned to working with sandplay. But 'post' music, the feeling tone of his play had changed markedly. At last there were a few ambulances, helping the soldiers and even things growing in place of the previous utterly desolate landscape resembling those awful WWI images.

One day he did a sandplay where everything was bombed apart from a little silver tower. I asked him about it. I knew Simon had strongly negative feelings towards his Dad. He said, *"My heart's under there. When the enemy goes far enough back, then my heart can come out."* I said slowly and gently, *"But Simon, the enemy never did go far enough back, did he? Your father kept hurting your mother. And so I guess your heart could never really come out."*

For the first time, Simon let my empathy in without being defensive. He responded by going over to the drums in the room. He said, *"This is what it was like to hear my mother being thrown across the room."* He just started to bang the drums, very loudly.

Now we know from Bushman (1999) that just discharging anger doesn't make people less angry. In other words, catharsis of angry feelings without cognitive processing is not healing, and can actually make people angrier. Many children are more than capable of physically expressing their angry feelings. What makes it healing is when the catharsis is coupled with cognitive processing (Scheff 2001).

So knowing this, as well as the fact that Simon had never been helped to think psychologically, as he banged the drums, I said loudly *"How dare you hurt my Mum, Dad. Stop hurting my Mum. I was only a little boy, I couldn't stop you. I hate you for that too. How dare you hurt her!"* I could see Simon was taking in what I said. One sign that your cognitive processing is helping the child to process is if they pick up on and then develop what you have said, in some way. Simon did just that. After he stopped drumming and I stopped voicing his protest (to make space for cognitive processing), he said, *"I need to draw the teeth."*

Simon then proceeded to draw picture after picture of his mother's broken teeth. I used core feelings words of 'utter helplessness, heart broken', enquiring whether this was right. I empathised with his shock, terror and grief. Again, with his permission, I asked if I could be him and talk to his Mum. I used the musical instrument feedback technique (*see* p.97),

Simon's mother's teeth

inviting him to ting the triangle if my words were something he might want to say: *"Mum, I'm so sorry you got so broken. Mum, I'm so sorry I couldn't help you because I was just a little boy. I really longed to help you, but I couldn't."* Simon was madly 'tinging' the triangle throughout.

At the end of many sessions, Simon was completely different. He had friends, and his autistic movements and obsessions with the army had gone. He said, *"It's weird, all the fighting inside me has stopped."* He did a drawing and called it 'ceasefire' because, he said, *"It's like the fire has gone out in my brain."*

Simon's ceasefire drawing

Simon had needed me to help him find the right words for his core feelings - and at the right time, after he had learned he could trust me. He would not have got there on his own. The words enabled him to move from raw sensation to thinkable thoughts and once he did so, he was able to grieve, rage and finally move on. But because no-one had sat down and had a healing conversation with Simon for over eight long years, his emotional, social and academic life has been at a standstill for all that time.

Chapter 5: Empathy troubleshooting

I What is failed empathy?

i. … *when it's parroting, not empathy*

> **Child:** *I feel sad.*
> ✗ **Adult:** *You are feeling sad.*

This is not empathy, but parroting (*see below* p.136). In other words, the adult has not made the effort to think about, feel into and imagine the child's pain in order to begin to understand how they are experiencing things. 'Mirroring or reflecting back … describes an activity that does not include the emotional depths of really taking in and feeling [the child's] pain' (Copley & Forryan 1997, p.195) .

ii. … *when it's sympathy, not empathy*

Sarah (8) says she doesn't know how she will survive when her Daddy leaves home to live abroad. The adult responds with a *"Poor you."* This is sympathy, not empathy, as once again the adult hasn't done that hard work of imagining and feeling into the child's experiencing of what has happened to her. Empathy is very different from sympathy. If you use pat phrases such as, *"You're feeling sad"* or, *"That sounds difficult"*, it's unlikely to have any impact on the child. Children and young people often sense that you have just trotted such comments out without in-depth reflection about their specific woes and pain. In fact, it may annoy the child, make him or her feel defined in some way, or the child or young person may dismiss you as inauthentic.

iii. *... when our motives are muddled ...*

It's not empathy if we haven't done the vital task of really thinking and feeling into a child's pain, and we just want to make the pain go away because it is making us feel awkward, uncomfortable, or in pain ourselves.

Of course, from time to time, listening to and being with a child's painful feelings will inevitably activate our own raw painful feelings, which means we are so busy trying to emotionally regulate ourselves or defend in some way against what we are hearing that we can't regulate the child (help him or her to regain a feeling of calm and emotional well-being). I have seen this happening so often. The adult literally doesn't hear the feeling content in what the child is saying. One time, for example, a little boy said to a school helper who was with him whilst he was playing, *"I miss my mummy"*, and he repeated this about 16 times in half an hour. Each time, the adult responded to his play, but she didn't say anything about his missing his Mummy.

So let's check we're not doing any of the following (adapted from Copley & Forryan's imaginative descriptions (1997, p.196 *passim*):

a. The 'sieve' ... 'A kind of pseudo-listening that does not really take in what the child is feeling ... 'in one ear and out the other'. (*ibid*)

> **Child:** *Sometimes when I'm at school I miss my Mummy so much it feels like I will die in pain*
>
> ✗ **Adult:** *Yes dear. I see. Shall we do some drawing now?*

b. The 'teatowel' ... '... a wiping away of feelings of distress, as opposed to paying attention to their possible meaning ... the adult avoids or evades the child's feelings by an imposed cheerfulness'. (ibid)

> **Child:** Sometimes when I'm at school I miss my Mummy so much it feels like I'll die in pain
>
> ✗ **Adult:** Just you keep yourself busy, that's the best thing to do

c. The 'nappy' ... 'very kindly maternal functioning, soaking up distress as a kind of 'nappy' or 'sponge', but which takes away some of its meaning'. (ibid)

> **Child:** Sometimes when I'm at school I miss my Mummy so much it feels like I'll die in pain
>
> ✗ **Adult:** There there, I'll give you a nice drink, that'll make you feel better.

I've added two more

d. The 'water in the chip pan' ... a spitting out response.

> **Child:** Sometimes when I'm at school I miss my Mummy so much that it feels like I'll die in pain
>
> ✗ **Adult:** Now it's time you grew up and be a big boy now. You are too old to still be missing your Mum.

e. Empathy (feeling and thinking about the child's pain)

> **Child:** *Sometimes when I'm at school I miss my Mummy so much that it feels like I'll die in pain*
>
> ✔ **Adult:** *It sounds so painful when you miss your mum, like you feel life will end because you're waiting so long for her.*

2 What should I do if the child spits out/rejects my empathy?

Give the child time

Are you moving too quickly into getting the child to process painful experiences prior to establishing a working alliance with her? The best way to build your connection is through relational play and fun, (*see* p.331) so that the child learns that you have a warm, kind presence. For the defended child, it's only once she feels safe in your presence that she will dare to let go of her protective shell and let you see the more vulnerable part of who she is. Give her time.

Speak indirectly

You may be using direct reference to the child's life when this particular child can only manage indirect reference. Convey your empathy through a story, or stay within the metaphors and images of her play (*see* Section 4).

Let the process come and go

The child may reject your empathy because you are keeping him in painful feeling for too long. If there is a sudden drop of energy in the child, or a lacklustre feeling, or sudden disinterest in his play, this can be a good indication that though your interaction may have started well you are unwittingly keeping the child too long in a painful place. Children need to be free to move away from difficult feelings and to come back to them in their own time. Let the process come and go. If the child trusts that you will be attuned to when he needs you to *stop* talking about the painful stuff, he will allow you to bring him back to it, all in good time.

3 How do I know if my empathic response is correct?

Don't expect the child to say: *"Wow, what an amazing empathic response, thank you very much!"* But you may feel one or more of the following:

- ✔ A sense of relief in the room
- ✔ A shift in the child's play
- ✔ A deeper sense of trust from the child
- ✔ More flow in the conversation between you
- ✔ The child will look at you more directly
- ✔ The child will say something that shows they are building on what you have said

4 How do I know when I have misattuned?

Again, you'll often feel a drop of energy in the room. Or the child will go silent or close off from you in some way (maybe even literally, like leaving the room). We all misattune at times. It's inevitable. When we do mess up, it's important we acknowledge this: *"I'm sorry Rick, I think perhaps I've not properly understood what you've been trying to tell me."*

Our acknowledgement can sometimes give the child the opportunity to work through painful misattunements in their past. This is called 'interactive repair'.

5 How do I empathise with the child's feelings when they are particularly painful ... without cutting off from them?

Some people realise that they feel threatened by one or more of the child's troubled feelings. They might, for example, be really good with a child's expression of sadness but not their anger, or good with their anger but not the child's despair or hopelessness. They may find themselves trying to persuade the child out of a feeling they are having, getting them to cheer up and move into happier or nicer feelings. Often it is the fear of our own unprocessed emotions that makes us unintentionally block a child's strong feelings. Without personal therapy, adults often think in too narrow an emotional range - the emotional range we know. If, for example, we are blocked on our own yearning, desolation, desperation, panic or distress, we will not be able to recognise and name these in the child. That's why, when talking to children about difficult issues, it's such a gift to go into our own counselling or therapy so we get the emotional support, time and space to feel and think about our own painful childhood experiences. We are then far better able to handle the child's pain and emotional storms and to think under stress.

6 Could it ever be dangerous to talk with children about feelings?

Yes - if it's not done well. Handled wrongly, some conversations with children can be harmful in that the child will feel worse, and not better after the conversation. In my experience, having no knowledge of the fundamental skills of therapeutic communication and the stages of empathy can mean some adults are offering the child an unfortunate mix of over-questioning, telling the child they are feeling something when they are not, or putting the child off asking for help with feelings, because the one-to-one time is misattuned, unintentionally patronising or a covert way of telling the child off.

Comments that can do damage

Damaging statements from a listening adult will be those that do one or more of the following: patronise, generalise, try to mind-read, mis-interpret, mis-attune, offer platitudes, fail to acknowledge or validate the child's experience of an event, accuse or assume what the child is feeling without asking the child what is happening. If any of these things happens, the children with a strong enough sense of self will manage to protect themselves by closing down, not talking about their feelings again.

Comments that infer a particular feeling or meaning

As I mentioned previously, it can be dangerous if you're told you're feeling something when you're not. It's often both infuriating and painful. A child is likely to shut the adult out and avoid emotional disclosure. If we tell an over-compliant child or one with little sense of self what they are feeling, they can all too easily take it on board as 'truth', and thus be more vulnerable to suffering psychological damage of some kind.

> Young children ....do not have the cognitive ability to say, *"Yes, this fits for me"*, or *"No, this doesn't fit me at all"*. [The child] believes everything she hears about herself ... if the child spills milk, the parent may say, *"Oh you are so clumsy"*. The child then thinks, *"I am clumsy."*   Oaklander 2006, p.11

Comments that shame

It can be harmful if the adult comes with a set agenda, for example, *"Now, today we've got to talk about your anger problem."* The child can feel shamed, exposed, belittled, humiliated.

Talking before establishing a sense of trust

It can be harmful if we open up a subject painful to the child before having established a good working alliance with him or her. We need to make sure that the child feels psychologically safe enough to talk with us - that there is a real connection between us.

Talking without sufficient care and respect

It can be harmful for a child to open up with an adult who does not offer empathy and understanding. Instead the adult stays silent, over-questions or moves into teaching or judgmental mode. If these things happen, the child is left alone with his feelings all over again. This can be extremely painful, and can convince the child that he is stupid to trust adults with his feelings. He is better moving into self-help, stiff upper lip, bottling things up, communicating through disruptive behaviour and so on.

A child's emotional disclosure must always be treated with care and respect. This is because when children talk about their feelings, they are opening themselves up, letting down their defences and so becoming vulnerable. This means that any uninterested or low-key response, any faded response, any judgmental, minimising, or critical response, any adult 'lectures' at this time, any talking a child 'out' of the feelings he is having, any changing the subject, any taking over what he is doing of saying, could hurt a child. When a child has felt pain too often because of such failed adult responses, he may stop wanting to share his feelings. He may become very defensive and decide that any openness, or daring to be vulnerable, is stupid.

Talking when we haven't sorted out our own 'baggage'

Some adults have just not received enough empathy, compassion or warmth in their lives, so it is very difficult for them to offer warm, empathic responses to a child. However, time in counselling or therapy can change this dramatically. Being on the receiving end of empathy and compassion means your heart opens and warms, and so you can emotionally warm a child.

7 How do I know if our 'feelings talk' has had a positive effect?

Look at the table called *The Feeling Rooms* (*see* p.412). It's a good idea to fill this in before and after you have had a series of feelings talks with a child. It describes the ability to feel life fully, which means having easy access to all the rooms and so being able to experience all the wondrous riches that life has to offer.

When a child is troubled, access into some of the rooms will be blocked by too many life experiences of blighting relational stress and/or relational poverty, which undermine a child's ability to trust, to play, to explore, to dare to try something new, to make mistakes, to be open enough to experience and feel what is awesome and marvellous in the world: and, most importantly of all, to be able to love in peace rather than love in torment, or not dare to love at all. You can mark or colour in some way the rooms the child has easy access into, and mark in another colour the ones they are blocked from enjoying.

After a series of talk-times with you, or rich relational times in other ways, go back to the Feeling Rooms table. Ask yourself, has anything changed? In particular, can you answer some of the following questions positively, whereas before you could not have described the child in this way?

- The child now has the capacity to experience states of joy, excitement, delight, awe and wonder, in a fully embodied way.
- The child can now talk about painful feelings instead of just discharging them (acting them out), bottling them up, cutting off from them or using quick fixes.
- As a result of the interactions with you, the child can share joyful moments with others. This demonstrates itself in the child's ability to play *per se,* as well as playing with words, and humour.
- The child is now able to trust in new ways.
- The child's emotional or physical symptoms have got better, partially or fully - for example, the friendless child has friends, the anxious child no longer exhibits anxiety symptoms, the aggressive child no longer bites other children, the cold, withdrawn child has the capacity for warm, enriching contact with others.

If the symptoms are still there, then it's best to keep having feelings talk-time if you can. Perhaps something in the child's behaviour is still not being understood in your times together, with some vital feelings not being addressed. That said, as Oaklander (2006) notes: 'When the child is doing well in his life, and our work has taken on an aura of just hanging out together, it is time to stop' (p.47).

3 Deepening the dialogue

Chapter 6: How to say it

Introduction

In this chapter we will start with the basics of how to say what we want to say in terms of offering a conversation which is truly therapeutic and empathic. Without these basics in place, some people all too easily feel inadequate or not good enough at helping children with their feelings.

But with simple adjustments in how we say things, the words we use, and how we say those words, the child can be enabled to feel psychologically safe, and so ready to and wanting to engage. Remember the intention is always to find ways to connect to the child so he feels a sense of *"Yes, she's really got it, and so I am no longer alone with all this stuff, these feelings, this pain."*

In addition, this chapter will cover common mistakes people make when talking to children, which can break or weaken the connection they have made, which puts children off, makes them feel unsafe. This is when children close down rather than open up.

That said, it's OK to make mistakes. We will all misattune from time to time. The important thing is to recognise when this is happening and then to find a way to mend things and reconnect as soon as possible. I will cover how to do this too.

I Don't expect a child to be able to find the words for feelings
Instead ... find age-appropriate ways of speaking psychologically

> A child's immaturity and incapacity to use verbal thought render impossible the use of more complex ways of dealing with overwhelming [emotional] storms, unmanageable [arousal] or mental pain. We see, therefore, that at this stage of [human development] what the psyche is truly deprived of are words.
>
> McDougall 1989, p.53

Because a child often doesn't have a rich range of words for feelings, it's important to recognise that there will be times when you will need to come up with the words for feelings rather than waiting for the child to do so. It is both unfair and often a waste of time to expect them to do this. When a child doesn't have words for their feelings, but is experiencing lots of stress in both his mind and his body, he will label his feelings with the language that he does know. In other words, children will label their emotional states according to the limitations of their own vocabulary. So for many children, words such as '*bored*', '*hate*', '*not fair*' will be used, when actually they are feeling '*hurt*', '*let down*' or '*anxious*'. In other words, what they feel will be channelled into the few words they know. Such vocabulary poverty blocks access to their deeper underlying feelings, so vital to the change process.

Adult: *So what do you feel about your Dad having to go to prison?*
Kevin: (silence - then) *I'm just bored. Shall we play football now?*

Where this is the case, we need to take a very active role in enabling the child to change troubled feelings into thinkable thoughts. This means helping them find the right words. Once you do this, they will usually 'get it' from your tone of voice and explanation, and so will be able to think and conceptualise with you with a more complex and sophisticated emotional vocabulary.

I re-visited Bollas' concept of 'the unthought known' in the last chapter, and what is happening with Kevin here is a good example. This little boy is in a state of raw pain, never translated into 'thinkable thoughts'. He needs help from an adult to be able to properly think about his feelings of desperately missing his Dad, his hurt and confusion about his father being in prison. Simply asking Kevin about his feelings will not help. He needs a mature adult reflective mind to provide the words, for example, something like this:

> **Adult:** *Your Dad had to go to prison. With some children, when a parent they really loved has to leave them in that way, they can feel lots of different things, such as confused, hurt, left, angry, scared and a deep deep pain of missing them so much. May be you feel some of that too or maybe it's something different for you.*

Aiden (7) was violent to other children. His father smacked Aiden a lot. Whenever another child looked at Aiden, he would become hyper-aroused and hit out. When asked by the headmistress why he hit other children, Aiden looked at his shoes and said nothing. For Aiden, his fear and rage had never been processed in the verbal centres in the frontal lobes of his brain. If they had been, then he would have been able to reflect on painful experiences in the here and now rather than move directly to primitive fight/flight reactions at the slightest stressor. So his feelings towards his father, now displaced onto other children, could not come out in words: it only came out in hitting.

With children like Aiden, one of the key roles for the adult is to move through the three stages of empathy (*see* p.43) and then offer words for their feelings in an enquiring, 'wondering' mode, rather than telling the child what he is feeling. In this way, we enable the child to link feeling to thinking.

2 Don't use too small words for a child's big feelings
Instead ... offer a rich emotional vocabulary

A person says, "*I feel depressed.*" Now I don't know what that means. It's empty. The word ... is a compromise with depression, which helps repress it, only admitting it in a vague, abstract way. So in practice I'll want to get precise, we are trying to get to the whole taste, body, image of the state of the soul in words. All that has disappeared and instead ... the big empty vapid jargon word, depression. That's a terrible impoverishment of the actual experience. Hillman 1983, p.44

Words can connect people or bring distance between them. With the right words, offered by the adult, the most healing emotional connection can happen for a child. With the wrong words, the child may not open up again. So we need to use 'powerful, resonant, full words' (Philips 2000, p.16) when helping children to speak about feelings and to throw what Stern calls '*affective magic*' (2004) at what we say. Affective magic is carefully considered use of voice, tone, volume, prosody, pausing, punctuation, in order to capture a child's emotional experience in a way that they can feel deeply understood. Put another way: our aim is to narrow the gap for the child as far as possible between 'experience lived and experience verbally represented' (Zulueta 1993).

Furthermore, we belittle children when we think they can only manage to understand and speak in simple concepts. We can expect so much more of children than '*sad*', '*scared*', and '*cross*', particularly if we give them art and play materials with which to communicate. If we only think in terms of '*sad*', '*angry*', '*scared*', '*happy*', we risk not hearing so many children's communications, which convey far more complex, multi-layered and subtle forms of feeling. In addition, we may end up trying to fit the child's communications, say, of desolation, betrayal, emptiness, feeling utterly wretched and so on, into a very narrow range of 'feeling words'.

Sometimes you may get a situation where the child is more emotionally eloquent than the adult, particularly when some children are free and able with the kind of language rich in the metaphor which naturally arises out of play and the use of art materials. Here is an example:

> **Brad (8):** grieving the death of his gran, draws a picture of a tree.
>
> **Brad:** Since Gran died, I am sad all the time, like a willow tree that silently weeps but inside its trunk there's a ginormous rainstorm …
> (beautifully emotionally charged language on behalf of the child)
>
> **Adult:** Oh poor you. What do you think makes you feel like that?
> (far too cognitive)

This is an example of the child being able to confront their pain far more effectively than the adult. The adult has failed to 'feel into' the child's beautiful analogy of the willow.

Here are some examples of misattunements between an adult and a child due to the adult using 'little words' for the child's big feelings. I provide possible alternative responses.

> **Lisa (10)** was put into care for a while as a toddler due to her mother suffering post-partum psychosis with the birth of Lisa's sibling.
>
> > **Lisa:** *In my dream, I was alone. I couldn't find Mum anywhere. I thought she must be dead. I ran and ran but I was just lost and running.*
>
> ✗ Avoid ... Unempathic response
> **Adult:** *Sounds a bit scary.*
> ✔ Instead ... Empathic response
> **Adult:** *How terrifying*
>
> ---
>
> **Kevin:** (*see* p.120: he has just heard that his father has been beaten up by some inmates in prison) They beat up my Dad.
>
> ✗ Avoid ... Unempathic response
> **Adult:** *Poor you*
> ✔ Instead ... Empathic response
> **Adult:** *Terrible, like a nightmare, the shock, the pain, for you as well as him.*

Just as in our response to children we can use words which downplay or minimise their experiences, of course children can do this too. They can use words that misrepresent or understate. As we shall see in the chapters on play and art, their play or art images often speak a far deeper truth. As Picasso said, 'Art is a lie that makes us see the truth'. So when a child voices a feeling about a trauma or loss, she may be downplaying the strength of her feeling, thinking that's it. If so, we need to make sure we don't just go along with what she says, but open up the possibility for her to speak further if she wishes to, and in more depth.

Remember Lamis on p.75 She was being bullied through horrible name-calling. Lamis told the teacher that the bullying, which had gone on for years, was 'a bit upsetting'. The research on the long-term effects on the brain of verbal abuse shows that it is far worse than 'a bit upsetting'. It can result in cell death in some of the key structures in the brain directly involved with social and emotional intelligence. As we saw on p.40, it can also adversely affect some of the verbal processing parts of the brain (Teicher, 2008).

So Lamis' use of language to describe what was happening to her was not serving her well: it didn't encourage other people to take what was happening to her seriously. Her teachers responded in a similar, low-key manner: *"You'll get through it, dear. Don't let it get to you. Just ignore them"*. Even if they didn't know the serious concerns resulting from the new brain research, these are deeply impoverished words in terms of the child's experience.

A vivid example of a failed response from a mother to her daughter is seen in the film *Lost in Translation*. Charlotte is speaking very openly on the phone to her mother. She says she doesn't know who her husband is anymore, and that she feels so lost. Her mother says, rather brusquely, *"Pardon?"* This misconnection crashes into Charlotte's moment of vulnerability. She closes down and replies *"Nothing"*. Once the phone is put down she bursts into tears - on her own.

One woman I worked with had been told as a child that she was depressed. It was a label she had carried with her all her life. It was the wrong word. The right word was *'raging'*. When she connected with her rage, at the age of 67, she was no longer depressed. The wrong word had contributed to her being stuck in deep unhappiness for over 60 years.

Benjamin (6) adores his Granny. He asked her to come to his birthday tea. She said that of course she would. His birthday came and went and no Granny. No card, no present. Nothing. Benjamin later found out that she was so caught up in seeing her new boyfriend that she forgot. He gives a smaller version of the big painful feelings he is having.

> **Benjamin:** *I am a bit disappointed that Granny didn't come to my birthday tea.*

✗ Avoid ... Unempathic response

> **Adult:** *Sounds disappointing.*

✔ Instead ... Empathic response

> **Adult:** *And my guess is that disappointment is one of your feelings and you have other feelings too that hurt a lot.*

Mia (9): Her parents have just told her that she is going to be moving to another part of the country and so changing schools all within three months. Mia has two very close friends she will now have to say goodbye to.

> **Mia:** *It's OK I am moving schools*

✗ Avoid ... Unempathic response

> **Adult:** *That's good you feel OK about it.*

✔ Instead ... Empathic response

> **Adult:** (here the adult gently opens up the possibility with the child that they might be downplaying) *And maybe part of you thinks it's OK and another part of you is really hurting.*

3 Avoid using adverbs and adjectives in your response to the child's play or art image

Instead ... be aware of using any leading words

Watch out for incorrect assumptions and references in the choice of words you use in response to a child's play or art image. Be careful you are not reading things into the image. The child might for example have drawn a cat with a down-turned mouth. Don't say - *"Tell me about that sad cat in your picture."* Instead, try saying *"Tell me about that cat"*, or, interview the cat: *"Hello cat, how are you feeling today?"*

Monster drawing

Let's say the child draws a monster (the child's word) with a tongue. The adult asks:

Adult: *Who is the monster sticking his tongue out at?*

The character may not be sticking his tongue out *at* anyone. The child may, for example, have seen a monster in a film (they often have their tongues out). Or he may have seen a dog with its tongue out. The adult is assuming an aggressive act regarding the active sticking out of a tongue at somebody. Also, the character might be a she. So instead, enquire here along the lines of, *"I wonder what the monster makes you feel?"* Or, *"I notice that the tongue is out"* (indisputable fact). Or, as before, interview the monster: *"Hi monster, can you help me understand what life is like for you?"* We always need to stay alert to how easy it is to make assumptions based on our own experiences.

If you do make a mistake here and assume something about a child's image which turns out to be wrong, many children will just correct you. They might say something like *"It's not a boat, it's a floating cup cake,"* or *"It's not sad, its cross."* This is great supervision, reminding you about the importance of enquiry rather than assumption when the child's meaning is unstated. No harm is done and the child stays interested and engaged.

If however the child withdraws, disengages from you or the play he is doing and you feel a deadness in the room, your misattunement may have been experienced as stress-inducing by the child.

If so, say something like, *"I wonder if I have said something wrong here about your drawing or play? If so, I apologise."*

4   Avoid speaking in lengthy paragraphs

Instead ... use short sentences and emotionally impactful phrases

Short, poetic sentences support a rich connection with the child, whereas long sentences and sophisticated, adult sentence construction often result in the child very quickly losing interest. Bear in mind that young children's concentration levels are not as good as adults', and the part of their brain that processes words is far less developed. A long-winded adult is likely to emotionally dysregulate many children. They will experience relational stress rather than soothing. Other children will just switch off.

Many adults tolerate clumsy sentence construction or meandering paragraphs from another adult who is helping them talk about their feelings, but with children you have probably lost them by about word eight! This is due in part to the fact that they are usually 'multi-tasking' when you are speaking to them (for example, playing with a toy car, fiddling with play-doh or something similar).

Noah (6) had watched his beloved sister being verbally abused by his volcanically angry father on many occasions. He talks freely about his pain and hurt and how he and his sister would walk on egg shells around their explosive father. He did this image which he entitled '*There are sleeping horrible things we mustn't wake them*'.

✗ An adult using too many words

Adult: *When you are showing me your picture I see that there horrible things as you say and that they are partly covered up. And it must feel so terribly unsafe living in a world where you are afraid of what might happen if the horrible things suddenly wake. Like how could you ever relax if you lived in a world like that, always waiting for the next horrible awakening?*

Noah's 'sleeping horrible things'

You will probably have lost the child's attention after the first sentence!! Over and above this, so many words can bombard the child, resulting in them just cutting off. In short it's a misattunement, and loss of connection.

✔ Instead ...

Adult: *Those horrible things in your picture (pause). They bring too much pain and fear*

Adult: *Having to be so so careful. Such pain, such fear*

Adult: *Waiting for next explosion - the pain of waiting and not being able to stop things happening after the waiting's over*

Here are some more examples of the power of short phrases in response to a child's pain. Sometimes you may find yourself making up new words like 'unhelped,' as you see below. You may find such 'language play' more accurately expresses what the child is feeling.

- So you were desperate.
- Too alone; too unhelped.
- And no-one knew. And no-one knew.
- You were so cross. Not just a bit cross.
- You so wanted your Mum to stay, not to go.
- You were so little to manage all that on your own.
- So brave when you let me help.

When a child is with an adult who is 'talkable to', and who is able to use short phrases not paragraphs, the child often speaks in succinct, deeply moving statements in response, as we see here:

> **Adult:** *So when your Dad left, your world collapsed.*
>
> **Pippa:** *Yes, the awful thing happened and no-one had stopped it.*
>
> **Adult:** (responding to Carla talking about her dad's depression, see p.76) *It felt like you lost your dad, because he slept all the time.*
>
> **Carla:** *Yep, like deadness takes over completely.*

We can learn a lot from children about the clutter of unnecessary words.

> **Ray (4)** His father had recently died from lung cancer after years of smoking. Ray took his mother's face in his hands and said, *You shouldn't have married him. You should have chosen another one. You should have chosen another one.*
>
> **Misha (8)** had watched as her mother's friend sank further and further into a very angry rage when drunk. The woman said angrily, *This is a nightmare.* Misha turned to her and with a steady calm voice said, *No, it is you who is the nightmare.*
>
> **Paolo (6)** looked at me one day and said, *I think I know what is wrong with nurseries, Margot. They take you away from your mother.* Paolo had not read the scientific research (Gunnar 2003) showing that in many nurseries, children experience a disturbing rise in brain cortisol levels in the afternoon which drops back to base rate when the children are with their parents again. Cortisol should go down, not up in the afternoon.
>
> **Jacob (5)** said to his mum who smacked him for the first time: *Mum, you could have used words not hands.*
>
> **Alex (4)** whose father had committed suicide, asked the doctor: *What happens in people's heads for them to hang themselves?*

5 Avoid using questions requiring a yes or a no (closed questions)
Instead ... use open questions

Closed questions are questions that ask for an answer, usually a yes or a no. Here are some examples: *"Does your Mum taking drugs again make you sad?"* or, *"Are you angry about Dad leaving?"* Such questions run the risk of bringing in our agenda and blocking the child's, closing down options, rather than being curious about the child's meaning of an event (*remember Stage 2 of Empathic Listening*, p. 52). Closed questions can lead a child away from what they are feeling. For example, if you've asked, *"Are you angry about that?"* and they are actually feeling sad, not angry, you are taking them away from their sadness in order to think about what you want them to think about - anger.

✘ Avoid

Susan: *I remember sitting in my room at lot when Dad and Mum were getting divorced*

Adult: *Did that make you angry?*

This closed question imposes the adult's emotional take on the situation, not the child's. The child has not mentioned anything to do with anger.

✔ Instead ...

Adult: *I wonder how you felt about that?*

or

Adult: *Wow, how did you deal with that?*

How to mend things when by mistake you ask a closed question

> **Ryan: (10)** *When my mum took drugs I had to do all the*
> *housework and look after my little brother and sister.*
>
> **Adult:** *Did you feel it was all too much?* (closed question)
>
> **Ryan:** (goes silent, the connection between them is lost)
>
> **Adult:** *I'm sorry, Ryan, I think my question wasn't right ... can you help me*
> *understand what that was like for you, with your words not mine?*
>
> **Ryan:** (looks up and engages with eye contact again) *It was hard but I*
> *felt so proud that I could help Mum like that.*

6   Avoid answering your own questions
Instead ... wait, empathise, and keep oriented towards the child's own meaning

It is tempting with children who are quiet and don't say much to fill in the word gaps, so to speak. It can be out of embarrassment, frustration or to keep the conversation going. In other words you ask a question, they don't respond, and so you come in with another question or a closed question. Here is an example:

> ✗ Avoid
>
> **Claire:**   *The girl with the big shouty mouth in my drawing is worried, she*
> *has been for ages.*
>
> **Adult:** *What is the little girl with the big shouty mouth worried about?*
> (Claire is quiet for some time). *Is she worried about the strength*
> *of her anger?*

133

Such questions can be 'crazy making', particularly when totally off the mark, and show a marked lack of curiosity about what something means for the child.

> ✔ Instead ...
>
> **Adult:** (interviewing the little girl in the picture) *Hi little girl, I wonder what you are worried about?*
>
> If Claire doesn't answer, empathise with the worry.
>
> **Adult:** *It's no fun worrying* (indisputable fact about the human condition) ... *and very painful when the worry goes on and on.*

7   Avoid asking several questions in the same sentence
Instead ... ask one question at a time

If you bombard the child with more than one question in the same sentence, they will quickly get distracted. Children are usually not at all interested in entering your complex thinking maze. Again, if you have misattuned in this way it is usually easy to spot - the child will lose connection with you, avoid eye contact, seem low, flat or disinterested. If this happens you can often re-engage them by moving away into relational play or correct yourself out loud: *"Oh my goodness, what was I thinking of? Far too many questions - I'm sorry!"*

Sandra (8) and her Daddy love each other very much. Sandra has just said that she stole a pound from her Dad's wallet and he got cross and called her a thief.

✗ Avoid

> **Adult:** *Do you feel that what you were doing was wrong? Do you feel your Dad was too angry with you? Do you feel hurt by what he said?*

Just like answering your own questions, this is 'crazy making' as well. It floods the child with the adult's possible meanings, bombarding her with closed questions, and shows no curiosity for the child's meaning of the event.

✔ Instead ...

> **Adult:** *I'm wondering what you wish your Dad had said or done?*

If Sandra doesn't say anything and you know she loves her Dad and his opinion matters to her, then move to Stage 3, Empathy (*Finding the right words and tone of voice to convey your empathy*), and refer to indisputable facts about the situation.

> **Adult:** *So painful when something horrid gets in the way of two people who love each other.*

If appropriate you might also add:

> **Adult:** *Maybe there is something your Dad didn't understand in all this, something you needed him to understand?*

Here you are opening a door for Sandra to reflect on what the communication to her Dad in the stealing might have been (*and see* pp.380-1 *on how parents can have non-shaming conversations with their children on stealing and lying*).

8 Avoid parroting

Instead ... paraphrase!

✗ Avoid

> **Child:** (enacting a teacher-pupil scene in her play in a very strict voice) *The teacher is saying, stupid boy, stop making such a mess on the floor right now.*
>
> **Adult:** *So the teacher is saying stupid boy, stop making such a mess on the floor right now.*
>
> *or*
>
> **Child:** *I feel sad.*
>
> **Adult:** *You feel sad.*
>
> **Child:** *Stop copying me!*

The child in this last example has given an excellent piece of supervision to the adult here. As I mentioned on p.107 (*in* Empathy Troubleshooting) parroting is just annoying! Instead, use paraphrasing. Paraphrasing in healing conversations means focusing on the key emotional charge in the child's statement, and commenting on it. It is *this* that is healing, in that it conveys to the child that you have really taken the time and effort to understand and grasp the central issues and emotional meaning of what they are saying.

✔ Instead ...

Paraphrasing 1

Child: (enacting a teacher-pupil scene in a very strict voice)
The teacher is saying, stupid boy, stop making such a mess on the floor right now.

Adult: *So the teacher is wanting the boy to clear up the mess, but she is being very unkind and attacking about it* (indisputable fact).

Paraphrasing 2

Child: (talking through her puppet, a crocodile) *Come over here teddy, it's lovely here, I'll help you get over the wall, look at the blue sky here, come play with me. Look at my awesome paddling pool.*

Adult: *Crocodile, you want teddy to come and share all the lovely things you have.*

Paraphrasing 3

Teen: *Dad works nights and Mum works long hours. So I don't get to see them much and Mum keeps saying be quiet because Dad is sleeping*

Adult: (knowing from previous comments that this is hard for the young person) *Sounds like you feel like there's not much lovely 'you and them' time at the moment. Painful and frustrating.*

In this last example, you can see the use of empathy, following the paraphrasing. These work well together and underline the sentiment the child is already expressing in his words and voice.

9 Avoid "Why...?" questions
Instead ... use open enquiry

> **Child:** *I feel angry with that monster* (in my picture).
>
> ✗ Avoid
>
> **Adult:** *Why do you feel angry with the monster?*
>
> **Adult:** *Why do you feel sad?*
>
> **Adult:** *Why do you miss your father?*

"*Why?*" questions mean that the child must make the shift away from what he is feeling into the thinking part of his brain, rather than getting there naturally. "*Why?*" questions means he is interrupted in having his feeling and then has to follow your agenda of wanting him to go into analysing what he is feeling. So "*Why?*" questions don't deepen the child's feeling, they detract from them. They close down the affect-led (feelings based) enquiry. Instead of "*Why?*" questions, use far more open-ended modes of enquiry such as interviewing the child's image or story character - for example:

> **Child:** *I feel angry with that monster* (in my picture).
>
> ✔ Instead
>
> **Adult:** *Would you say that to him? Monster, I feel angry with you because...?*
>
> **Child:** *Because you always frighten me and so I never feel safe even in my own home.*
>
> **Adult:** *Wow, how awful. Every child has a right to feel safe, particularly in their own home.*

10   Avoid platitudes

Instead ... let yourself be moved by what is specific to this child's emotional pain

It's important not to trot out platitudes. In order to avoid doing so, as before, follow the three stages of empathy. If you really let yourself reflect and feel what the child is saying, imagine into their pain, and let yourself be moved, you will offer healing empathy and not trite statements which can alienate the child. Otherwise, the child will pick up on your inauthenticity, and lack of imagining into what is specific to their life experience.

Lauren is talking about how much she loves her mother and how worried she is about her getting ill or dying.

✗ Avoid

    Adult: (using a platitude) *Love is a wonderful thing, so no wonder you worry.*

✔ Instead ...

    Adult: (validating empathy) *You love your mum so very much but that makes you fearful of how much it would hurt to live your life without her.*

Cameron describes his rage at his Dad for saying he would come to see him that weekend and then not doing so.

✗ Avoid

    Adult: (using platitude) *Ah yes! Anger can be a strong emotion.*

Cameron ignores this but continues. He says that as well as his feelings about his Dad, his dog is ill too.

✗ Avoid

> **Adult:** *Well there is clearly sadness and anger in the room today.*

✔ Instead ...

> **Adult:** (validating empathy) *No wonder you were angry, I imagine you were really looking forward to his visit and then on top of that to see your dog being ill.*

99

11 Avoid patronising statements

Instead ... ensure you are not talking down to the child, just because she is young

It's really important that we don't talk down to children. If we do, the child may just talk over us, switch off, move into a protective silence, and so on. Adults don't like patronising statements and children don't either. It may not have been our intention or how we actually feel, but children and young people quickly sense the 'power over' feel of patronising responses such as, "*I think you need to look after yourself*", or, "*I think your feelings are very important,*" or, "*In a quiet moment think about what I have said. You will realise I am right.*"

Being spoken to like this offers a very empty connection with a child. This is usually because such statements are easy to deliver, without any of the hard work needed to imagine in to how it is to be this child with these life events, and what he feels and thinks about them. So instead, give the child the gift of taking the time to imagine into the feelings specific to him in this particular situation or with this particular experience.

Jordan's mother was neglectful, smoking cannabis and getting drunk most days. She would often lock Jordan in the house at night alone, and go out clubbing. So Jordan was placed with her Gran. It is clear from the files that Jordan loves both her Gran and her Mum.

> **Jordan:** *My Mum didn't want me. She left when I was four. So now I call my Gran, 'Mum'.*

✗ Avoid

> **Adult:** *That must be difficult for you, dear.*

Such a patronising statement is minimising and belittling of Jordan's real pain. Instead, think and feel about what it must be like to be a little girl and to lose your Mum, and for you to believe all your life, rightly or wrongly, that she abandoned you because she didn't want you. This is a profoundly painful story and one that should move you deeply. So you won't be giving the child a quick response but a considered response after taking the time to reflect on what she has just told you.

✔ Instead …

> **Jordan:** *My Mum didn't want me so now I call my Gran 'Mum'.*
>
> **Adult:** *So although you have a lovely Granny/Mummy, how painful to think that your Mummy didn't want you, when it was actually* *the drink and pills she took, she couldn't look after you, love you in the way that you needed her to.*

12   Avoid over-questioning

Instead ... use questions for the purpose of informing your empathy

There is nothing wrong with questions per se. But questions asked with a monotone voice and which do not come from a genuine place of concern, curiosity and compassion for the child can be entirely non-therapeutic at best, and very invasive and stress-inducing at worst. Furthermore, a question or a series of questions which are not followed with empathy are pointless: they bring the risk of asking the child to open up, only to abandon him in a vulnerable state having done so. Over-questioning leaves no mental space for the child's own spontaneous expression or sense of wanting to tell.

Steph (10): Steph's Mum has MS. She contracted the illness when Steph was eight. Mum has had to go into hospital frequently. Steph loves her mother deeply and is worried about her. She is often a young carer in the house, looking after her Mum, particularly when she comes out of hospital.

✗ Avoid

Adult: *What do you feel about your Mum being in hospital?*

Steph: *Sad.*

Adult: *And if sad was a colour, what would it be?*

Steph: *(Sighs)*

Adult: *What do you think you will feel at home without your Mum?*

Steph: *Sad.*

Adult: *Your Mum has been in hospital before. Some children worry that their Mum may never come back. Do you?*

Steph: *I guess so.*

Adult: *How do you manage that?*

Steph: *Can I go to the toilet please?*

This barrage of questions is intrusive and bombarding. As a result, Steph needs to protect herself by saying she wants to go to the toilet. Other children with such a misattuning adult may just comply, or say anything they think you want them to say to get you off their back. Worse still, a child can come to believe that it's not a good idea to talk about their feelings, because it's too stressful.

Always hold in mind the purpose of questions, which is to find the meaning a child has given to an experience and the feelings he has about it, so that you can then connect with him through understanding and empathy. So in the case above you would acknowledge and empathise with the sadness (Steph has twice said she is sad). You would not go on to another question (here about worry) before doing so. You might simply say something like this:

> ✔ Instead …
>
> **Adult:** *I understand your Mum is in hospital again. Wow, that must be so hard. Could you help me understand what that's like for you?*
>
> **Steph:** *I miss her so much but when she comes home, sometimes I find that difficult too, because I have to do all the helping and the housework.*
>
> **Adult:** *So when she's away, you long for her, but then when she comes home, it's like having to be a mum for her. That is such a lot for you to have to deal with. You do so well with all this.*

13   Avoid thinking concretely

Instead … reflect on possible symbolic meaning of what the child is telling you

When a child tells you about some painful event in their life, don't just think literally. Perhaps there is some symbolic meaning in what she is saying too.

Stella (7): (witnessed parental violence) *My knee got hurt. It gets hurt a lot you know* (shows the adult a little cut on her knee)

Think of the possible symbolic as well as literal meaning for all the hurting that Stella has witnessed and been subjected to in her life. If the adult doesn't reflect on possible symbolic meanings here, she might reply like this:

✗ Avoid

Adult: *Poor you. I think I have a little plaster in my bag. Would that help?*

Hold in mind what the child is telling you and what you know about their life story and think of the emotional themes that are common to both. Then once you have done this reflective work, offer your empathic intervention.

✔ Instead …

Adult: *And perhaps you are also letting me know that you are often in pain and maybe people don't really know that so they've never helped you with your hurt.*

The adult tells Stella a story about a family of animals full of hurting but where there were no doctors or people that helped, until one day, one of the animals howls, "*Enough! Stop the hurting!*" in such a strong powerful voice that the goblins from the North Winds hear and visit the family to help them find their kindness.

14   Avoid talking all the time

Instead ... know the power of pause and silence

> By intervening too quickly, the [adult] missed the chance of listening for
> further leads.   Casement 1985, p.11

Know the power of pause and silence: to give both you and the child the space and time to think. Is the air so full of words (yours or the child's) that there is no time for you or the child to think, feel, reflect?

We need to remember to always leave enough silence for children's feelings to 'fill-out', and leave ourselves enough time to think and reflect, instead of rushing in with an ill-thought comment or question. In fact, the 'verbal aspect' of your therapeutic conversation with a child may at times not be the most important part of the healing process. Instead, it may be the non-verbal elements - your soothing voice, your smile, your enthusiasm, your warmth, your ability to 'hold' the silence, in which the child finds a way to show you what she feels.

It helps to listen to the quality of the silence in the room and pay attention to what you are feeling. For some children, periods of silence in your time together can feel a great relief. It can be experienced as not crowding them with your words, and instead, waiting for their words, giving them space. For another child, your silence can be experienced as oppressive, a too difficult or too embarrassing experience for her. She is perhaps re-experiencing feeling alone or not reached out to.

We need to learn to tell the difference between the different effects silence can have. With children who find silence hard, make sure you are in charge of the conversational flow. Structured activities can really help here, for example using 'emotion worksheets' (*see* p.180, p.326). After explaining the subject matter on the worksheet, offer the instructions without any hesitation or doubt in your voice. It's not helpful to be tentative and wordy, for example, "*I wonder if you would mind, I mean, I've got these things that we could do, er, um is that OK with you ... ?*"

Just say, *"OK, here is a picture, would you colour in the bits that sometimes feel like you or your life ...?"* - clear and confident.

15 Avoid burdening a child with your feelings
Instead ... be aware of your impact on the child

> **✗** Avoid
>
> **Adult:** *I feel scared about the things you have told me.*
>
> **Adult:** *I feel really hopeless about what you have said.*
>
> **Adult:** *I am worried about you now.*
>
> **Adult:** *I am sad because you are sad.*
>
> **Mum:** *I can see you are unhappy and that makes me unhappy.*
>
> ***
>
> **Child:** *You need to find me a Daddy.*
>
> **Mum:** *I am sad too that I don't have a partner. In fact it's been one of the saddest things of my life that I don't have a partner.*

The comments above may seem harmless enough, but they're not. They bring the adult's feelings into the conversation: they shift the child from what *they are feeling* to what *we* are feeling. A child is busy with what he or she is feeling, and so having to think about what is happening for the adult is distracting, intrusive and confusing.

Many children will feel anxious, dysregulated or even disturbed if you say that you are worried about them or feel hopeless about something in their life, or say you are frightened for them, or that something they have said frightens you. Helping children to speak about feelings is to provide them with the richest possible experiences of emotional regulation: what we do should never add to their emotional dysregulation.

Moreover, if we say something like *"I feel scared about what you are telling me,"* we are really saying we cannot contain the child's anxieties. Psychologist Heinz Kohut used the term 'over-burdened' to describe children who have had to deal with their parents' disturbing feelings as well as their own. So the last thing we want to do as listening adults is to over-burden children with our feelings as well.

> ✔ Instead ...
>
> Rather than saying *"I am sad because you are sad"*, just empathise.
> For example:
>
> **Adult:** *Such a very sad thing happened to you then. So painful, and you were just a little boy.*

16 Avoid reassurances

Instead ... have the courage to stay with the child's painful feelings

The kind of reassurance to avoid is when you don't know if the child is right or not. For example, the child might say *"I don't know if my Mum likes me."* To say *"I am sure she does"*, would be wrong. The child might be right, her Mum might not like her and she is picking up on this. So this sort of reassurance assumes knowledge you don't have. Many people are tempted to reassure over such things, as they are unable to stay with the pain of what the child is saying.

In addition, reassurance rarely works. This is because a child's fears and fantasies about themselves, other people and the world, are likely to be far more entrenched as an established life view compared with your reassurances, which are, after all, simply opinions. Also, reassurance, however well intended, can be an empathic failure. The child presents her reality and you just present a different one. Often she won't correct you on this: rather she will just be less motivated to tell you her feelings in future. In this sense, reassurances often comfort the adult and not the child!

✗ Avoid

Peter: *I love my Mum so much, but she doesn't like me anymore.*

Adult: *I think she does dear. Don't worry, and anyway, I really like you.*

Use validating empathy and in so doing connect with the child, rather than misattune as in the example above. Peter's Mum might indeed love him very much, but for some reason he can't feel it or she can't show it. But we do know Peter doesn't believe it. And note the words "... *you think* ..." used below.

✔ Instead ...

Peter: *I love my Mum so much, but she doesn't like me anymore.*

Adult: *It must be very painful loving and needing a Mum so much, who you think doesn't even like you.*

✗ Avoid

Child: *I don't think anyone thinks I am special, not anyone.*

Adult: *I do.*

Child: *You don't.*

Adult: *You don't believe me that I think you are special?*

Child: *Yep, you're right, I don't believe you.*

✔ Instead ...

Child: *I don't think anyone thinks I am special, not anyone.*

Adult: *How painful to have lived your life feeling that grown-ups you have known have failed to see just how special you are.*

The one form of reassurance that is OK is when it's in the form of psycho-education, addressing a child's negative self-referencing about some painful life event, where factually we know she is wrong. For example, a teenage girl says something like: *"It was my fault that my uncle sexually abused me."* You can respond with a gentle challenge. But this challenge won't be just a bit of quick, *"There there dear"* kind of comforting, but it will include information about the human condition, and in this case, the law.

Adult: *I really disagree here. Many children who've been abused think like that because they have the idea that adults always know best, so it must be their fault. Also letting themselves know they've been hurt by the people who are supposed to protect them can be too difficult to think and feel. But the fact is that it was your uncle doing something wrong, not you, and it's a crime for adults to touch children in this way.*

Even this sort of psycho-educational reassurance may not work. For example, after this, if the young person still says *"You are wrong, it was my fault,"* she is letting you know that she can't hear the facts right now. So get curious about why she feels like this. Ask her to do an image with all the pictures and/or words that show how she feels it is her fault. Then empathise and try psycho-education again when she is ready to hear.

The final section in this chapter cover very common sticking points in therapeutic conversations with children that can all too easily throw the listening adult.

17 What to do and say when a child moves into long periods of silence in a talk-time

> It was a lonely, unsatisfactory encounter where the questions I asked were left unanswered. I had a very clear picture from this of Zoe's own experiences. Hunter 2001, p.95

If a child moves into long periods of silence in your first talk-time together, ask yourself: did I really lay down clearly enough the reason why we are spending one-to-one time together? Did I say clearly enough that the sessions were for helping with feelings that hurt? When an adult doesn't do this, the child, through no fault of their own, may start to structure time in the way they want, in order to feel safe.

If you feel sure the child does know what the talk-time with you is for, and still remains silent, reflect on what this communication of silence might mean: how the child might be conveying to you something painful that he has experienced in his life. For example, a child's silence or refusal or lack of desire to answer questions may be saying something about the emptiness, or desolation that she has experienced in key relationships in her life.

Daniel (10) had a mother who, when drunk, was no longer emotionally available to him. His father also no longer lived at home. Daniel had emailed and texted his Dad lots of times, but his father had not replied. When Daniel met with Rachel, his key-adult, he would just stare out of the window for long periods. He still came to sessions but would not engage visually or verbally. Rachel reflected on what Daniel might be communicating about his life, by unconsciously 'making' her, Rachel, feel what he has felt.

Rachel: *(doing a Big Empathy Drawing of two people separated by a big wall). Will you let me know if this rings any bells for you? This is me and this is you, and sometimes it feels as if there's a big wall between us, with me trying to make contact with you through the wall. But perhaps part of you doesn't want contact. Maybe you're letting me know what it's been like for you, trying to reach out to someone who doesn't respond? But I might have misunderstood something, so will you change the picture to be right for you?* (Rachel hands the pen to Daniel)

Rachel's Big Empathy Drawing

> **Daniel:** (takes the pen and makes the wall even bigger) *My Dad has a wall around him that means he can't even hear his son calling out to him.*
> **Rachel:** *So you call and call, but all you meet is a brick wall? And when you meet that wall, you feel ... ?*

Daniel's response

18 What to do and say when the child throws lots of feelings at you at the same time

> **Tina (6):** (as she plays with the toys in the room) *I'm worried my cat might die, he's old you know and this spiderman has lost his rope, do you know where it was, it was here in the toy box last week? It's like, my friends hate me, don't know why. Look at how this gun fires, Pow! Pow! Pow! I could kill my teacher because I got into trouble again and it wasn't my fault. Mum drinks you know, I'm worried about her too. Ah, there is*

> *spiderman's rope. Now can we play that game with him*
> *climbing up the biscuit tin?*

Firstly, be compassionate with yourself - it would be hard for anyone to still keep thinking when this happens. Pick up as many 'balls' as you can. The common pitfall is to just pick up on 'worried about mum', because it's the last one on the list. Remember the others that Tina has spoken about:

- » Worried cat might die
- » Friends hate me
- » Kill the teacher
- » Got into trouble unfairly
- » Worried about Mum who drinks

With so many themes it may be best to respond using the Big Empathy Drawing technique (p.79), which will help you gather up all the themes in a way that the child can then process.

> **Adult:** *You've very bravely told me about some very painful feelings here.*
> *Thank you. You've told me how you are worried your cat might die,*
> *how you feel your friends hate you and you don't know why - that*
> *must be so painful because they are your friends. You've told*
> *me about how angry you are with the teacher because she told*
> *you off for something you didn't do and finally you're worried*
> *about your mum because she's drinking. So many things. Wow,*
> *life's hard for you right now. I'm so sorry. I'm wondering if one or*
> *more of the things in this picture are the hardest for you right now?*

Tina's worries

And if you have dropped one or more of the 'balls', well, you can say something like this:

> **Adult:** *So many feelings, fear of loss, worry, anger ... and I'm wondering if one or two of these feeling are the hardest for you right now?*

19 What to do and say when a child rushes on in their play from one thing to the next

It's also very common for children (particularly under ten years of age) to rush on from one thing to the next in their play. It often leaves the adult listener breathless, deskilled and not being able to hold in mind all of what the child has said.

One important thing you can do in this situation is to say to the child that his stories are important and special: so, is it OK with him for you to write down bits as he speaks, so you can remember them? If he agrees, whilst the child plays, you can write down the key phrases and emotionally charged images and themes in his play or play story. This will prevent you being flooded by all you hear and it will help your processing.

Secondly, you don't need to respond immediately to the child's outpourings. After hearing the story, you might say something like, "*I am having a feeling about your special story and when I have had some thoughts about it I'll let you know.*" This allows you to respond when you've had time to properly reflect on and process what's gone on, perhaps later in the talk-time. If you need yet more time to think, you can always come back to him in a future talk-time and say, "*I've been thinking about your story from our last time together … can I see if I understood it?*"

20 The Big Empathy Drawing

Finally, as I've mentioned above, one of the best ways of responding to emotionally-packed play or speedy storytelling from the child is the Big Empathy Drawing intervention, *see* p.79.

FREQUENTLY ASKED QUESTIONS

"What if children get in too deep?"

By and large, children will not open up to someone whom they sense will not be able to respond to them with compassion and warmth. In all my years of practice, I've never seen a child start a conversation about painful feelings unless they sensed that the adult was 'talkable to'. I would argue that a child's self-protective mechanisms are, for the most part, better than those of many adults. So with an adult with whom they feel psychologically unsafe or judged, children are usually marvellous deflectors into action or 'just playing' away from feelings, fiddling with something or saying something like *"Can I go to the toilet/back to the classroom now?"*. Similarly, if you are being too direct they will let you know. They will usually just change the subject or overtly say, *"Don't talk to me about feelings"*.

Children will communicate about a painful feeling when they sense it is safe to do so, because the adult is warm, understanding, non-judgmental, non-lecturing, and an excellent listener: someone who can provide the safety for them to feel and think about what they need to feel and think about. Children will work at a level they feel comfortable with. If a child feels safe with you, they will go deeper.

That said, if a child has felt deeply about something with you, then make sure you allow a really good length of time to reflect on this. You may need to summarise what's been said before you end your talk-time together, so they really 'get' that you have understood what they have needed you to understand. Remember too that it is vital that you only work within the limits of your competence. If you worry that a child is going away too distressed, make sure you get appropriate supervision and support to work out what to do next to ensure the child is safe.

"What do I do if a child gets so upset, angry or anxious they can't seem to hear my words anymore ?"

Bessel Van der Kolk (1999) and Dr Bruce Perry (1995), both eminent child trauma researchers and clinicians, found that if very stressed out children are going to be able to listen to our words, we need to calm their bodies first. If this doesn't happen, their frontal lobes (the key part of the brain for attention and concentration) will not be able to register what you are saying. This is because with high levels of arousal, which we see in trauma, the frontal lobes are flooded with too high levels of stress hormones, cortisol, CRF and noradrenaline in particular. This results in very poor functionality in this part of the brain.

This state of alarm also triggers high activation in more primitive parts of the brain - the old mammalian brain (the limbic system) and the brain stem. This is the reason why children overwhelmed with feelings move into far more primitive behaviour - usually some form of fight (aggression) flight (running away or hiding) or freeze (emotional numbing or dissociation).

When we calm the child's body physiologically, their calm body sends calming messages to their brain (brain-gut interactions). As a result, the frontal lobes can start to function again. Often playful things work best to calm the child's body. Try blowing bubbles together, or use a breathing together game, or work with Tibetan bowls (a powerfully relaxing musical instrument). Drumming together can also work well. Remember if you don't calm the anxious, agitated or angry child's bodily arousal level before starting a conversation about painful issues, you may as well be talking to the wind! And also remember that a soothing melodic voice is nearly as powerful at activating oxytocin (anti-anxiety chemical) as physical contact (Seltzer et al 2010).

Soothing and touch

If your own child were distressed and agitated, you would naturally offer cuddles and the warm security of your body to comfort and regulate them. However, of course the professional context is different, with varying protocols in place about touch, or an outright ban.

Therapeutic use of touch, in my view, is vital in situations where abstinence would actually be inhumane. Examples include the empirically backed beneficial use of touch in the comforting of a child who is in an acute state of distress. Not to reach out to the child in such circumstances could actually be re-traumatising and neurobiologically damaging. Abstaining from touch in the face of some intense emotional reactions, such as grief or anxiety, can lead to a state of hyper-arousal, in which toxic levels of stress chemicals are released in the body and brain; the severely damaging long-term effects of this have been intensively researched worldwide and are well documented.

Moreover, in such states of distress, touch can often be the only means of maintaining a connection with the child when he or she can no longer hear or make therapeutic use of our words or soothing tone/eye contact, and therefore is in danger of cutting off or trying once again to self-soothe, with all the detrimental effects that this can bring. So we need to be very aware of and able to recognise when a child is so emotionally dysregulated that touch must precede words, otherwise our words are rendered useless.

There are some important recent neuroscientific research studies showing the power of simple handholding to quickly regulate a person's dysregulated arousal systems, and bring stress chemicals back to base rate (Field, 2006: Perry, 2007: Coan et al, 2006: Coan et al, 2013). Some people might argue that they will just wait and then offer their empathic verbal statements once the child becomes regulated. For so many children, this just won't work. If I had waited until one desperate little boy, who knew his Daddy was about to die, became regulated, I would have been waiting forever. The same is true for Millie.

Millie (10) was suffering from post-traumatic stress after she had seen her mother crashing the car and ending up in hospital needing plastic surgery to her face. Sometimes, when she was deeply distressed, I would sit next to her and put my arm around her. When I did that, a remarkable thing happened to her use of language. Her verbal communications became very clear, coherent and emotionally literate, often poetic. She talked about the horror and pain of seeing her beloved mother so broken and still on the pavement and how it felt like her world had ended. I remember Lowen's (1967) statement that, 'The more you are held, the more you can let go'. Probably the increased level of psychological safety from my human touch had a dramatic effect on her frontal lobe functions and left-right brain co-ordination, resulting in the two sides of the brain working together in a beautifully co-ordinated way. As a person, Millie simply felt safe.

All this being said, it is vital to think long and hard about both the impact of touch and the impact of lack of touch for each particular child. Always ask yourself, based on her past experience, how is this child likely to read my intentions? Will she think that your intention is to seduce her or to control her, rather than to comfort her?

We need to be very aware of damaging and unnecessary uses of touch in a therapeutic context, for example, touch as an avoidance of the child's feelings and emotional pain, as an avoidance of real contact, as a block to painful memories, as an ill-thought-out or impulsive act of futile reassurance/gratification, as a block to important therapeutic work and conflict resolution.

The practitioner also needs to be aware of touch which is posing as healing, but which is actually being used to satisfy the practitioner's need for contact rather than that of the child's. Naturally, we need also to be aware of touch that could be experienced by the child as invasive, confusing or traumatising, or experienced as eroticising in any way whatsoever. So before reaching out with touch, it is best to think ten times in contrast to once or twice as we might before using a verbal intervention (Fish 1992).

In summary, I hope this chapter has helped you to recognise the rich array of verbal tools we have available to us for conversational connections. As with a poet, the use of carefully considered words in talk-time can have such a powerful impact, and when words are not enough to reach the child consumed with unbearable levels of stress, we also need to carefully consider the use of appropriate touch.

Chapter 7: Getting to the painful stuff

Introduction

> It is our [conversation with the child about their experiences], our
> complex, meandering, stirring, surprising, painful, and moving dialogue
> - that enables [children] to begin the process of transformation.
>
> Hughes 2006, p.92

This chapter and the next will offer you ways of being and key interventions to help your conversation with a child flow. When there's flow, the connection between you will deepen. You will be supporting the child to reflect on his life, his relationships, and his feelings in a more meaningful way.

After the initial opening of a conversation with a child, setting the scene and explaining things, some people feel de-skilled, embarrassed, not knowing what to say or what to do next, particularly after a child has spoken about something important. So this chapter will support you to think about how to deepen the dialogue in ways that make the child feel psychologically safe and maintain their interest in talking about themselves and their life. There are several resources here, offering many options for children, from the most defended to the most emotionally articulate.

An analogy that always comes to mind when I think of the deepening process of adult-child therapeutic conversations is the door at the back of the wardrobe in CS Lewis's famous book, *The Lion, The Witch and the Wardrobe* (1950). Sometimes, when helping a child with troubled feelings, an adult goes into the wardrobe, and the wardrobe is just a wardrobe. In other words, lots of things are said but all the words never result in a powerful connection between adult and child. At other times, the back of the wardrobe leads both adult and child to an amazing land beyond. This is when the adult is able to develop and sustain a conversation with the child in a meaningful way. Some adults may be forever 'stuck in the wardrobe', meaning that they rarely enable a child to experience empowerment, resolution or real positive change. This chapter is about helping you go beyond.

 What research shows ...

Research shows that if we take people deeper in our response to what they are saying, they are far more likely to reflect at a deeper level themselves (Greenberg 1997, p.57). People are ten times more likely to shift to an internal focus after a therapist's response focused them in this way than when the therapist stayed with the client's focus (Adams & Greenberg 1996, p.132). This is all the more so with children who just don't have the resources or knowledge on how to reflect on their feelings in depth.

So just waiting for a child to talk and reflect at a deeper level might mean you wait forever, as I mentioned on p.96. Hauser's famous study (2006) showed that resilience and thriving in teenagers are all to do with the capacity for psychological thinking. So if we want children to think psychologically, we must model how to do it in the way we talk with them.

A 10-year-old girl, after being helped to speak about feelings, sat in a state of deep contentment and said with wonder, *"I never knew that I thought that. But I do. And I know that I thought that for a long time, but I never knew I did."* Hughes 2011, p.175

Personally I've also been very impacted by Grotstein's (2005) statement that when adult and child are in powerful conversational connection, 'something holy happens'. This is meant not in a religious sense; but my experience is that the quality of connection between them is something quite beautiful, as both appreciate on some level that it is a moment of profound and genuine meeting from which some form of internal change is inevitable.

How to ensure that deepening is therapeutic and not troubling for the child

Deepening a dialogue can bring about a profound connection between adult and child. The problem can be that some adults are frightened of this level of connection, of what is indeed intimacy, and/or frightened of the deeper feelings they themselves have encouraged the child to access. As Grotstein (2005) says 'The [child] is dependent on the [adult's] courage to feel what he cannot feel so it's safe [for the child] to feel it.'

So we really need to avoid helping a child to open up, and then leaving them there, analogous to opening up a wound and then not treating it! The child would arguably be in a worse state than before the conversation, and, once again, alone and abandoned with their painful feelings.

Tess (7) was caught shoplifting powdered milk for her new baby sister when she was four years old. Mum was depressed, Dad was an alcoholic and both were addicted to drugs. Her parents were then charged for drug trafficking and Tess was taken into care. Tess still loves both her Mum and Dad deeply. She is allowed several supervised visits a year to see them, but many times they don't show up.

163

In therapeutic conversation with the child professional, this is how the discussion can go:

> **Tess:** (using playdoh) *I've made a beautiful den for a fox. I've made her a lovely bed of leaves and moss.*
>
> **Adult:** *And if someone made a lovely den for you, who would you invite into it?*
>
> **Tess:** *Everybody in my special family, my tummy mummy and my real dad, not my carers.*
>
> **Adult:** *Just your special family.*
>
> **Tess:** *Yeah.* (fiddles with a wind-up music man) *I don't know how to wind this up, make it work - can you help me?*
>
> **Adult:** *OK how about you hold it and I will turn it. So that's a pretty cool den.*
>
> **Tess:** *That's for the fox.*
>
> **Adult:** *Are there other creatures in the wood too, that the fox can make friends with?*
>
> **Tess:** *NO.*
>
> The two get on and play. No feelings are referred to again in the time they have together.

The adult has helped Tess go deeper but in ways that are troubling, not therapeutic, in the sense that "*You have reminded me of how much I miss my family - how much I desperately want them back, but you have not helped me with that.*" As Van der Kolk (1999, p.18) says: 'Exploring trauma for its own sake has no therapeutic benefits unless it becomes attached to other experiences, such as feeling understood'. What is missing in this example is an empathic response from the adult to the child's courageous expression of emotional pain. Hence I re-iterate the importance of following all three stages of empathic listening (*see* Chapter 3 *The Art of Empathic Listening*) before embarking on how to deepen therapeutic conversations with a child.

So let's try it again, and see how Tess's courage in talking about her painful missing of her birth family can be acknowledged and met with empathy,

Adult: *And if someone made a beautiful den for you who would you invite into it?*

Tess: *Everybody in my special family, my tummy mummy and my real dad, not my carers.*

Adult: *Just your special family.*

Tess: *Yeah.* (fiddles with a wind up music man) *I don't know how to do this - can you help me?*

Adult: (feeling into the child's pain, and what comes to mind is Shakespeare's phrase - 'untimely ripped') *Yes I will help you with that, but I would also like to help you with the awful pain of missing your mum and Dad.*

or

Adult: (not going with the child's deflection about the music man) *What a lovely thought to imagine your first family all together again, but this time in a beautiful place, not a place of so much pain, like it used to be at times.* (if the child is able to stay with this - the adult may continue ...)

Adult: *Perhaps sometimes you long for it to have been different - for you to have been able to stay with your Mum and Dad who you still love so very very much. And for someone to have helped them to care for you better.*

Here's another example of an adult who gets a child to open up and then abandons him there. When **David** was five (now age ten) his mother left. She separated from Dad and now lives in another country with a new man. At age seven, David's Dad died so David now lives with his paternal grand-parents. The family thinks it's best not to talk about the painful events of David's past. Encouraged by the adult to 'explore' his feelings, David made painful reference in metaphor and indirect expression to the traumatic separations he had experienced.

> **David:** *The animals are going too far away and they are never going to come back and then Mum and Dad really miss them.*
>
> **Adult:** *And where do they go to when they go far away?*
>
> **David:** *To an apple shed.*
>
> **Adult:** *Ah, an apple shed. What's it like there?*
>
> **David:** *The apple shed's OK except the far away animals don't want the apples. In fact they don't want anything. They just lie still and dull in the mud.*
>
> **Adult:** *It is squelchy mud or another sort of mud?*
>
> David says nothing. After a long silence he says, "*Let's play chess.*" His painful missing and the too far away animals who lie 'still and dull' in the mud are not referred to again.

So this conversation has not been therapeutic for the child: there has been no empathic response, so no emotional regulation or help to process or deepen connection through the acknowledgement of his pain. Again it's simply a sense of "*You have reminded me that my mum and dad are gone - how much I am hurting about it - you have not helped me with that.*" As Meltzer says (1969) 'Yes, tiptoe up to a [child's] pain but do tiptoe, don't freeze or walk the other way' (p.58).

So let's try it again where deepening means helping the child with his pain, not abandoning him in it.

> **David:** *The animals are going too far away and they are never going to come back and then Mum and Dad really miss them*
>
> **Adult:** (direct response - if David can manage it - *see* Chapter 2)
> *And I'm thinking it's like your Dad and Mum who both went too far away ... and you were such a little boy, made all the worse perhaps because no-one helped you with all the too painful missing.*
>
> or
>
> **Adult:** (indirect response) *So in your story the going too far away and never coming back is so painful, so much hurt and so little help to manage all the pain.*
>
> **David:** *The apple shed's OK except the too far away animals don't want the apples. In fact they don't want anything. They just lie still and dull in the mud.*
>
> **Adult:** (direct response) *... and I'm thinking that perhaps sometimes you feel so low and sad like the animals because of all the pain you have known.*
>
> **Adult:** (indirect response) *Maybe life's been just too hard for the far away animals and so it's spoilt their enjoyment of the good things in life.*

So in summary, what factors are involved when an adult gets a child to open up and then abandons them there? I've discussed the following factors:

- The adult may not have undergone any (or sufficient) personal therapy or counselling to address her own emotional baggage, so the child's pain is too much for her to feel; it may be reminding her of something in her own life that she is trying not to feel.
- The adult doesn't have the empathy skills, so she literally doesn't know what to say.
- The adult doesn't appreciate the power of empathy, which can so profoundly emotionally regulate and give children the ability to reflect on and feel what has happened to them, in ways that heal.

Finding words to help the child access their core feelings underneath the surface

Many people try to help troubled children but they go with what's on the surface - namely their troubled behavior. When they address this with rewards or sanctions, it often doesn't work. The behavior persists or another troubled symptom takes its place. We have got to go under the surface to enable the child to get in touch with their core feelings, which are fuelling the troubled behaviour. In other words, we need to deepen the dialogue.

Core feelings are the deepest, most authentic feelings we have. We often avoid acknowledging them as they can be so painful. Yet if we are to heal, core feelings must be accessed, and worked through. So firstly, go to the table entitled *Common Themes for Painful Childhood Experiences* (*see* p.382) to keep in mind the core feelings that a troubled child may well be struggling with, remembering what you know about their history.

Both children and adults can think that the feelings they are having are their core feelings, but often they're not. Instead, they are defences against core feelings, protecting them from the pain of what they are really feeling deep down. Many children, for example, tell themselves they are angry or bored, that they hate someone, or that "*It's all rubbish*", because these feelings can be experienced without much or any pain. When defences inhibit the child from experiencing their feelings in depth, they will not be able to move on and emotional and social development can come to a standstill.

What it's like for a child to be enabled to access their core feelings (in a safe way)

When a child is enabled to feel what he really feels deep down (because he is with an empathic adult who has made it psychologically safe to do so), it can be a great relief. There's often a feeling of deep connection between you and the child as a result: that it's a place that needed to be known and dwelt in for a while before moving onwards. Remember Greenberg's comment that we have to arrive at the place in order to leave it (2014). Furthermore, a core emotional state always holds important information for reflection or action; for example, the child may realise that they need to make a protest (empowered anger, Greenberg 2014), or to grieve, or to get help to confront someone.

Examples of common child or teenager defensive feelings and statements

What we may get (defences)

Hate	*Bored*
It's all my fault	*Depressed*
Stupid	*Can't be bothered*
Don't care	*It's rubbish*
Smash him up	*He/she is rubbish*

Core feelings which may lie under the defence

Hurt	Helpless	Betrayed
Sad	Hopeless	Anger
Fear, terror	Alone	Mistrust
Loneliness	Rage	Shock
Desolation	Shame, disgust	Grief
Not belonging	Empowered	Overwhelmed

- **Michael (10)** was stuck in tormenting guilt for three years after his father left home. Michael was convinced the leaving was due to his bad behaviour. He needed help to get to his core feelings of grief and protest through anger, necessary with the processing of any traumatic loss. Once he did this, he started learning at school and emjoyed good friendships for the first time in his life.

- **Dylan (12)** was stuck in hate because of a cruel father. He took it out on younger children by hitting them. With talk-time with an empathic adult, Dylan was helped to get in touch with his core feelings of hurt and impotence in the face of his father's harsh treatment. His parents split up. The courts listened and respected Dylan's wish only to see his father very infrequently and under supervision (UN Convention on the Rights of the Child, Article 3). Dylan was a different boy. He knew his voice had been heard.

- **Mary (14)** kept saying she didn't care about anything or anyone. She became physically violent to her mother. Her mother went to social services because she said Mary was too hard to look after anymore.

Mary ended up in residential care. As with Michael, an empathic adult helped Mary access her core feeling, which was grief. She was grieving a period in her life when her mother had to go into rehab and nearly died because of alcohol abuse. At age six, Mary had been left with strangers (foster parents) not knowing whether she would ever see her mother again. Her social worker spoke of the fear, terror and desolation the six year old Mary may have felt, and Mary broke down in tears. With the adult's help, Mary voiced her anger with her mum in a supervised session. *"Why did you prefer the bottle to me, Mum? Why didn't you think of me when you nearly died?"* Her mother explained and apologised. Mary cried and cried, softened and moved by her mother's non-defensiveness. The two of them started to live together again, their relationship healed because core feelings had been accessed and shared.

In helping a child access their core feelings, we need to adhere to all the fundamental principles discussed so far in the book. It's crucial never to tell a child what we think their core feelings are. Instead, we need to help them to get there on their own with our empathy and with dialogue deepening interventions. Otherwise there can be the patronising tyranny of *"You think you're sad, but actually underneath that you're angry"*.

In the next chapter I will explore key interventions to help you deepen the dialogue when you and a child are having a convers ation that matters.

Chapter 8: Dialogue deepening interventions

1 *"Show Me"*

By and large, everyday language is not the child's natural language for feelings. But, with an adult they trust, children and teenagers can often show, draw or play out their feelings very well indeed. So when a child is trying to communicate something, giving them a piece of paper and crayons with the simple request, "*Show me*", can be highly effective. It also ensures that the child knows you are intent on understanding the meaning he is ascribing to a feeling, event or relationship, rather than straying into the dangerous territory of inferring meaning.

How to use this intervention

Mark's drawing

Mark: *(10) I hate that Wayne in the playground. When he shouts awful things at me, he makes me feel awful inside.*

Adult: *(Steven)* Will you show me the awful feeling inside? (produces large piece of white paper and some felt pens)

Mark: (draws the pain lines coming from Wayne's shouting mouth piercing Mark's heart and his head and his tummy).

Steven: (more able to empathise now) *So the shouting gets right inside you, into your head, your tummy and your heart. You have helped me see just how horrid your awful feeling is.*

Mark: (feeling met by the adult - continues to draw) *Yes it's like pricking me all over with pain.*

Steven: *So it really, really hurts you, all over, everywhere. And I am thinking, how alone you have been with this and how brave you are for telling me now.*

Later in the session:

Steven: *Grown-ups must keep children safe. So let's work out a way to make that happen.*

Mark agrees that Steven can speak to Mark's teacher, who takes the bullying seriously and intervenes effectively.

"*Show me*" is also great to use when a child says things like "*I'm cross about that*", or "*I'm a bit scared*", and then runs aways from the feeling into some form of action. "*Show me*" can be an active way of re-engaging them. The adult can simply say, "*Will you show me what your 'cross' feels like?*": "*Will you show me what 'a bit scared' feels like?*"

When the child 'shows you' - often they express something far more profound than 'a bit scared', or a generalised "*I'm cross*".

When Claire asked **Lauren (7)**, to show her 'a bit scared', she did a sand picture. Claire then asked Lauren to give the sand picture a title. Lauren's title was *'Death in my head, my bed and my dreams'*.

Lauren's sandplay

This led on to Lauren being able to talk about her fear of her Mum dying. All this had come about because, when she was six, Lauren saw her Mum faint. For a time, she thought her Mum was dead. Using *"Show me"* had opened the door to a far more profound conversation than just hearing that Lauren was '*a bit scared*'.

2 'Finish the sentence'

> With sensitive accuracy, the [adult] expands the [child's] hints into an elaboration of feeling or experience. Greenberg 1997, p.8

Many children say something profound, but then leave it hanging in the air; they don't finish the sentence or move quickly on to doing or saying something else. If we're not careful, we may collude with this, and key communications will be lost. It's as if the child opens an important little door, metaphorically speaking, and if we don't hold their hand to help them walk through it, the door can slam shut, perhaps not to be opened again.

Such children need help to stick with a feeling so as to get to a point of awareness or insight. Otherwise, they can move into safe, 'distracting' play, or simply change the subject. So use the 'unfinished sentence technique', as in the examples below.

How to use the intervention

Your help can come in the form of some simple encouragement to finish the unfinished sentence.

> **Child:** *I know what the worst feeling in the world is. It's fear.*
>
> ✗ Avoiding the feeling
> **Adult:** *I see.*
>
> ✔ Instead … (use unfinished sentence technique)
> **Adult:** *And the worst feeling in the world is fear because … ?*

Marvin (7) is in a family where people argue and fight a lot. Twice, he has watched his teenage brother hit his Mum. Marvin loves his Mum very much. Marvin's schoolwork has deteriorated and he is often seen staring into space. The fighting at home is clearly affecting him. This is his comment after some toy soldier play:

> **Marvin:** I don't like soldiers, they fight too much.
>
> ✗ Avoiding the feeling
>
> **Adult:** (Javid) They do, don't they?
>
> ✔ Instead (using unfinished sentence technique to deepen and develop the dialogue)
>
> **Marvin:** I don't like soldiers they fight too much.
>
> **Javid:** Because when they fight too much what happens is … ?
>
> **Marvin:** When they fight too much the watching people badly want it to stop but are too scared to make it stop.
>
> **Javid:** What are they scared might happen?
>
> **Marvin:** That they would just become smashed up too, too smashed up to help the wounded ones and that would be just awful awful, awful.

The adult now has enough information to move into an empathic response. His response holds in mind how Marvin's play story speaks of the emotional themes of his home life (*see* p.48).

> **Javid:** How awful for the watching people - so desperate for it to stop but so frightened that they would get so hurt themselves they couldn't help the wounded ones. I guess they care so much for those wounded ones.
>
> **Marvin:** Oh yes, the wounded ones need the watching ones.
>
> **Javid:** So, the watching ones feel helpless to stop the fighting but they really matter to the wounded ones.
>
> **Marvin:** That's right.

Sometimes you can start with the unfinished sentence but then follow it on with other ways to deepen the dialogue. In this next example, the unfinished sentence leads on to the intervention I talked about on p.173 - *"Will you show me ?"*

> **Tiffany:(14)** *I feel so fed up about school.*
>
> **Robert:** *You feel fed up about it because ... ?*
>
> **Tiffany:** *Because I am always letting myself down.*
>
> **Robert:** *And that makes you feel ... ?*
>
> **Tiffany:** *Like screaming.*
>
> **Robert:** *Will you show me what that feels like by drawing it?*

Tiffany's drawing

After Tiffany has done this, Robert looks at the picture with her. Robert tries some psycho-education (*see* p.97). He says that people who keep criticising themselves have often had grown-ups in their life who haven't been good enough at giving them encouragement, and instead have too often discouraged or criticised. Robert then continues:

> **Robert:** *If the scream could talk what might it say?*
>
> **Tiffany:** *Say more nice things about me, you're so mean.*

Tiffany is no longer feeling defeated. Because she really took in Robert's psycho-education, she has moved into a place of healthy protest. She has a new insight about how she has compliantly taken in too many discouragements she has received in her life without any "*Stop!*" or "*Enough!*" or "*It's not OK for you to treat me in this way.*"

Here is another example of a child who is helped to deepen and explore what she is feeling. **Ellen (10)** makes a statement with emotional charge but needs help to expand and develop it.

> **Ellen:** *I will be a zookeeper and I will be a bank robber when I grow up.*
>
> **X** Avoiding response
>
> **Adult:** *That sounds interesting.*
>
> **✔** Instead (ask the child to expand on what they have said by a simple question)
>
> **Adult:** *What sort of zookeeper will you be? What sort of bank robber?*
>
> **Ellen:** *A really bad bank robber and a zookeeper who lets the animals out, because he just keeps forgetting everything. I am just so fed up of being told I am such a good girl all the time.*
>
> **Adult:** *Like part of you wants to break out and be free to … ?*
>
> **Ellen:** *To scream and shout and do something bad.*

3 Emotion worksheets

Emotion work sheets are drawings or charts which show specific feelings or feeling states with short captions or statements (*please see* pp.326-9). Children are simply asked to look at the pictures and read the captions (if they can), and draw or write on them if anything in the picture or series of pictures resonates with what they feel. You can design and use your own work sheets, as I'll describe below.

The use of structured exercises and 'emotion work sheets' is a really good intervention for children and teenagers who don't want to talk about their feelings; I've worked with them quite often. This is because they don't require the child to say anything; just colour something in or mark with a tick or a cross. Worksheets can be a great aid in acting as a springboard for those children/ teenagers who need support to take that initial step into the world of 'reflected-on feeling'. In other words, resistant children can start with emotion worksheets and, in so doing, often find thinking about their life, their feelings and relationships in this way, very interesting. This motivates them to subsequently enter into a meaningful dialogue with you through more symbolic work, for example through the use of sandplay or drawing.

How to use this intervention

Whether you are making up your own worksheets or using ones already devised (*see also Draw on Your Emotions,* Sunderland 1997, and *Draw on Your Relationships,* Sunderland 2008), the ones that are most effective are those informed by psychology and/or brain science. So, for example, worksheets about loss should be soundly informed by what we now know from research about loss and what life can feel like when you lose someone you love.

With the worksheets I have previously designed on loss, I have used concepts from Freud's paper *Mourning and Melancholia* (1917), which comments so profoundly on the world that has lost all its interest for the bereaved person: 'the world cannot recall you'. I have also used Panksepp's research papers on the pain of social loss (Panksepp & Watt, 2011) in terms of what we now know about the terrible, debilitating pain people experience, which results in part from opioid withdrawal in the brain. So the worksheets provide the child with psychological concepts and knowledge of the human condition *in a format that speaks to them.* Spending time thinking this through and researching key psychological concepts for each worksheet also ensures that we don't make worksheets which simply reflect our own experience, or our own personal biases about what 'should' happen.

When choosing already published emotion worksheets, I suggest referring to the tables on p.382 (*Common Emotional Themes for Painful Childhood Experiences*) to really reflect on what the child is grappling with. On the basis of this, select worksheets that are relevant to the child. I usually have three or four worksheets for, say, an hour's talk-time, although of course I may end up not using them all.

When devising your own sheets, you might also like to pick some statements under specific headings from the table and then do some simple drawings to support them. Then offer your drawings to the child with this instruction, or something similar:

> **Adult:** *Have a look at the drawings in this picture. If you have any of the feelings in the picture, tick the picture or colour it in. If you don't feel any of the things in the picture, you could use the final square to draw or colour in what you do feel.*

Some children will naturally talk to you about what they've done. For others who remain silent, if you know enough of their life story and there is a clear tie-up between what has happened to them in their life and what they are drawn to in the worksheet - you can make an empathic intervention, directly or indirectly.

4 Reflective summaries

Often during a talk-time in which an adult is helping a child to talk about feelings, the child will cover many themes: for example, failing my maths test, a dead cat, bullying, worried my Mum is going to die. It can be so easy to just respond to the items at the end of their long list, and fail to pick up on their other important issues.

So an end-of-session summary is always important to deepen the reflective process. It just isn't OK to say something like, *"So you have told me some very important things today. See you soon/next week."* Remember such a lot of the healing properties of a therapeutic conversation come in enabling the child to reflect on feelings. The end of a conversation about feelings is a key opportunity for this. In addition, when the child has covered several important issues, or emotional themes part-way through a talk-time, consider a mid-session summary.

How to use this intervention

Basically as you progress through the talk-time, hold in mind the various emotional themes covered by the child and then find the right time to summarise them. This can often be carried out most effectively by doing a quick drawing/ diagram of the themes on a big piece of paper with felt pens, or you can use other media such as puppets, or miniature objects in the sandbox.

The mid-session or end-of-session summary will show the child that you have really listened to everything she has said. It will help her to reflect more clearly on what she's drawn, made, said or enacted. In the summary, it's important you don't just describe the child's story or play but that you comment on the key emotional themes, and convey your empathy. Here are a couple of examples.

Adult: *So, in your story today a big fish came and swallowed lots of ships and all the people were frightened and their houses got knocked down* (description). *How frightening, no-one to help them take on the big fish and say, "Stop."* (empathic comment)

Adult: *So your story today has been about creatures in a terrible storm who were asking for help, but people just ignored them and walked straight past, so they all gave up* (description). *I can imagine just how lonely they felt, and how easy it would be to think that, because some people in the world are so uncaring, everyone in the world is uncaring* (empathic comment on emotional themes)

A big fish came and swallowed lots of ships ...

You might then say, "*I'm wondering if I've missed out anything important or misunderstood anything?*", just as you would with the Big Empathy Drawing (p.79) giving the child opportunity to add their own comments and thus create a more complete picture. This co-created reflective process can enable the child to leave the session with a far more satisfying feeling of completion and wholeness.

With children who have spent the whole session conveying feelings through play, metaphor and story without at any time referring directly to actual people or events in their life, you might consider: "*I'm wondering if any part of the story feels a bit like something in your life?*". But this would only be appropriate for a child who has willingly talked to you about his life before, and/or with a child who you sense is now relaxed enough and trusts you enough to talk about her life without the protective shelter of the metaphor. If you have got it wrong, the child will simply ignore your question or say "*No*". If this happens, you'll know it's not yet time to move in any closer.

And finally, you can invite the child to talk about any thoughts or feelings they are taking away from your time together. You might say something like,

> **Adult:** *So today you talked about your step-brother and his illness and then we did some sandplay, and your feeling of aloneness over what is happening at home for you, seems so hard. I wonder if you are thinking or feeling anything about what I have just said, or indeed about anything that has happened today in our time together?*

5 The "I'm not ready to go on yet" response

"Wait ... wait ... what you said ... what you said seems so important!"

Hughes 2007, p.85

Many children have a habit of dropping powerful feeling statements into a conversation with a trusted adult. The child can then quickly move away from the comments they've made, into busy playing. Many children behave in this way to avoid staying with the pain or intensity of what they have said. They may do so because they have little or no experience of the wonderful sense of relief they can feel as a result of an adult's empathic response. This can particularly be the case with children who want to take total control of a talk-time, as a way of managing their anxiety.

When this happens, you might need to gently interrupt the child. Say something like, *"I'm not quite ready to go on just yet. You have told me some most important things. Can we stay here for a moment?"* Then you can go over what the child has said, adding validating empathy.

> **Susie: (5)** (her mother has recently been given a prison sentence for six months) *Oh look a blue butterfly in the toy box. I wish I could take that home, I miss my mum. Butterflies are my favourite and the colour blue. Can I do a blue painting today? Here now I will get the paints ready.*
>
> **Sam:** (speaks in a gentle, slow voice) *Hey Susie, I am not quite ready to go on yet. You've just told me a most important thing. You are missing your Mum. Of course you are, you love her so much and she loves so much* (based on known fact). *I'm so sorry that you are hurting so much right now.*

> **Susie:** *I am, I really am (starts to cry). Mummy come home, come home, please please.*
>
> **Sam:** *Susie, you long to be with your Mummy again so much, you long to be with your Mummy again. The visit next week I guess feels like just too too long a time to wait. You want her now, "Mummy come back now", you want her to hear. You want her to know.*

If, on the other hand, the child really doesn't want to go back to what she has said, then naturally let her continue deflecting, until such a time that she feels psychologically safe enough to return.

6 "Will you help me understand this?"

For some children, challenging behaviour is the only 'language' they have to express their feelings. They cannot tell us what is happening for them in any other way. When such children are helped to find a different language for feelings, the challenging behaviour often ceases.

How to use this intervention when a child has caused hurt or damage

i. Let the child know you know what has happened, but in a calm, non-punitive tone. For example: *"I hear that you kicked a teacher yesterday"*.

ii. Find a way of telling the child that this talk-time is not about telling them off or giving them a consequence (this may well have been handled elsewhere). Instead, you want to understand what the event meant for them. This is with the hope that the feelings they had, which precipitated their aggressive or hurtful act, can be communicated, fully addressed with you as an empathic adult, and worked through. The behaviour may not stop straightaway - none of us learn a new language immediately! But the more we help the child learn that their feelings are valid and can be communicated openly, without fear of judgment or reprisal, the less likely it will be that challenging behaviour will be their language of feelings.

iii. Lots of children think their bad behaviour is because they are bad, so it's often such a relief that an adult is interested in understanding *why* they behave as they do, rather than just criticising.

> **Adult:** *Will you help me to understand what made you kick your teacher? I'm asking you so we can work out why things are going wrong and then we can think how to do things differently, so you don't keep getting into trouble.*

The Big Empathy Drawing can be particularly helpful to facilitate this discussion. Since his Dad left home to live with another woman, **Tim (8)** (*see* p.21) is often found shouting at little children in the playground. He sometimes hits them. He has been endlessly disciplined about it but the problem is not improving. Reya is Tim's teacher. He likes her very much and trusts her. He has started talking to her about what's going on at home and how his Dad left to be with someone else.

> **Reya:** *Tim, will you help me understand what might be going on for you that means you keep getting into trouble? I wonder if it's a bit like this (draws Big Empathy Drawing) ... Someone says or does something and you fill up with anger, and lash out. But when that happens we only see the angry Tim. Is that right?*
>
> **Tim:** *I suppose so. Like a switch goes on in my brain and then that's it, I see red.*

Reya: (draws a figure on the picture and writes the words next to it - lost and hurting) *No-one sees the Tim who is in pain because he's missing his Dad so much.*

Tim: (heated) *That's right, people need to give me a break because my Dad screwed things up by leaving us.*

Reya: *I know, they don't understand how much pain you are in. Did you know that when animals lose someone they love, scientists have found that they can get angry too, because a chemical that triggers anger is released in their brain? It's the same for us. But the scientists also found that if we dare to feel sad feelings with a grown-up who wants to help, then the anger starts to go away.*

Tim: *Well in that case, I am glad I told you about my Dad.*

Reya: *So am I. What a brave thing to do.*

Reya reads him *The Day The Sea Went Out and Never Came Back* (Sunderland, 2003) a powerful story about grieving and yearning and how to do it.

Reya's Big Empathy Drawing

Here's another example of asking for help in understanding what's happening.

> **Claire:** *Will you help me to understand what is was like for you when your Dad was coming home angry all the time?*
>
> **Susan:** *(14) I was scared of him.*
>
> **Claire:** *Yes so scared that you told me you hid under the bed when he walked through the door. What a sad thing for such a little girl to have to do with her Dad, instead of waiting for him to come and give you a great big warm hug.*
>
> **Susan:** *I thought there was something wrong with me. That if I was different, erm, better or something, he would be happy, not angry.*
>
> **Claire:** *You took it so personally. How painful to think that you were the cause of your Dad's misery. You were too little to know that it was probably something totally different that was getting him down and nothing at all to do with you.*
>
> **Susan:** *I just wanted to please him but I could never find the key to do that!*
>
> **Claire:** *Of course you did - just to get your Dad to smile, to see him light up because of you instead of all that frowning and shouting.*
>
> **Susan:** *Yes and the awful thing was when I went to my friends' houses and their Dads used to play with them.*
>
> **Claire:** *And I guess you watched and as you did, you hurt so much inside to know what you were missing.*
>
> **Susan:** (looks down and tears roll down her face)

7 The '*Finish the Story*' technique

This is an interactive, 'working together' activity. Basically, you and the child make up a story together. It is a 'drawn story' on a large piece of paper. Each of you takes it in turns to tell the next bit through drawing and talking.

Phase 1

You open the story with empathic indirect reference to the child's issues. Set the scene by introducing disguised characters and events - nothing direct.

Phase 2

After this initial opening, the idea is for the child to bring the next phase of emotional content to the story and for you to support that content by keeping the story moving, but not adding emotional content of your own. Using this process will often reveal key emotional issues in the child's life, what is troubling them, and the meaning they have given to important life events. This is because like many of the other interventions in this chapter, this is a *projective technique*. This means that as soon as a child draws a picture or makes up a story, he is likely to be communicating about things that really matter to him. As Carl Jung (1982) said 'Everything unconscious in projected'.

Also you following and not leading in Phase 2 will bring out whether the child has psychological resources, for example wisdom, the ability to assert themselves (in the story at least), the ability to recognise their needs. Or the story might take the child into some pit of underlying despair.

But how do we prevent ourselves from leading the story? Basically, each time that you draw and say something, what you provide will be a filler, a 'treading water', as opposed to taking the action or feeling content forward in any way. Your words, however, can be an empathic underlining of what the child has said in their turn-taking. You might want to try practising this technique with a friend, colleague, or a child you know well at home, and ask for feedback as to whether they thought you supported them in their narrative or took over in some way, or tried to lead.

Phase 3

Once the child's emotional content, psychological strengths, underlying core feelings have come out in the story, and you have given good time to this, you can then choose how to respond. Think what will be most therapeutic for the child - a summary of what they have said and done? Psycho-education, key psychological messages, spoken through one of the characters? Acknowledgment of the characters' concerns, strengths, despair and so on?

Using the Finish the Story Technique

i. Suggest to the child that you make up a story together on a big piece of paper.

ii. You begin the story. Draw as you tell. Make sure the story opens with some of the key emotional issues in the child's life, but make sure they are suitably disguised.

iii. Pass the pen to the child. They draw and talk about the next bit.

iv. When they've finished their bit they pass the pen back to you.

v. You draw the next bit, and so on.

vi. At the end of the story, you summarise what happened in the story, focusing on the emotional themes.

Ground rules for the 'Finish the Story Technique'

✔ You can offer empathy to the characters as appropriate

✔ You can offer empathy for emotional themes the child introduces

✔ You can underline what the child has said in some way, so they know you have understood their meaning

✔ In Phase 2, you can take the action forward with bland statements such as *And then …, When all of a sudden …, And what happened then was …*

✔ In Phase 3, gently introduce psycho-education and key emotional themes where appropriate, voiced through a character.

Melissa (7) worries about everything, but she tries to manage her feelings all on her own. She bottles up her feelings about Mum's depression, about Dad being away from home so much, about whether they can pay the mortgage, about her little sister's bedwetting problem and so on. She carries the world on her shoulders. It is affecting her schoolwork, her friendships and her sleeping. But she doesn't tell anyone about her worries, because her Dad trained her to be his 'big strong girl'.

Karen, who knows about Melissa's worries and home situation, starts the story. She opens with emotional themes from Melissa's life: being over-burdened with adult concerns, worried about Mum. The story is suitably disguised through indirect expression, as it is about a small creature called Oggie. Such indirect expression protects the child who is frightened of direct reference to actual life events and who may dysregulate too easily if you talk directly.

Phase 1

> **Karen:** *Once upon a time there was a small creature called Oggie who had some problems. The problems went everywhere with Oggie. So wherever Oggie went, so did Oggie's problems. They got under her pillow, and into her dreams and sometimes turned into nightmares. They even got into her homework books, so she kept making mistakes. Friends tried to help Oggie. The help didn't help. Some said, "Look, everything will be better if you just put on a happy face." They didn't understand Oggie's horrid problems. Only Oggie did.*

Phase 2

> **Karen:** *Then one day ...* (Karen passes the pen to Melissa)
>
> **Melissa:** (Melissa draws a picture) *Then one day, Oggie was so full of problems that she wandered off on her own into a deep dark wood ...*
>
> **Karen:** *She wandered around the deep dark wood feeling ...*
>
> **Melissa:** *...feeling that she never wanted to feel anything ever again!* (passes the pen to Karen)
>
> **Karen:** *Poor Oggie. Too painful for Oggie to feel those painful feelings anymore. Try just not to feel anymore. Then, all of a sudden ...* (passes the pen to Melissa)

Oggie's story

> **Melissa:** *Then all of a sudden, a bird flew overhead.*
>
> **Karen:** *It kept flying around until …*
>
> **Melissa:** *It saw Oggie and it swooped down to her.*
>
> **Karen:** *The bird said … (passes the pen to Melissa)*
>
> **Melissa:** *I would like to be your friend. You are too on your own.*
>
> **Karen:** *So what happened next was …*
>
> **Melissa:** *They went to have ice-cream in bird's tree house.*
>
> **Karen:** *… and then Oggie felt…*
>
> **Melissa:** *Well she likes tree houses and she likes pink ice-cream - so it was OK.*

Oggie's story (continued)

Phase 3

Having listened carefully to Melissa's development of the story in Phase Two, and after several more minutes of Melissa elaborating the story, Karen decides that maybe the most therapeutic intervention will be psychological messages and then a summary:

Karen: *A little grey sparrow on the next branch had been listening to all this. He said, "Excuse me for butting in your lovely ice-cream time together, but I used to try to manage all my problems on my own, but it made me very unhappy. Someone said it was brave to ask for help. Now when I have a problem, I go and speak to the Big Owl, and I feel much better."*

Melissa: *But I thought it's far far braver to do it all on your own?*

Karen: *"Not half as brave and smart as having the courage to tell someone who can really listen", said the bird. "Big Owl showed me that a problem shared is a problem halved."*

Karen: *(offering summary): So in the story, Oggie was convinced he had to do all the 'worrying' about things in his life all on his own. What a sad thing, but then he met a lovely bird and my guess is that Oggie started to feel better … then in comes sparrow and said he had learnt that worrying alone wasn't good, that the smart thing is to share his problems. Is there anything you want to say about the story Melissa?*

Melissa: *Can you be my Big Owl Karen?*

Karen: *Melissa I'd love to be.*

8 The "When x happens, some children feel ..." technique

This is a great technique for children who don't want you to talk directly to them about their feelings, because they find it too shaming, embarrassing, intrusive or exposing. So this intervention is a form of indirect expression, because you are referring to what *other* children feel in circumstances similar to those of the child you are working with. Your sentence, *"When x happens, some children feel ..."* can be packed with psycho-education, empathy and understanding for the child, whilst neatly side-stepping direct reference to events in the child's life.

As this is a story intervention, the word limit I talked about earlier does not apply. That said, check if the child is becoming disengaged at any point. If that happens, accompany what you are saying by drawing what you are talking about.

How to use this intervention

Shaun (9): has been bullied by two older kids who messed up his PE kit (Shaun is a very good runner). They also called his Mum (who is depressed) a 'nutcase'. Shaun is aware the adult (Aileen) knows about all this.

> **Shaun:** *I don't care. They're stupid. What they do doesn't matter to me.*
>
> **Aileen:** *I hear that. And I also know that sometimes, when children are bullied they try so hard not to let it get to them, but it does. One boy I knew was bullied because children were jealous when he kept getting top marks at school. They said his mother smelt and was the fattest mother in school. Like you, the boy tried to just get on with things. But one day he realised that he felt furious about what had happened, because all the shock and pain was making him really unhappy. He just couldn't stop thinking about what had happened to him.*

> *So he told his mum and together they found out the school bullying policy (every school has to have one). Lots of teachers helped. One teacher was really good and said in a very strong voice, "Alan, I am so sorry that this dreadful thing happened to you. You have an absolute right to feel very very safe in this school and we must make sure you do." So in the end the boys had to apologise and they never bothered Alan again. They didn't dare because all their parents knew what had happened and the teachers were always watching.*
>
> Shaun looks thoughtful, and seems to relax a bit.

9 Empty chair work

This technique was devised in the 1950's by Fritz Perls, a famous psychotherapist and founder of Gestalt Therapy. Gestalt therapy is in part about heightening a person's psychological awareness of themselves and others. Empty chair work is essentially a role-play, to explore our relationship with ourselves and with others. If you are using it to explore relationship with others, you can imagine someone important in your life is sitting in a chair in front of you. You then talk to them, with the support of the listening adult who can often help. People find that what they say to the person in the 'empty chair' is often far more coherent and emotionally charged than simply having thoughts about this person in their head.

It's a powerful technique. We know from science that vividly imagined experience activates the brain in similar ways to the real thing. In other words, you can feel like you are really talking to the person you have chosen to talk to and that they are really sitting there. As it can be so powerful, don't use this intervention with a child at the end of your time together. This is because you always need to spend a bit of time coming out of the role play, being back in the reality of the room and reflecting together on what has happened.

How to use this intervention

With children and young people, it can often be easier to ask them to choose a puppet or other large doll to put on the chair to represent the person they want to talk to, rather than leaving it completely empty. In the following example, Peter (adult) and Gaynor (child) have been having important conversations together for a while. Gaynor really trusts Peter. So using this technique, Peter is able to help Gaynor onto a new level of awareness. Note how he combines it with the unfinished sentence technique.

Gaynor: *My Dad messes me around. Every since he moved out, he promises to come and visit. But then so many times, he rings up and says he has to cancel because of work.*

Peter: *OK can you find something in the room, a puppet maybe to be your Dad and can you put it on that chair?* (Gaynor does so. She chooses a lion puppet). *OK, let's imagine your Dad is in this room sitting in that chair, can you say to your Dad, "Dad, you mess me around".*

Gaynor: (facing the chair): *Dad, you mess me around.*

Peter: *And what that makes me feel is ... ?*

Gaynor: *Sad.*

Peter: *Sad because ... ?*

Gaynor: *Because you say you will come and visit me and then you don't.*

Peter: *I guess that makes you feel really sad and really hurt too.*

Gaynor: *Yes it does, it's like I don't matter to him enough.*

Peter: *How about saying that to him as well?*

Gaynor: (angrily) *Dad it's like I don't matter enough to you. You call yourself my Dad. You don't deserve that name.*

Peter: *So many feelings about your Dad letting you down, sad, hurt*

Peter: *and now you are letting yourself know how angry you are about it.* (building in important time for reflection) *OK let's take Dad off the chair for now* (puts lion puppet on the floor) *and see how you feel now you've let yourself know these things.* (invites Gaynor to sit back down on the cushions opposite the lion puppet)

Gaynor: *I'm going to write a letter to him and tell him about all this.*

Peter: *Good idea - what will you say?*

Gaynor: *You don't love me Dad otherwise you wouldn't treat me like this.*

Peter: *Ah, so you think that his not coming to see you is a sign of his lack of love for you.*

Given how well Peter and Gaynor know each other by now, Peter feels he can have a go at helping Gaynor move away from a position of certainty about her Dad's motives and actions, to more sophisticated mentalising (*see p.78 on mentalising*).

Peter: *I'm just wondering Gaynor? Maybe you're right, but could it be something else, do you think? Some Dads don't see their children enough because it's too painful to say goodbye all over again. Others, because they think their children don't want to see them. And others because they don't realise how much it matters to their son or daughter that they keep in regular contact, and that they keep their word.*

Gaynor: (interested) *Really?*

Peter: *We just don't know what's happening in your Dad's head. And that's the hard bit … the not knowing: but you could always*

> ask him. I'm wondering if you'd like to tell him in your letter what it feels like for you when he doesn't come?
>
> **Gaynor:** (animated, and clearly feeling empowered and curious) Could I say, something like, "Dear Dad, when you're coming to visit, and then you don't, it makes me feel like you don't love me." Can we do the letter now? I mean, and send it for real?
>
> **Peter:** Of course.

Alternative for children who can't do the role play themselves

What if Gaynor or another child for whom you think this intervention would be useful is not prepared to do the roleplay? Perhaps too shy, or perhaps because she's just not aware what she feels about her Dad letting her down: in other words, her feelings have never been formed into coherent thoughts. Where this is the case, it can really help the child to hear you putting feelings into coherent thoughts instead.

You can set it up like this, using the drum and triangle technique I described on p.97. Here, Gaynor seems happy to use the instruments as Peter suggests.

> **Gaynor:** My Dad messes me around. Every since he moved out, he promises to come and visit. But then so many times, he rings up and says he has to cancel because of work.
>
> **Peter:** OK can you find something in the room, a puppet maybe to be your Dad and can you put in on that chair? (Gaynor chooses the lion puppet) OK, let's imagine your Dad is really sitting in that chair. Are you OK if I pretend to be you and I talk to your Dad? (Gaynor nods). If I say something that you feel is true for you, ting the triangle. If I say something that isn't what

you are feeling or thinking, bang the drum. If you are not sure just do nothing. OK?

Gaynor: *OK.*

Peter: (talks as Gaynor to the Dad puppet on the chair) *Dad, you mess me around.*

Gaynor: *Ting*

Peter: *When you don't turn up when you say you will, it makes me feel I'm not special to you anymore.*

Gaynor: *Ting*

Peter: *When you don't turn up when you say you will, it makes me feel you don't love me anymore.*

Gaynor: *Ting*

Peter: *I feel really hurt about it.*

Gaynor: (silence)

Peter: *I feel really angry about it. I feel really angry with you Dad when you let me down like this.*

Gaynor: *Ting ting ting*

Peter: (building in important time for reflection) *OK let's put the Dad lion puppet on the floor opposite us. So it seems that you feel angry with your Dad and not special and unloved when he lets you down like that. But when I said hurt - perhaps that's not right for you?*

Gaynor: *Just so cross. Calls himself a Dad, huh!*

Here are a couple of examples of deepening the dialogue using the techniques we've explored. The first is again about a child's hurt resulting from poor connection with a parent. But unlike Gaynor in the example above, Tom is ready to go a bit deeper into the hurt beneath his anger.

Tom (9) has told Ed that he gets really fed up about Mum being on her computer all the time.

Enquiry about the child's meaning (here using unfinished sentences)

Tom: *I feel fed up about my Mum being on her computer all the time ...*

Ed: *(Tom's teacher) You feel fed up about it because...?*

Tom: *Because I think she finds her computer more interesting than me.*

Ed: *And that makes you feel ... ?*

Tom: *Like smashing up the computer and smashing up the whole world*

Deepening the child's experience through creative intervention

Ed: *Will you draw a picture of that? (after he has done this, Tom looks very sad) So after the smashing you seem to be having a different feeling.*

Tom's drawing

Empathic response to the child's image/feelings

Ed: (does a Big Empathy Drawing) *I wonder if it feels a bit like this - all the smashing angry feelings mixed up with hurt feelings, like silent tears and your Mum perhaps too busy on her computer to notice.*

Ed's Big Empathy Drawing

Tom is invited to make his own changes to Ed's image

> **Ed:** (gives Tom the pen) *Will you show me where I have got that right or wrong?* (Tom scribbles out the tears and draws what he says is 'a sad gap that never used to be there between us'.)

Tom's response

Ed empathises with and validates Tom's response

> **Ed:** *I see it's not so much silent tears but this gap between you, which hasn't always been there. How painful.*
>
> **Tom:** *Yes, I think when I was a little boy she did find me interesting.*
>
> **Ed:** *What a painful thing to believe that your Mum being on her computer means she doesn't find you interesting.*

Ed and Tom have been in real dialogue. Tom feels relief because at last someone knows, really knows, the pain he has been going through with his Mum. Before this, it had been too lonely, no-one knowing.

What happens next? Ed is concerned that Tom is building up a view of himself as boring and dull. Ed decides to challenge Tom's certainty about what is going on in his mother's mind, and in so doing, models a more mentalising stance (*see* p.78). He introduces doubt, and other theories of motivation, in a wondering way.

> **Ed:** *It may be true that your Mum being on her computer means she finds you not interesting. But I'm wondering if it might be something else? Maybe it could be lots of different reasons instead? What do you think?*

Ed suggests to Tom that they think together about what other possible reasons there might be as to why Mum might be spending more time with her computer than with her son. They come up with: no-one played with mum when she was a child; Mum doesn't realise sons need lots of mum-time: Mum is really busy at work at the moment: Mum doesn't know how to approach Tom now he is getting older. She is more comfortable with younger children: now Tom is getting older, Mum doesn't think Tom really likes or wants so much quality time with her.

Tom begins to feel a bit better and is less certain that his mother finds him boring. Ed and Tom discuss how Tom might ask his Mum to spend more time with him.

Here's another example of combining interventions, where the reason for the mother's absence is rather different. I was seeing **Toby's (8)** Mum. Mum thought that Toby needed help. Mum told me that Toby had had a lovely relationship with her for the first five year of his life. Then Mum's Mum had died and she fell into a bad depression. Despite being on anti-depressants, she admitted that she no longer felt like playing with Toby or going out with him to the lovely places they used to go to together. It all seemed such an effort. But when she didn't play with Toby, he seemed to get very frustrated and sometimes hit her. He appeared to feel awful afterwards and was really down and withdrawn. Mum went on. Despite Toby feeling bad about hitting her, she understandably hated him for it. How could he be so selfish, she said, when surely he was old enough now to see how much she was suffering. She admitted that their relationship didn't feel good anymore.

Before I saw Toby, and beginning with *Stage 1 of Empathic Listening* - feeling, thinking and imagining into what life must be like for him, I thought a lot about what it must be like for a little boy to have a mother he loves so deeply and with whom he shared such lovely times, only to lose her (in the way he knew her) to a mental illness, based, although Toby couldn't know it, on his mother's own loss.

I understood that whilst it was not acceptable for Toby to hit his mum, how desperate a child must feel when the connection to their beloved mother is blocked or lost for some reason. I knew the brain science; that grief can trigger too high levels of acetycholine which makes animals violent with each other. However, I also knew that when I met Toby I must get *his* meaning on all this.

Enquiry about the child's meaning

> **Margot:** Toby, I hear from your Mum that sometimes things get very difficult at home and that you get cross and she gets cross and then everything gets sad and too hard. I'm here to see if I can help things go far, far better at home. I understand that your Mum and you had five lovely years and then she got ill and sad. But sometimes grown-ups get things wrong; so can you let me know if I have got anything wrong here?
>
> **Toby:** (quietly) *It's right.*

Toby's drawing

Deepening the child's experience through creative intervention

> **Margot:** Wow, that must have been so hard for you. Can you help me understand - how was that for you? All those years of a lovely mummy and then a sad ill mummy. Will you show me? Here is some paper. (Toby does drawing on previous page)
>
> **Toby:** Like a bulldozer comes and smashes into the wobbly house until it's just dust

Empathic response to what the child has done or said

I now had to think about the emotional themes common to Toby's life story and play story. I knew that the change in his mother's mental health must have hit him very hard. I also knew that he hit his mum (maybe the bulldozer) and then felt very bad about it. His drawing suggested that Toby worried that he might have damaged Mum, which would fit with her saying he felt awful after lashing out at her when she didn't play with him. I also held in mind the pain of lost connection, as I have described above. Bringing all this together, I did the following drawing as an empathic response. I respected the fact that Toby had responded in metaphor and so I also communicated in metaphor with him.

> **Margot:** Toby, I wonder if the bulldozer might feel one or more of these feelings when bulldozing the house. It would be so understandable if it did. Some smashing ups in the world come from angry feelings but some smashings come from panicky or hurt feelings or other feelings too. If you don't know what one of these words means let me know. If you do, and you think that's what the bulldozer might feel, would you circle it?

Margot's response

Child invited to make his own changes to the adult's image

Toby was clearly thinking. He circled 'smash it up,' heart-broken,' 'panic' and 'wanting to make it all better but ending up making it worse instead'.

Toby's Response

Adult empathises with and validates the child's response

> **Margot:** *Poor bulldozer, and my guess is that he sometimes feels so bad about the smashing, when inside he is hurting so much.*
>
> **Toby:** *Yes bulldozers have feelings too you know.*
>
> **Margot:** *I know I know…. (pause - then quietly) .. especially when they have lost or feel they have lost the most precious thing to them in the whole wide world.*

I included some psycho-education (*see* Chapter 2, Empathic Listening *for more on this*) talking about how when people are not getting (or not feeling they are getting) attention/connection from people they love, they often lash out in panic and pain (Johnson 2004, on the normality of attachment protest). I invited Toby's mother back in to do some parent-child sessions. I also helped Toby's mother to set clear limits for Toby to prevent him from hitting her, and to spend more fun time together. The little boy was immensely relieved. He stopped hurting his mother. Spontaneously in one session, he threw his arms around my neck and said, "*I love you*". Deep gratitude often engenders loving feelings.

4 Talking about feelings through drawing, play, sandplay, and stories

"I knew that's what I felt, but it was vague and confusing until I did a drawing of it."   Ebele, 12

Everyday language is not the natural language of feeling for children. Their natural language is that of image and metaphor, as evidenced in their love of stories and make-believe play. When, as adults, we attempt to connect with them using everyday language, it may not work. Everyday words may not be enough to get to the heart of the matter. Because of this 'language problem', many children/teenagers fail to get the help with their painful life experiences that they often desperately need.

If we want to reach out to children and teenagers and motivate them to speak freely, we are far more likely to be successful if we do it through 'their' language. Thinking and using everyday language can and needs to follow, as we help the child reflect on what's happening and how he or she is feeling. But for many children, it cannot be our starting point

In this section, I'll cover key tools and ways of being with children that can unleash the healing powers of image, art and metaphor. I'll look at the play techniques that can enable even very young children to convey the subtleties and complexities of key emotional experiences in their life. I'll explore how both art and play can offer the protection of indirect expression, via, for example,

"It's not me who feels this, it's the pig in my drawing". I'll show how working in metaphor supports even the most defended child/teenager to explore their experiences when otherwise they might avoid or deny. I'll start with a chapter on how to use puppets and sandplay: then I'll give you 20 key strategies for this kind of work, including enactments (*all the strategies are listed for quick reference opposite)*: and then I'll talk about storytelling.

Overall, I want to demonstrate the healing process that is made possible from communication through art and play: the capacity for reflection that a child or young person can develop, in place of previous primitive emotional discharge through challenging behavior: the relief she may gain when sharing what she has been dealing with all on her own, for too long: and the often profound insight she can have, born out of creative imagination.

Some adults may have been put off using art and play with children, feeling that 'they've never been good at art' and wouldn't know what to do. My aim is to show that you don't have to be good at art in the slightest. If you are warm and playful and empathic, the child's imagination will flow, and all you need to know is how to respond to the child when she does!

Through reading this section, I hope you'll be feeling inspired to try using many different kinds of creative media, and also to find your own materials. I hope you'll also discover that such interventions are indeed some of the richest and most direct roads to the creative unconscious needed for healing.

Creative Techniques

1	Following the child's focus, not your own	231
2	Commenting on what is absent in the child's play, as well as what is present	233
3	Talking directly to a character in the child's drawing or play	236
4	Identification - asking the child to speak as one of their play or art images	238
5	Dialoguing - getting two or more people/images in the child's play to communicate with each other	245
6	Finding out who's who in the child's play, and what they're like	248
7	The 'Nosy Seagull' technique	251
8	Dealing with a flood of images, and deciding which of them to work with	252
9	*"What would happen next?"*	254
10	Not rushing on - allowing space	256
11	When there's lots of action - building in reflection time	256
12	Asking for a title	257
13	Directive use of drawing, play and sandplay	258
14	On not pressing for happy endings	260
15	Knowing when to invite potency and protest	262
16	Rehearsal of the possible	266
17	*"Do it"*	268
18	Working with the 'eleventh hour' happening	270
19	When the child keeps repeating the same play story week after week	272
20	Enactments	274

Chapter 9:   Using puppets and sandplay to ease conversation

1   Helping children speak about feelings through puppets

Puppets in action

The particular therapeutic potential of puppetry

Working with puppets is ideal for circumventing a child's reluctance to speak about feelings. Puppets offer children and young people sufficient psychological safety through disguise and distance. As a result, many children find themselves able to speak more spontaneously and freely than they would be able to without a puppet on their hand. They are given a protective sense of *"It is not me speaking, it's the puppet!"* This is similar to - *"It's not me, it's the role I'm playing,"* in enactment. And yet the little characters created when animated are very real. It is easy to suspend disbelief both for the child and the spectator.

Through the use of puppets, the listening adult can give the child the powerful experience of having an audience, witnessing, sometimes, vitally important emotional statements about key interactions with key people in their life. Importantly too, through puppets, children can convey their feelings about the emotional energy states of significant people in their past or present.

> There is no doubt that gross events - such as births, death ..., the break-ups of families, the child's prolonged separations from the significant adults ... and so on, can play an important role in the factors that lead to later psychological illness. But clinical experience tells us that in the great majority of cases it is the specific pathogenic personality of the parent(s) and specific pathogenic features of the atmosphere in which the child grows up that account for the mal-developments, fixations and unsolvable inner conflicts. Kohut 1977, p.187

What using puppets can convey

i *Mood states*

By using puppets to show particular movement, gestures and energies, children can convey the moods of key figures in their life,which have really impacted them. **Rueben (8)**, for example, conveyed his father's depressed mood through a dog puppet's droopy arms, hanging head, and slow, lifeless movement. It was clearly cathartic for him to show me what he was living with day in day out. **Chrysta (14)** had a parent who suffered from panic attacks and phobias. She picked a meerkat puppet and used it with sharp and jagged movements, arms and head rigidly held. The meerkat swooped down on other little puppet people and insisted on making them stand correctly and be tidy. I empathised with the little puppet people that meerkat's actions perhaps made them feel tensed up and tidied away at times, just when they wanted to be free and play.

ii *A child's feelings about key relationships in his or her life*

A child might play out her relationship with a frightening teacher, with a needy parent, or two arguing parents, or with a bullying sibling. She can play out key interactions, superficial, conflictual, anguished, failed connections and misconnections, or indeed, loving tender connections.

iii *The qualities and energies of specific self-states*

Through puppets, a child might need to show you her really frightened self, or her hopeless defeated self: a harsh inner critic, a be-positive-best-foot-forward self. These can be very hard to put into words. Puppets can reveal so much in terms of how they move, speak, listen, relate, and use silence.

iv *Aspects of self in conflict with other aspects of self*

These aspects of the self can then dialogue with each other, using two or more puppets. For example, **Leon** suffered from chronic low self-esteem. He had very strict and blaming parenting. Using puppets, he chose to enact the following conversation:

- his 'weak' self, arguing with his 'strong' self
- his 'persevering' self in conflict with his 'defeated and shamed' self
- his 'self-blaming' self arguing with his 'put-down' self

> **Self-blaming self/Critic:** *You're so stupid for doing that.*
> *You make such a mess of everything.*
> **Put-down self:** *Yes but look, I am trying.*

The adult, whilst hearing both sides, can join in with a voice, 'with playfulness, acceptance, curiosity and empathy' (Hughes, 2009) (*and see this book,* p.236) and psycho-education.

In addition to all the above, through puppets the child can play out key relational moments in his life; the time when Mum announced she was splitting up from Dad, a betrayal, the time the Head teacher shamed the child is assembly in front of everyone, and so on.

What you need when using puppets in therapeutic conversations

A range of puppets. Ones with moving mouths are by far the best.

- *Mythical characters: dragons, witch, unicorn*
- *Monsters*
- *Defenceless animals: lamb, baby pig*
- *Animals who can be powerful and/or attacking: lion, crocodile*
- *People: range of professions relevant to children, for example teacher, lollipop lady, police, and fire person*
- *Family members: Mums, Dads, Grandma, Grandpa, other adults, boy child, girl child, baby*

How to work with puppets

i *Working indirectly*

You can work indirectly, not referring to the child's life. If this is how you decide to start, simply ask the child to choose a puppet or puppets and play with them or speak as them, or create a spontaneous play. If you have a puppet theatre, you can offer this. They will soon get the hang of it. Or they may initiate such play themselves. You can then begin to relate to the puppet(s) in terms of what the puppet/s say or do.

ii *Working directly: structured tasks*

Ask the child to pick puppets to represent people who have been important in his life (either for bad or good reasons). Ask the child to speak as that puppet on its own, or to another puppet who represents himself. **Thomas**, for example wanted to use Mr Fox to represent grandfather. I interviewed Mr Fox, asking him why he never smiled (Thomas' grandfather often had a very still face). Thomas found it a great relief to explore different reasons and came to believe that his grandfather's apparent lack of warmth wasn't something to do with him being bad, but more about how his grandfather was feeling.

Ask the child to enact a familiar conversation between two or more characters (for example, a typical row with Mum, if that's the current issue). Find out about who the person or character is. Give each character equal airtime. Be like a couple's therapist! After a dialogue of conflictual exchanges between two puppets, summarise the feelings and thoughts of each character and feed that back to them. Then a good question can be, "*If you had three wishes of the other character, what would your wishes be?*"

You can then move from asking the puppets to talk to each other, to you talking to them individually. Ask them how they are feeling and encourage them both to really express their needs clearly. After this, ask the child to put the puppets down in front of you both and still facing you, then summarise with empathy what has happened.

This will enable the child to stand back from a painful relational experience in their life and really clarify their thoughts, why something really matters to them, really gets to them, really hurts them. It can also be another route to 'rehearsal of the possible', helping children consider any action or conversation they may want to initiate with a person in their life with whom they are having the conflict.

Sometimes this exercise can end up with you asking the child if they want you to ask the other person (for example, Mum) into the next talk-time together. The child may be so relieved to have a referee, as it takes courage to face a 'big person' and sometimes a 'controlling or even frightening big person' on your own. In the meeting you can do some conflict resolution for real, and model how to do it into the bargain!

Another way of helping a child or young person think about feelings is to ask them to choose a puppet to be an emotion they have frequently and call it that emotion, such as Mr Sad, Mr Angry, Miss Frustrated (the child can choose the gender). You can then interview the puppet, using the kind of questions I suggest for talking with an image (p.240)

Mr Angry and Mr Sad

Adult: *Hello Mr Angry … What is life like for you? What do you need?*
(*and so on*)

Telling the puppet something as a way of getting the child to hear it

One way of getting a child to hear something is to tell it to someone else, and who better to do this than a puppet, who can whisper things back in your ear? So with **Charlotte (6)**, who finds me just too big and bold, I do a lot of the therapeutic communication and empathy through a chimp puppet called Dexter who has a wonderful moveable mouth.

> **Margot:** *What's that Dexter? (Dexter whispers in my ear) Oh you are saying Charlotte has had a too difficult time in her life with no-one helping her? (Dexter nods) Yes you are right.*
>
> **Dexter:** *(whispering in Margot's ear again) Oh OK Dexter, you say you feel so cross and sad that she had to deal with all that frightening stuff with her mummy and look after her baby brother at the same time and that she was just a little girl.*
>
> **Dexter:** *(nodding and whispering again) You want to say to Charlotte you are so sorry that all that happened to her?*
>
> **Margot:** *(to Charlotte) Charlotte, Dexter wants to say he's really sorry about what happened to you and that things have been so hard for you sometimes (Dexter whispers again)*
>
> **Margo:** *You want me to ask Charlotte if you could give her a cuddle?*
>
> **Margot:** *(to Charlotte) Is that OK, Charlotte? (Charlotte nods. Dexter gives Charlotte a cuddle)*

Processing puppet work

Whether you are working directly or indirectly, after the enactment, always lay the puppets down and sit slightly away from them. This is to make a clear differentiation between the enactment time and space, and the reflecting time and space. You might start by doing a Big Empathy Drawing so that you can show the child what you have understood about what they conveyed through the enactment. And remember, always encourage the child to change your drawing until it is right for her. This is the route to the co-created empathy we have talked about before. (*See* p.392 *for puppet play in schools*).

2 Helping a child to talk about feelings through sandplay

The particular therapeutic potential of sandplay

Sandplay is an incredible technique for helping children to speak about feelings. It was first devised by Margaret Lowenfeld in 1927 and was initially taught at the Institute of Child Psychology from 1931. Sandplay enables children to convey complex emotional experiences, self-states and sense impressions, and to present an in-depth multi-sensorial view of key aspects of their inner and outer world all at the same time.

Benefits of using sandplay to enable children/young people to speak about feelings

✔ Through sandplay, the child can convey multiple meanings and different aspects of the same experience simultaneously. He can, for example, convey feelings about 'my father' and show many different aspects, different feelings, different personal meanings of 'father' all at the same time.

✔ Through the molding and shaping of the wet sand, the child can convey the terrains of his emotional 'landscapes'.

✔ Through sandplay, the child can convey the feeling tone of his inner world of thoughts, feelings and perceptions, with exactitude, through the complex relation of forms, the moulding and shaping of the sand, the choice of the miniatures, in terms of their size, body build, colour, their positioning and placing, and distance from each other in the sandtray.

✔ A sand picture also provides you with a very clear view of the child's perception of himself/others/life in general. You can really imagine yourself into his view of the world. Looking at the sandplay world, you can ask yourself, what would it be like for me to be in this world? For example, a world where everyone is looking away from everyone else, or a world where there are lots of critical faces.

✔ The sandplay technique can offer a real sense of safety. This is because few children/teenagers have negative associations around playing in the sand, as opposed to, say, bad school experiences with music or art.

✔ Unlike painting, the miniatures are easily moveable, so the child or young person can re-arrange them, try out all different placings, add things, take things out, until he is satisfied that he has 'said' in the sand what he wants to 'say'. He can try out different things, study them visually, rehearse different endings, or solutions. To play out one's problems rather than just talking about them can be extremely fruitful, in bringing about remarkable changes often in a short amount of time. The powerful change process however, will only happen when sandplay is done by the child with a real sense of thought and contemplation, as opposed to just plonking miniatures in the sand tray over a few minutes. The level of absorption is tangible in the former and clearly absent in the latter.

How it works

Children choose from a whole range of miniature objects (usually a mix of small toys and little ornaments) which, ideally, are arranged in categories on shelves, although you can produce a jumble from your bag and just spread them on the floor (standing them up) if you're working in a more ad hoc setting. The child is then asked to place the objects of their choice in the sandbox, either in free play or in response to a specific suggestion from the person working with her (*see* p.299).

What you need

The important thing is to have some miniatures from each of the following categories:

- *People figures: angry, cruel figures as well as figures who are stereotypically warm, kind, concerned*
- *Family members: Dads, Mums, children, Granpa, Grandma, siblings, babies, and others as appropriate to the child*
- *Professional people: policeman, doctor, fireman, lollipop lady, teacher, farmer and so on. Human figures should be in a range of different ethnicities and nationalities in terms of skin colour, features and dress*
- *Monsters*
- *Mythical characters: for example, wizard, fairy, witch, unicorn*
- *Animals: Farmyard and jungle*
- *Dinosaurs*
- *Buildings: houses, school, barn, prison, castle, church, mosque, tower block, palace, park and so on*
- *Transport: train, aeroplane, boat, car, bus, truck (including emergency service vehicles)*
- *Furniture*
- *Food (a variety)*
- *Treasure/coins*
- *Nature: trees, flowers, hedge, stones, shells*
- *Outside man-made: gate, fence, road, tower, lighthouse*

Sandplay is also known as the 'world technique', so the best thing is to have objects which represent most things in the world (*see* Lowenfeld 1991 *for much more on sandplay therapy*). This is a tall order, and you can get completely addicted to car boot sales for a while. Having said that, children and teenagers often produce amazing things if you have limited resources, for example, only 30 items, as long as they cover a range of categories.

In an ideal world you'd have two sandtrays, one with wet sand and one with dry sand. A sandbox is usually about 23 x 29 x 3 inches (*57 x 72 x 7 cm*). Any smaller, and it is hard for a child to represent a complex psychological landscape. The box should be painted blue on the bottom to represent water. Children often use the sandbox as their theatre or film set. Another great thing about sand is that things can stand up in it, thereby giving an immediate 3D environment. Things can be hidden, exposed, camouflaged and so on. Wet sand can easily be used to make structures, buildings, caves and so on, forming any landscape/backdrop for the miniatures chosen.

How to introduce a child to sandplay

Show the child the miniatures and the sandbox. Put your hands in the sandbox and show the blue on the bottom, telling her that it can represent water. Demonstrate how you can wet the sand, then mould it into a building, a wall, a dam and so on, so that you create a setting. Show her how you can then put miniatures in the setting to make up a story, or a play or a film set. The miniatures are easily moveable so the child/teenager can rearrange them, try out different placings, add things or take things out, until they are entirely satisfied that they have conveyed exactly what they want to. This is a non-directive use of sandplay, rather like 'free association' in psychoanalysis. Sandplay can also be used in a more directed way. Some children find a clear instruction (such as one of these below) makes them feel safer than the open-ended instruction of, "*Make a picture, anything you like.*"

Introducing a teenager to sandplay: *"I'm not playing with toys. That's for little kids."*

The initial response of teenagers can be one of *"I don't want to play with toys."* So we need to be very careful to say that the objects might look like toys but they are actually symbols, in other words, they can be used to stand for something: for example, *"Someone might pick this dragon to stand for his anger, or this chipmunk for his fearful part."* I have never had a teenager not work in sandplay after this explanation.

How to respond to a child's sandplay

Think about the inner world being represented in the sand. Instead of getting hooked on detail, think what you would feel like if you lived in a psychological landscape like this for a day. Is it, for example, a very unsafe world, unpredictable, confusing? Or is it a mixed place with aspects of real human warmth, but with aspects of human coldness as well? Is it a place of unthinking cruelty? Or a place where things are very wobbly and fragile? Are there lots of contrasts? There will probably be some aspects and details of the child's sandplay world that we may never understand, but that doesn't matter. What matters is that we are able to grasp and empathise with the central emotional themes the child is trying to convey.

Leon (*see* p.217) had two shouty parents, who would not tolerate anything less than 100% compliance. As a result, Leon was a far too good child. He did this sandplay, a psychological landscape of domination. He used it to make a story about being attacked by every sort of monster and fierce animal, who are also attacking each other. Leon said, *"If you were there you wouldn't survive."*

Richard (13) lived in care. When he was 11, his Mum said she couldn't manage him anymore. He was heartbroken and often ran away from his foster placement to hide in the garden and gaze at his mum as she did the washing up (he could see her through the window). On one occasion, he ran away and was

Leon's sandplay

found several hundreds of miles further north - he was extremely clever at getting himself around the UK! He did this sandplay of himself sleeping in a graveyard, a psychological landscape of desolation and abandonment. When asked why, he said, *"Because for my mum I may as well be dead."*

Richard's sandplay

When planning your empathic response, notice what is absent in the sand picture as well as what is present. For example in Leon's and Richard's pictures there is an absence of human warmth, of home, comfort, safe shelter, of any helping figures. Comment on such absences (*and see commenting on absences* p. 233).

Sadly, these heart-breaking sandplays are typical of children whose parents have not been good at loving children, as their parents weren't good at loving them when they were children. But one of the advantages of using sandplay is that this awful impoverishment becomes so apparent. This means that the child need no longer be left so unbearably alone with it all. Now your acknowledgement, empathy, attunement and correction of any "*It's all my fault*" myths are part of the healing process.

As a result of your therapeutic response, it is amazing to see how the sandplays of such children start to change. Because of your response, their inner world begins to feel a warmer, kinder place, and their sandplays begin to reflect this too. Often where before there was just desert, now there are things growing. Where before there was just death and war, now there are ambulances and nurses. Where before there was utter chaos, now there is some degree of order. It is a sobering reminder that unless we are social workers, we cannot change the child or young person's outer world: but we can help them change their inner world of thoughts, sensations, self-talk and images, to a warmer, kinder, richer place.

The 'Line down the Middle' exercise

(Adapted from '101 Play Therapy Techniques' Kaduson & Schaefer 1997, p.100-2)

Start by saying to the child: *"Make a line down the middle of your sandtray, and show one of these each side."*

Your hopes	Your fears
A loveliest day in your life	A horrible day in your life
Your biggest losses	Your biggest gains
Happy for you	Sad for you
Memory of a horrid alone time	Memory of a lovely together time
Good things about my Dad	Difficult things about my Dad
(or Mum, or other significant	(or Mum, or other significant
people in the child's life)	people in the child's life)

In the same way, the theme of 'before and after' can be played out on either side of a sandtray line.

Before Mum	After Mum
and your Stepdad got married	and your Stepdad got married
Before new baby was born	After new baby was born
Before you went to the new school	After you went to the new school
Before Mum took drugs	After Mum took drugs

Obviously these are just examples. Choose a 'before or after' that is relevant for the child or teenager with whom you are working (the 'line down the middle' work can also be done using paper and crayons).

3 Helping children with feelings in other media

And of course as well as puppetry and sandplay, you can also use clay, painting, drawing, enactment, play dough and so on. *You can use your own imagination to extend your range of options.* So to finish, here are just a couple of examples of what sorts of conversations you can have with a child using other media ...

◆ Make all your family members in clay. Then talk to each one in turn.
   "What I like about you is ..."
   "What I find difficult about you is ..."

◆ Make a figure in clay of someone you don't like.

◆ Make a figure in clay of what it feels like to be you when you are feeling good about yourself.

◆ Make a figure in clay of what it feels like to be you when you are feeling bad about yourself.

◆ Draw or make in clay your family as animals.

◆ Using clay and miniature figures, make a place that feels unsafe for you and a place that feels really safe.

◆ ... other ideas?

Chapter 10: Twenty creative techniques to use in conversations that matter

TECHNIQUE 1: Following the child's focus, not your own

When a child has made an amazing image in play, sandplay, clay and so on, it may be tempting for you to draw attention to the images in the picture/sandplay that interest you, perhaps because they seem to be very strong emotional statements, or simply because they arouse your curiosity. But in so doing, you may be failing to follow the child's own focus. The following, is an example of this common pitfall.

Dan (6) suffered years of sibling verbal abuse at the hands of his older sister. When he went to his parents about it, they dismissed it as attention-seeking and just said he needed to learn to stand up for himself. In fact, sibling verbal abuse is far from 'just attention-seeking'; whether it's loud rants, sarcasm, or put-downs, they all have the corrosive effect Teicher et al (2011) describe (and *see* p.40).

✗ Unempathic response

Dan: *In my drawing, the fox is eating the chickens.*

Martina: *Hmm. I'm interested in the pink pudding you've drawn in the corner of your picture. Tell me about that?*

Martina has let her own curiosity interrupt where the child is. This gives the message to the child, *"I'm not really interested in what you are saying about the fox and the chickens"*.

✔ Instead …

Martina: *Would you help me to understand what that is like for the chickens? (Stage 2: Empathic Listening: see p. 52)*

Dan: *The chickens have been scared of the fox all their lives, and so when the fox finally gets them, they felt terrified But they knew it would happen one day.*

Think about the emotional themes common to the child's play story and life story.

✔ Instead …

Martina: *(sticking to indisputable facts about the drawing) So, in your drawing, there is no-one helping the chickens, no kindness, no safety - so alone, so scared.*

or

Martina: *How dreadful to live with that level of fear, and no-one helping to make the world safe for them.*

TECHNIQUE 2:   Comment on what is absent in the child's play, as well as what is present

This technique can be used when there is a very clear tie-up between 'the psychological landscape' of the child's life story and the psychological landscape of play story.

a. *Their life has included significant loss and/or relational poverty and their art or play image is desolate and barren*

b. *Their life has been full of conflict and arguing and their art or play image is full of fighting, aggression and persecution*

c. *Their life is chaotic and their art or play image is of a confused, upside-down world*

In your imagining into the child's world, as depicted in their sandplay or drawing, comment on what is absent, as well as what is present. Consideration of what is *not* there in the child's depiction of a psychological landscape can be as important as what is there. There is no danger of inferring meaning, as you are commenting on indisputable facts about the child's image. Here are some common absences which often seem to appear in drawings and sandplay of children who have known significant relational stress of some kind. The absences you may comment on might be:

* Absence of safety
* Absence of home
* Absence of warm, caring people
* Absence of kindness
* Absence of gentleness
* Absence of anyone helping
* Absence of comfort
* Absence of friends
* Absence of togetherness
* Absence of potent protectors
* Absence of any warm human connection between the two characters

Here are some examples of such worlds and how you might comment on absences.

a) Persecutory worlds

Craig (10) had witnessed parental violence on several occasions. He made a sandplay image. He gives it a title: *Mess of hate and scream.*

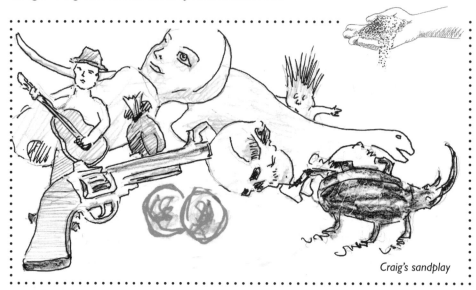

Craig's sandplay

Here is what you might say in response to Craig's sandplay, which really would be a direct comment about his life as well. This is not about putting words into his mouth or inferring meaning: it is speaking about indisputable facts about the picture and the truth about his life (as verified by Craig in his first session with the adult). And Craig can choose to respond, or not.

> **Adult:** *And in your sand play I see that there is*
> *No-one helping*
> *No safety*
> *No kindness*
> *Nobody who is understanding*

b) Bleak worlds

Rachel (14) was emotionally abused by her stepfather. Despite this she loved him. He then walked out on Rachel's mother, and Rachel had to care for her younger siblings. It is easy to see, in her sandplay picture, these key traumatic life events.

66

Rachel: *The cockerel pecks the child and then leaves her for dead*

99

Rachel's sandplay

So here the adult comments on the absences in Rachel's picture:

66

Adult: *So in your picture, there are no warm, caring people to help the child.*

Rachel: (passionately) *Duh, you think? There never is, there never was.*

Adult: (after a short pause: gently) *Too alone, too unhelped.*

99

TECHNIQUE 3: Talking directly to a character in the child's drawing or play

When a child engages in imaginary play, the characters he or she depicts are often key aspects of self and/or key aspects of important people in his life, past or present. So if the adult interviews a character/s in the child's play, it can heighten the child's awareness of particular 'self-states' and/or help the child to reflect on their feelings towards key figures in their life. Furthermore, interviewing a child's image from their play or painting can show the child that you are really interested in what they are doing, and so heighten their sense of psychological safety with you. Also, making this connection is really useful if you are unclear about the child's meaning of an image they have drawn or played out. Hence, at times, interviewing one of the child's images with open-ended questions is appropriate, before coming in with your empathic response. Without interviewing, you simply may not have enough information to offer the child an accurate empathic response.

Dragon down the toilet

> **Child:** *I've drawn a dragon down a toilet.*
>
> **Adult:** (looking directly at the dragon) *Hi dragon, how does it feel at the bottom of the toilet?*

Once you have interviewed/talked directly to a character in the child's drawing or play, based on what the child says, you can then offer empathy.

Esther (8) was adopted after three years of neglect with her substance-abusing parents. Esther draws a lovely bright baby bird who she says fell into a too silent hole in the ground and no-one heard its cries. The adult interviews the baby bird. Here is the child's response and the adult's empathy that follows:

> **Esther:** *He nearly dies because he is so lonely.*
>
> **Adult:** (talking directly to the lovely bird in Esther's picture) *I'm so sorry lovely bright bird that you have known this silent people-less world so early in your life, and no-one helped when you so needed them to.*

Through the protection of the metaphor, the adult is referring to the child's experience of relational poverty.

TECHNIQUE 4: Identification - asking the child to speak as one of their play or art images

When a child has emotional 'charge' (strong feeling) around a particular image or character in their play or art, ask them to imagine *into* the image and speak *as* the image. This process is called identification. Identification helps children really enter into the feel of their images, emotionally engaging with them rather than just *talking about* them. Speaking as their image or a character in their play bypasses the censoring, over-rationalising part of the brain, and helps transport the child firmly into the realm of imagination and feeling. It often helps them reach a far deeper level of clarity and truth. Of course very young children tend to do this in their imaginary play without needing to be asked!

> I asked Billy to stand up and imagine that he was the volcano and to tell me about himself. *"Pretend to be the volcano, be its voice.* Start by saying, *"I am a volcano ..."* So Billy said, *"I am a volcano."* To my questions he added, *"I have hot lava inside me. I haven't erupted yet, but I will ..."* I then asked Billy to paint a picture of what he thought his anger looked like. He painted a large, thick red circle with various colours inside the circle [and said], *"This is Billy's anger inside his stomach ... I get mad when my sister messes up my room and when I get in fights, and when I fall off my bike."*　　　　Oaklander 2006, pp.84-5

You can even help a child find meaning in a seemingly random painting by 'interviewing' the shapes and the lines.

Alfie (8) had a very intrusive mother. Ken, a teaching assistant is sitting with Alfie as he does a painting. Ken knows that Alfie needs the safety of indirect expression. After Alfie has finished, the following conversation begins.

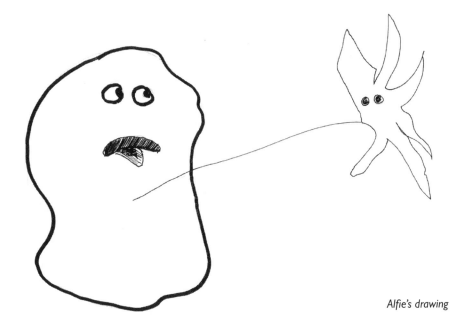

Alfie's drawing

Ken: *Tell me about your painting*

Alfie: *The red line is crashing into the blue blob.*

Ken: *How does the blue blob feel about that?*

or

Ken: *I'm wondering, what's making the red line crash into things?*

or

Ken: *If it could talk, what would the blue blob say to the red line about being crashed into? (use of identification)*

Alfie: *(responds best to the latter) You always interfere. You always barge in.*

Ken: *Blue blob, how do you feel now you've told the red line about how it interferes and barges in?*

Alfie: *About time!*

(i) *Good 'interview' questions for identification*

Once the child is readily telling you about a character's experiences (even when the character is a blob or a line, as above), you can ask her to use *"I"*, not *"it"* in her reply. This deepens the child's emotional engagement. Here are some good interviewing questions to choose from which you can put to a central, emotionally charged figure in a drawing, or to an object. Importantly, and as a way of continuing to give the child the protection of distance, all these questions are addressed to the child's image, not the child. So make sure you look at the image, and not the child, when you interview.

Adult: *Hi Cornflake Packet in Nathan's picture ...*

What is life like for you?	*What frightens you?*
What do you need?	*What threatens you?*
What are you feeling at the moment?	*What pleases you?*
How do you feel about your life?	*What is the best thing about your life?*
What do you want from life?	*What is the worst thing about your life?*
How do you feel about your size?	*What or who do you like/love?*
(if this seems like a relevant issue)	*What or who do you dislike/hate?*
What do you like to do most in the world?	*What are your innermost secrets?*
What do you like to do least in the world?	
What do you dream about doing with your life?	

Obviously you wouldn't ask all of these! Otherwise, likely as not, the child would feel bombarded and invaded. The list is just to give you a sense of the range of possible questions. Just use the ones most relevant to the child's image and issues. Also remember, these are just sample questions. Each question can lead to further development. At the end of the interview, offer an empathic summary to process the reflection (*see* p.182).

'**Child:** *There's a big bad hand in the swamp, squashing all the little elves until they hurt like crazy.* "

The squashing of the elves.

When we don't have much experience, we may rather naively assume that the Big Bad Hand is an abusing figure in the child's life, when the hand could just as easily symbolise the child's own raging or destructive feelings. Our idea may be completely inaccurate. So there's the need for appropriate enquiry and curiosity into what the images might mean to the child, to avoid inaccurate interpretation. It's important not to imagine we can 'intuit' or mind-read what's happening - it can be dangerous; hence the need for this interview technique. If you are at all unsure of the meaning for the child, ask only open-ended questions.

> **Adult:** *Hello Big Bad Hand, what is it like to be you?*
>
> *or*
>
> **Adult:** *What do you feel about being in this swamp?*
>
> *or*
>
> **Adult:** *What makes you want to squash the little elves, until they hurt like crazy?*
>
> Then the adult can interview the elves:
>
> **Adult:** *Hi there little elves, what is it like for you being in the swamp with the Big Bad Hand?*

Sammi, (8) lost her mother, who had died after a prolonged illness. In this talking session, Sammi has drawn a little flame, flickering in a dark empty room (her words). In this example, Mark has the sense that Sammi is ready to identify with the flame and no longer needs to refer to the flame as 'it'.

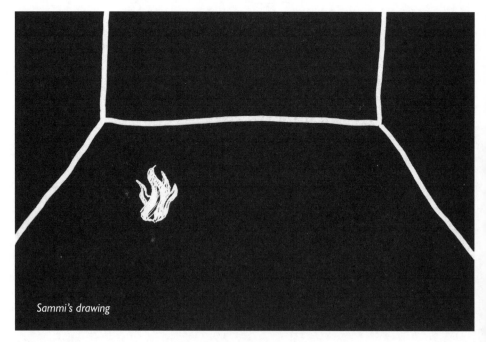

Sammi's drawing

242

> **Mark:** So, little flame, tell me about yourself. Will you finish this sentence? -"I am a little flame and what I feel is, or what I need is ..."
>
> **Sammi:** I'm a little flame, and I need a safe shelter otherwise a gust of cold wind through the open window could blow me out - so easily.
>
> **Mark:** What would it feel like if you were blown out?
>
> **Sammi:** Like the world had gone totally dark, like the world has lost its light and warmth forever.
>
> **Mark:** What might happen then?
>
> **Sammi:** I would live in a dark, dark world, alone in a dark, dark room for the rest of my life.

Sammi is talking most eloquently about her sense of absolute bleakness, desolation after Mum died and her despair of ever finding a warmer brighter world again. Mark can now - and only now - after having understood Sammi's meaning of the flame (as opposed to dangerously mindreading what it meant for Sammi, as he had previously!) move on to empathise with Sammi's feelings. He stays in indirect expression, knowing that Sammi still finds it too difficult if he refers to actual events in her life.

> **Mark:** (to the drawing, and very much holding in mind Sammi's pain at missing her mother): Wow, little flame. How painful and frightening to be in this world where you feel your own light could go out so quickly and you would be plunged into such terrible darkness.

243

A little later, Mark might make a comment like this:

> **Mark:** (to Sammi, about the flame, again speaking indirectly about Sammi losing her mother): *I guess right now the little flame doesn't know that even when the worst thing in the world happens there are always people who can come and warm the room again and make the sun shine through the window, when the flame is ready to see it.*

Here Mark is providing the psychological message that the world does indeed go cold and bleak when you lose someone you love, but that there are always warm and caring adults in the world who can help children heal their pain. Mark is not rushing into happy endings, but simply planting a seed of hope for Sammi that there is an 'around the corner', and she does not need to grieve on her own.

It's important that we avoid getting into a long apologetic request to interview a child's image. In other words, don't say something like this:

> **Adult:** *It's useful for us to learn more about the little flame in your picture. I wonder if you would be prepared to enter into this image more, to identify with it, and for me to interview the flame?*

or

> **Adult:** *Would you mind, I mean I think it would be a good idea if you try to be the flame in your picture and then what I'll do, if it's OK by you, is to interview the little flame?*

Instead, just say confidently to the child, *"Be the little flame in your picture. Can you finish the sentence, "I am the little flame and what I feel is ..." ?"* If the child lapses and say *"it"*, gently guide them back to *"I"*. However, if your instruction is clearly dysregulating the child, don't insist: the child may be showing through his or her unwillingness to say *"I"* that this degree of identification is too much, too soon. Saying *"I"* when the time is right will show that the child's emotional engagement is deepening.

TECHNIQUE 5: Dialoguing - getting two or more people/images in the child's play to communicate with each other

Dialoguing is where two or more images or characters in a child's picture or play story clearly have an important relationship or connection (either conflictual or supportive), and you ask the child to get them to converse or 'dialogue' with each other. This is a way of deepening awareness about self and others, often to the point of resolution and/or action for change.

In their play stories, younger children will often tend to enact a conversation with two images or characters who are connected in some way without any prompting from you, and will give a natural running commentary about events!

Jake (9) repeatedly witnessed his father issuing painful put-downs to his mother. So in his play he is conveying, through dialoguing, the awful dominance/submission interactions he has seen. In his play, the big lorry comes and goes crash, crash into the little car.

> **Little car:** *Help help!*
>
> **Big lorry:** *I'm going to smack right into you. You deserve to get smashed up, you are such a wimp of a car.*
>
> **Little car:** *You are right, I'm just a silly little wimp of a car. I can't help it. People always say that to me.*

Older children may need supporting to enact a dialogue between important images or characters that they have presented as being in some kind of relationship. Asking them to enact a conversation between the two can reveal the deeper meaning when, for example, a monster is frightening a squirrel. The adult could ask: *"Would you be the squirrel, and talk to the monster?"* Or offering the 'unfinished sentence' technique (*see* p. 175), *"So, as the squirrel, could you finish the sentence, "What I feel about you, monster, is ... "?"* Then the adult can invite the child to switch, and ask him to be the monster and talk back to the squirrel and so on, back and forth in conversation. It's important to be aware that these two characters may be different aspects of the child, different self-states or sub-personalities, or they might be two different people in his life. We can't know until the child makes it clear.

Ella (9) has drawn a little crushed ladybird under someone's big foot. This is clearly a portrayal of an important conflictual connection.

Ella's drawing

> **Jenny:** OK Ella, be the ladybird and talk to the big foot. Can you finish the sentence: "I am ladybird, and what I feel about you, foot is ... ?"
>
> **Ella:** I am sick of being trodden on by you.
>
> **Jenny:** OK foot, what do you want to say back?
>
> **Ella:** I am a bully and so I go around just stamping on people's feelings
>
> **Jenny:** So ladybird, what do you feel when foot says to you he is a bully and that's what he does.
>
> **Ella:** Very cross.
>
> **Jenny:** Tell him.
>
> **Ella:** You are so unkind. You do not know about gentle. I can never love you, you don't see this. You want me to love you, but how can I? (Ella has tears in her eyes)

After Ella has dialogued in this way, Jenny remembers that Ella has spoken previously about how her father often shouts at her, particularly when he's had too much to drink. Jenny doesn't refer Ella to this reality. She recognises Ella's need for the protection of the metaphor, so empathises, using indirect expression, with Ella's feelings of ambivalence towards her father.

> **Jenny:** Yes, it is never right that big feet hurt little ladybirds. I understand that it can kill off love and respect.

After this session, however, Ella starts to talk more openly about her father. As a result, Jenny asks Ella if she would like help to speak with her father. Ella said she would. Jenny helps Ella to say to her father that she finds his shouting after drinking really awful.

A word of caution, however, about using 'dialoguing' as a technique. If a child is already feeling something very strongly and vividly with an image or story they have created, using 'dialoguing' and identification would be inappropriate and an interruption to the child. This is because 'dialoguing' and identification are an aid to help the child go deeper into their imagination. If they are already there, they don't need this kind of support.

TECHNIQUE 6: Finding out who's who in the child's play, and what they're like

We need to stay open-minded about who the 'goodies' and 'baddies' are in a child's play story. Some children's play stories are very clear in terms of who the bad guys are and who the good guys are, and which characters represent the child and which represent other people in her life. Other stories are not clear at all about any of these things.

A persecutory figure in a child's play story is not necessarily someone the child is frightened of. It could be an image of the child's feelings of rage, her wish for revenge or something else. Similarly, we can't assume that just because there is a small child and a big monster in a child's story, the child is identifying with the small child. Lots of children, for example, have nightmares of monsters on the day they have had a temper tantrum or furious outburst, because in a state of intense rage, they can feel they are a monster. It is also very common for children with depressed or exhausted mothers to tell a story in which the 'little hen', 'little duck' or the 'little cow' is attacked by a bad monster. The bad monster may be a symbol of the child's anger towards her 'emotionally fading' or less lively mother. Alternatively, the child may fear that her anger and/or frustration about what is happening might damage or destroy a 'weak' parent.

So we need to find out. This is a way you can get the child's meaning rather than projecting your own meaning.

When Dan was born, (*see above* p.231) his older sister Joanne, then aged ten, had hated the fact that her Mum had this lovely little baby. Joanne called Dan awful names and told him time and time again that he was ugly and stupid and smelly, so much so that Dan developed a stutter. Dan did a sandplay about a woman being attacked by monsters while lying on a grave.

Dan's sandplay

So who is who? Is Dan conveying what he would like to do to his sister, namely kill her off and then still attack her with monsters, or is he conveying what it felt like being with his frightening sister? It could be either, or both. Freud talked about 'condensation', meaning that in dreams, a single character could be 'a plurality of people' and one place could be 'a plurality of places'. So this story may be a 'condensed' image of Dan's feelings about the cruelty he experienced and his expression of rage at that cruelty. Without asking Dan for his meaning of the picture, we will never know.

So here's what to do. You can ask Dan overtly, "*Who is good and who is bad in your picture?*" or, "*Do you think the woman deserved such an attack?*". Or you can interview one of the characters:

249

> **Martina:** *Hello monsters ... tell me what you want to do.*
>
> **Dan:** *I want to tear the woman's body into a thousand pieces.*
>
> **Martina:** *Because...?*
>
> **Dan:** *Ever since I was a baby she made my life a misery.*
>
> **Martina:** *And that makes you feel ... ?*
>
> **Dan:** *So much hate, feeling so angry. We have had enough.*

For Dan, the sandplay became a 'rehearsal of the possible' through which he began to find his courage to seek help (*and see below,* p.268).

Izzy (5) had spent several years watching her parents have bitter arguments, until eventually they split up. At school she often bullied other children. In her sandplay stories she always enacted fights where knights would be left wounded and dying.

Each time, the adult assumed (without checking) that Izzy was identifying with the wounded knights. Repeatedly, Izzy played the same story with no development, and so the adult realised she must be failing to read something properly. One day she decided to switch tack and said, *"Wow! What a scary dragon you are!"* Izzy's face lit up - *"Yes, yes!"* she said with glee, dancing round the room.

The adult had eventually got it right about who was who! Izzy had felt so unbearably impotent watching the war between her mother and father that, in her imagination, via story, she needed to experience herself as potent, hence seeing herself as a powerful dragon. The adult then read Izzy the story of *A Wibble Called Bipley (and a Few Honks)* (Sunderland 2001). It's all about a little creature who felt so hurt and impotent that he turned to bullying to feel big and powerful and get away from his too painful feelings. The story offers empathy to children like Izzy, about how people who have experienced impotence often need to move into feelings of power 'over' others.

Eventually Izzy could communicate to the adult how she had felt helpless and frightened when her parents fought all the time. After a while, she found a way to be powerfully creative as opposed to powerfully destructive, via her real success at art and design at school.

TECHNIQUE 7: The 'Nosy Seagull' technique

This technique was devised by Sue Fish, an eminent founder of humanistic child therapy in the UK. After the child has told his story or played something out, and you're still confused as to who the goodies and baddies are and which character the child is identifying with and so on, then nosy seagulls can fly in. You will need to find some little toy birds or puppet seagulls, or something equivalent, for example, nosy neighbours or nosy chimps. They settle down by the side of the child's sandplay or picture and start having a conversation. Often the child is so entranced by this unexpected piece of theatre, enacted by the adult (via puppets or toys) that he tells the seagulls who is who in his story, who is good and who is bad, and so on.

> **Dolly Seagull:** *Well what do you think, Ethel Seagull? Was that big giant in the story good or bad? Because it did seem to be helping the little boy?*
>
> **Ethel Seagull:** *But Dolly Seagull, didn't you see it had enormous teeth? I never trust giants myself.*
>
> Often the child can't resist.
>
> **Child:** *You are so silly - of course the giant is a good giant!*

TECHNIQUE 8: Dealing with a flood of images, and deciding which of them to work with

One of the most common challenges to the adult helping a child with feelings is the 'child in extremis', who, because of your provision of well-chosen art materials, pours out a myriad of profoundly moving images in a painting, puppet-play or sandplay. All manner of Greek mythic-type images are presented: depictions of falling forever, being taken over, catastrophic impotence, death and dying, fire, flood, smashing, tearing, and horrific acts of betrayal.

The challenge is then, how on earth should you respond? A simple "*Um*", or "*I see*" or "*Looks horrible*" just won't do. Imagine: through art media, the child has created extremely powerful images of pain, and nothing of any gravitas comes back from you. It is equivalent to the baby 'who throws out cries of panic and nothing comes back from the mother' (Schore 2005). So what do we do?

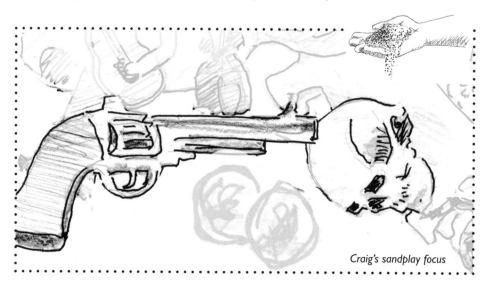

Craig's sandplay focus

If a child's drawing, play story or sandplay is very full, it may be impossible (and indeed unnecessary) to pay attention to all the images. If you only deal with one or two images in depth, that is fine. In his image, (p.234) **Craig (10)** was drawn to the relationship between the skull and the gun, and did

252

not refer to the other images, the monsters, man with the guitar and so on. So be it. If the other symbols are important to the child they will appear again in future sessions. So take the lead from the child regarding which are the most emotionally charged images for him. In some cases, it is best to simply ask the child which images are most important to him. Corrine knew that Craig had suddenly become very aggressive at school.

> **Corrine:** So, with all these images in your sandplay picture which are you most drawn to, what's most interesting?
>
> **Craig:** The skull and the gun.
>
> **Corrine:** So tell me skull, what is life like for you in this world (of the sand picture)?
>
> **Craig:** All I know is the gun pointing at my head.
>
> **Corrine:** And skull, that make you feel...?
>
> **Craig:** Not a lot, I'm dead.
>
> **Corrine:** OK, so be the gun. Gun, skull says he is very aware of you pointing at his head.
>
> **Craig:** Yes, although skull is dead, I would still like to shoot his brains out.
>
> **Corrine:** (knows Craig can tolerate direct questions about his life) Wow, such passion ! Does that remind you of any feeling you have in real life?
>
> **Craig:** Yes, it's what I want to do to my father.

This led to a very important conversation about Craig's fury towards his father (who had died of cancer) for leaving him, made more complex by his feelings about the violence he had witnessed between his father and mother. After important grief work, there were no more images of violence in his play and his aggressive behaviour became a thing of the past.

TECHNIQUE 9: *"What would happen next?"*

Sometimes when you say to a child, *"Would you tell me about your drawing/ sandplay picture?"* they shrug and say nothing. This can be the case particularly with teenagers, so take a different tack and ask, *"What would happen next?"* or *"If it were a film set, what would happen next?"* Many teenagers who do not respond to, *"Tell me about your picture"* will respond to this because there is no pressure for them to say anything. They start to move the miniatures around to develop their scene or story. So the still 'picture' becomes a piece of drama in the theatre of the sandbox. Or, if they have done a drawing, give them another piece of paper for them to do *"What would happen next?"*

Ella's father, who shouted at Ella when he was drunk (*see* p.246), had witnessed awful atrocities whilst on active duty in the forces, but no-one in the family talked about it. Since her father returned home with his regiment, Ella became very anxious. When a parent does not work through their own 'emotional baggage' left by trauma or loss, it can impact strongly on their child. Since children have such super antennae around their parents (because they need them so much), they can pick up on what is happening in their parents' inner worlds. Carl Jung, a famous analyst, called this 'participation mystique' - the mysterious participation. This sensitivity can result in the child developing actual physical or neurotic symptoms in response to the parent's distress. Ella was sure that the monsters she dreamed about were actually real. She started to see them in the curtains. Ella did the sandplay opposite. It was about the spiders inhabiting the house.

> **Ella:** *They are everywhere.*
> **Jenny:** *Can you tell me what that feels like?*
> **Ella:** *It just is.*
> **Jenny:** *What would happen next?*
> Ella took the spider from under the sofa and got it to attack the baby.

Jenny: *How terrifying for the baby who is all alone. The scary spider seems to have all the power and the baby to have no power.*

Jenny: (knowing that Ella can tolerate direct expression to what is happening in her life) *I'm wondering if it's a bit like that for you. That sometimes it feels like your fears have all the power.*

This led to Ella spontaneously picking up the baby, cradling it and throwing the spider across the room.

Jenny: *How do you feel now you have done that?*

Ella: *Look this baby is fed up of spiders. Spiders should not live in my house. (pause) Sometimes when my Dad looks at me, he has spiders in his eyes.*

Jenny: *Will you draw them?*

Ella's sandplay

From this Jenny and Ella had a really frank conversation about Ella feeling frightened of her father. Jenny invited Ella's father to meet her and found a way to open a discussion about his own need for support and counselling.

The question, *"What would happen next?"* has been a lifesaver for me on several occasions with some troubled and inhibited older children and teenagers. Have a look at the example on p.323 of a girl who wouldn't talk to me but she would show me 'what would happen next'. It was rather like session after session of a silent film. Eventually she told me verbally the story about her life that she had enacted in metaphor for so long in the sand.

TECHNIQUE 10: Not rushing on - allowing space

Avoid the pitfall of rushing in to say something in response to what a child has told you or in response to a child's image, rather than giving the comment/picture/sandplay/clay object time to really have impact, on both the child and you. This will also give the child the experience that you are reflecting on what they have said or done, rather than quickly commenting because you think you must say something. Sometimes it may be appropriate to say something along the lines of: *"I'm having a feeling about your picture, what you're saying and when I've had a thought about it, I will let you know what that is."*

TECHNIQUE 11: When there's lots of action - building in reflection time

With many children, a lot of *action* often happens in a 'talking about feelings' session where the child is given play and art materials. So make sure you build in sufficient *reflective non-action* time as well. Action alone is unlikely to lead to change. Without sufficient reflection time, the child may be unable to fully think about and process what he is playing out. It is not enough just to say *"So you have told me a very important story today. See you next week!"* Instead, pick up some of the key emotional themes in the session, and reflect on them. This can be in the form of mid-session summary, or an end of session summary, or both (*for more on these summaries, see p.182*).

> *"So in our time together today, your story was about a boy who got bullied everyday. People saw, but just walked on by. He kept dreaming of dying a lonely old man, all forgotten, under a bridge."*

Then the empathy and the psycho-education:

"I can imagine how terribly alone he was feeling, his pain of no importance to anyone. But there are always people with kindness in their hearts. Perhaps we need to help the boy find them, because maybe until we do, he will not trust that such people exist."

TECHNIQUE 12: Asking for a title

Some children will not tell you about a picture they have drawn or created, but if you ask them for a title, they will give you one, often a very powerful one. With teenagers, it can sometimes help to say, *"If your picture were a film, what would the title of the film be?"* Often the title the child gives is very poignant, and says a lot about their core feelings or a central emotional theme in their life.

This is a sandplay picture created by **Maeve (13)**. Maeve had been beaten by her mother on many occasions (her mother was mentally ill). Maeve was taken into care. When asked to talk about the sandplay, Maeve just shrugged her shoulders and said nothing. But when asked to give it a title she immediately said, '*The Cave of Bad Mothers and Dead Babies*'.

The title enabled the counsellor to have a clear tie-up between life story and play story. From this, using indirect expression, she could empathise with what a terrible place the cave was, and how terrifying for the babies, who had no-one there to protect them; and how the mothers in the story, who were supposed to be protecting the babies, were actually frightening them to death. The communication from Maeve to adult and adult to Maeve was all done in metaphor. If Maeve had wanted to say what had happened to her overtly, she would have done so. However, after this, in the next session, Maeve felt safe enough to refer directly to her physical abuse, saying,"*I felt like I had died many times.*"

TECHNIQUE 13: Directive use of drawing, play and sandplay

Some child counselling approaches advocate always following the child's play. However in some circumstances, with some children, this will not bring about positive change. Instead, it can sometimes be more effective to give them a focused task using play materials. This can really help those children who are clearly wanting to talk about something in their life directly, and do not need the protection of 'staying in the metaphor'.

Here are some examples of directed tasks, which can be used in these circumstances. They are of course to be used according to what is right for the particular child you are working with. Your tone of voice is important, so the child hears you issuing a suggestion, not a command. So speak gently and warmly. Here are a few suggestions - obviously not all of them at once!

Adult: • *Will you make a picture of what the problem you've been talking about feels like?*

• *Will you show me with a drawing/a painting/sandplay - whatever you like - what if feels like to be you at the moment?*

• *Here's the sandbox and the miniatures - would you make a picture of the good things in your life and the things you'd like to change?*

> • *Will you draw a picture of the people in your life but as animals?*
> • *Can you put yourself in the picture too?*
> • *Pick a sandplay object to stand for how you feel right now*
> • *Will you make a sandplay picture/ painting? On one side, would you show me what hell on earth is for you and on the other side - what heaven on earth is for you?* (suitable for older children)
> *In the sand, or on this paper, show an important dream you've had.*

99

As ever, it is never OK to ask a child to open up in this way and then not connect with them afterwards. So the child will need an empathic response after they have shared their picture/sandplay with you. They will also need relevant psycho-education if they have said something that indicates that they have a belief about themselves which is inaccurate (the negative self-referencing I discussed earlier).

The different 'you's

This is another directive use of play, sandplay or drawing. Look at the list below and pick one of the statements appropriate to the child or young person and their life issues that you are working with. So then you can say, *"On this piece of paper, or in the sandbox, can you show me ... "*

> » The sad you   » The excited you
> » The frightened you   » The stuck you
> » The angry you   » The you when everything's going right for you
> » The powerful you   » The you when everything's going wrong for you
> » The guilty you   » The inner critic in your head
> » The happy you

Alternatively, you can show this list to the child or teenager and ask them to choose the 'yous' they often feel. You could then ask the child to get their different 'mes' to talk to each other. This is dialoguing (*see above*, p.245, *and for more on using puppets, sandplay and other creative media, see* Chapter 9)

TECHNIQUE 14: On not pressing for happy endings

When an adult has not sufficiently addressed her own painful life experiences, for example losses, trauma and so on, she may be unable to be fully present when the child talks about painful feelings directly or through play. She may try to move the child towards a happy ending in their play. This is particularly the case if the adult hasn't had personal experience of healing connection through therapeutic conversation.

So make sure you acknowledge the pain as portrayed in the child's play or art image, otherwise you risk serious misattunement with the child. When a child has had a really difficult start in life, talk of happy endings feels alien to what they have experienced.

Instead, when an adult attunes and empathises with a child or young person's hopelessness, despair or desolation as it shows up in their play or artwork, the child is no longer alone with it. The adult is metaphorically holding their hand, regulating them and helping them reflect on what has happened in a new way. This process gives the child fresh perspectives, and a deep sense of security, of being both held and understood.

Here are examples of adults pressing for a happy ending, and what they could have done differently.

Rosa (11) is the fifth child in a large family where Mum and Dad, due to drug abuse, are under scrutiny by social services as to whether their children should be taken into care for neglect. Rosa draws a lonely crying mole in a dark forest with many big trees. Anna the teaching assistant uses the identification technique (*see above*).

X Unempathic response

Anna: *So if the mole could speak what might he say?*

Rosa: *Nobody loves me.*

Anna: *Yes they do little mole. I love you!*

Rosa: (thinks to herself - this adult just doesn't have a clue!)

✔ Instead …Rosa draws a lonely crying mole.

Rosa: *Nobody loves me.*

Anna: *You feel so unloved, little mole.*

Rosa: *Yeah I do actually.*

Anna: *Because …?*

Rosa: *Because sometimes it feels like no-one even notices me.*

Anna: (holding in mind Rosa's life story which informs this
intervention) *So little mole has known a kind of dark forest
without enough love, people don't even notice him. It's like he gets
muddled and thinks the fault is his, rather than with the people who
are not able to show him love in the way he needs.*

Ami's (8) mother died a year ago. Her schoolwork has gone downhill dramatically. All the teachers know she needs help to grieve. Frances is there for Ami to talk to, when she is ready. Ami does a sandplay of just a head with no body in the middle of lots of sand and rocks, which she says is like an empty desert.

✗ Unempathic response

Ami: *My body lives in my head now. Who wants a body if it has a broken heart in it?*

Frances: *How about doing another picture, Ami, of your heart being all mended. It might really help.*

✔ Instead:

Ami: *My body lives in my head now. Who wants a body if it has a broken heart in it?*

Frances: *And I'm thinking when your mother died, it may have felt like the world became an empty desert, as if all that's lovely in the world has gone. I understand how living in your head might feel easier than being with your broken heart. It can be so painful to let yourself know how much you miss someone who has gone.*

TECHNIQUE 15: Knowing when to invite potency and protest

When a child is feeling hopeless or helpless, there can be times when it's difficult to know whether and when to help them find their potency, their psychological strength, and their healthy protest, and when to enable them to stay with their pain. The important thing is to ask yourself, are you running away from the pain in the room towards an ending of potency? Is this for your benefit or theirs?

If the adult finds the child's helpless, hopeless feelings too threatening, she may push (consciously or unconsciously) the child to a more hopeful place, when he is not feeling at all hopeful! The child may go with the adult's suggestions simply out of a need to comply; but, in so doing, he may forgo his need for her to really understand how defeated and miserable he feels about something in his life. Here's an extreme example of when it would have been far more appropriate to stay with the pain and not think of potency and protest.

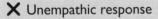

✗ Unempathic response

Child: *My Mum likes the new baby best. I can never get her to love me like she loves the new baby.*

Adult: *So let's think together now of all the ways you could get her to love you as much as your baby brother.*

This question leaves unacknowledged the pain the child feels, and the grief at feeling she has lost her Mum to the new baby.

When used well, inviting potency and protest is not a denial of the child's feelings of helplessness or hopelessness, but rather an intervention that helps the child think about options, find their voice, allow the protesting and/or potent self to speak. It can help them move from unquestioned passivity to being able to think about choices. This is the case when the practitioner has double-checked with herself that she is not using the technique as a diversion tactic, because she is finding it hard to stay with the child's painful feelings.

Using the technique effectively

i) When a child tells a story in which a character is feeling stuck, hopeless, unsure and so on, at times it may be appropriate for the adult to encourage potent thinking about options. So in a story about a bee who's very hungry, she might say something like, *"So I am wondering if there is anything the bee could do about being in a flowerless place?"*

ii) Ensure you use open-ended questions which do not contain a covert 'happy ending' suggestion in the question. Here is an example of an adult's open questioning. It gives the child, Chloe, an option, at a time when Chloe is struggling with despair or hopelessness. Chloe can comment further on the bird's horrid feelings, or, as happens here, Chloe may indicate that she's ready to move on and find her own positive resolution to the situation.

Chloe (7), who has been sexually abused, enacts a play story about a small bird that gets all yuk in her beak from the slime of a jelly snail. It means no birdsong, and the bird used to love singing. The adult empathises with how horrid the bird must feel about the yuk and also the loss of how things used to be.

> **Chloe:** Yes, yes, the bird stays at home now not even talking, not even singing.
>
> **Adult:** Is there anything the bird wants to do or say about that? (open question using the language of potency)
>
> **Chloe:** She wants help to get the yuk off
>
> **Adult:** I wonder what that help might look like or feel like? (Chloe takes the bird lovingly in her hand and uses wet wipe after wet wipe until she sinks back in her chair).
>
> **Chloe:** It's all over now.
>
> **Adult:** What does that 'all 'over now feeling' feel like? (the adult marks the moment of potency, by asking Chloe what she feels, having acted in a proactive way).
>
> **Chloe:** So good. And if another jelly snail comes her way, she will peck him so badly and squark so loudly that the jelly snails everywhere will never go near her again.

Some children need both empathy for their hopeless/despairing feelings *and* help to find their potency. Pippa draws a picture of Ted the toad being 'hopelessly stuck in a swamp'. Should the adult, Chris, empathise with how awful it is to be in the swamp or should he say, "*Is there anything Ted wants to do about being stuck in the swamp, or to say about it?*" Is Pippa's primary need for Chris to hear and recognise how hopeless she is feeling, or does she need him to help her appreciate that she does have some smart problem-solving skills? In some cases, a child may have both needs. If Pippa doesn't respond to the language of potency, this may be evidence that she needs Chris to stay with her pain. So what does Chris say?

Chris: *So how does Ted the toad feel about being stuck in the swamp?*

Pippa: *Horrible.*

Chris: *How awful to have all that toad hopping power and yet find himself so powerless to use it.* (empathising)

Pippa: *Yes, Ted is just miserable. Like you say, Ted is used to being able to move about very well - and now he's just a nothing.*

Chris: *How awful to feel like he is nothing after being able to get along in life* (empathy). *I'm just wondering if there is anything Ted wants to do about it?* (language of potency)

Pippa: (Answer 1): *Well, he might call out to the little people in the tree at the other side to help him.*

Pippa: (Answer 2): *No, he feels he will just have to stay there until he dies.*

Pippa's answer will determine Chris' next intervention.

TECHNIQUE 16: 'Rehearsal of the possible'

> If you always do what you've always done, you'll always get what
> you've always got.   Henry Ford, 1863-1947

'Rehearsal of the possible' is an intervention which enables the child or young person to rehearse a different way of being or a resolution to a problem through play, rather than just through talking about it. We know that our thinking when we are moving is actually superior to that when we try to work out a problem when sitting still. This is because of the strong networking links between the cerebellum (responsible for motor related functions in the brain) and the frontal lobes (responsible for decision making) (Schmahmann & Caplan, 2006).

As Watchel (2008) says: 'So many therapeutic interventions offer narratives of description, but no narrative of possibility' (p.272). He goes on to state:

> The [child] needs to imagine and dare to pursue greater possibilities, to
> see the path toward an alternative way of experiencing himself and an
> alternative way of living. And he also needs experiences that help him
> develop the wherewithal to live differently in the way he is beginning to
> envisage.   Watchel 2008, p.274

So with this intervention, you suggest to the child that they rehearse (in drama, sandplay or through art) a way of being that is different to how they are usually. So for example: you might ask them to speak confidently, to make a protest, or try being naughty (when they are too good). Sometimes you may have to model for them how to do these things!

I once had 'helping with feelings sessions' with a teenager I'll call **Freya**. Before I saw her, she was deeply depressed and had virtually stared at the walls for the last two years. She was an only child. When she was 12 her Mum had taken in a lover, who started hurting Freya. Social Services found out, and said Freya's Mum would have to choose between Freya and her lover. She chose the lover.

As a result, Freya was taken into care. *"I couldn't get my Mum to love me. I couldn't get her to choose me. I couldn't get him to stop beating me up"*, she would say repeatedly. Freya's Mum rarely visited her. I knew I needed to acknowledge and empathise with her catastrophic sense of impotence. But I also had to consider whether Freya had other core emotions, which had been eclipsed by two years of feelings of utter defeat and despair.

One day she did a picture where a dinosaur (she said it was her Mum's lover) was drinking all the water from the waterhole and the little chimp (representation of herself) could not get any. *"Did you know that chimps have far bigger brains than dinosaurs?"* I said. *"Is there anything the chimp could do?"* Freya was clearly thinking. On the back of this new sense of potency, she tipped over a nearby boat, distracted the dinosaur and got to the water. I suggested she did a role-play in the sand of standing up to her mother's lover. This is inviting rehearsal of the possible. Freya did this week after week, and pushed the man out of her life. Knowing how angry Freya was with her mother, I suggested using the sandbox to rehearse standing up to her mother as well. Again she found this useful and told her (rehearsing in fantasy) about how angry she was at her brutal choice of choosing her lover over her daughter.

Then one day she rehearsed in sandplay taking her mother to court to divorce her. After rehearsing this in several sessions, she did just that. She went to court and became a ward of court! She told me *"Now I can get on with living my life rather than being tied to a mother who doesn't want me."* She went on to do very well in life.

TECHNIQUE 17: *"Do it"*

Sometimes, through their play or artwork, children are on the verge of acting in a potent creative way and yet, without encouragement, they pull back from doing so. Often this is because of critical voices in their head, or from a fear of being shamed or disapproved of. So watch out for statements that start with "*I feel like …*" (doing something potentially *free, big or protesting*), or the equivalent: "*I feel like …*"

- Running round the room
- Telling that horrid teacher in my drawing to go and bully someone his or her size
- Saying 'NO!' in a big loud voice

If you hear the words "*I feel like*" or "*What I feel like doing is …*" or something similar, make sure you say, "*Do it!*" Hopefully the child will 'do it' - symbolically through play of course! After they've done it, it's important to ask, "*How do you feel now you've done it?*" Often the answer is very important, and sometimes even vital for the healing process of reflection and assimilation. If you don't say, "*Do it!*" in such circumstances, you could miss a vital opportunity for change *(and see Winnicott's comment below).*

Remember Dan (*see* pp. 231, p. 249) whose sister Joanne was so abusive?

> **Dan:** (after drawing a big bad snapping-teethed mouth) *I feel like sticking the snapping teeth in a hole in the ground and saying to it "No more!"* (He pauses. Without encouragement, all this potent, taking-charge energy could simply have faded away).
>
> **Martina:** *Do it. Try it. Tell it again: "No more! No more!"*

> **Dan:** (screws up his picture of the snapping-teethed mouth, and grins from ear to ear) *No more! No more!! Yabadabadoo!!!*
>
> **Martina:** (after a short appreciative pause) *So, Dan, how does it feel now you've stood up to the snapping-teethed mouth?*
>
> **Dan:** *Like the best sort of day ever!*
>
> **Martina:** *Yes I can see that. I loved your "No more!" Your voice was so strong. I wonder if perhaps you would like to play your "No more" on the loud drums too?*
>
> 🙾

an does, using the percussion instruments in the room. After several more ssions like this, and with the help of the adults in his life, Dan is able to confront s sister and the bullying stops.

This exchange shows the importance of being encouraging, and witnessing e child's potent action, spending time with it, so the child can experience his vn potency in a really embodied way. For a child who has been shamed or ained into total compliance and obedience, to then experience feeling potent not ipotent, active not passive, is a very important moment.

So an "*I feel like ...*" moment is far too important to leave unused. Rather, ay with it, draw attention to it and encourage moving from desire, want, interest d so on into action.

Abdullah (6), (depressed, shy and far 'too good') had a lovely warm ENCO called Claire, who was helping him with his feelings. One day, Abdullah :ew a picture of a magic helicopter.

> **Abdullah:** *It flies into the highest clouds. It makes them twinkle with magic dust. I feel like getting in the helicopter and flying round the room.*
>
> **Claire:** *OK, Abdullah, go for it! Would you like to wear these special helicopter goggles? (She digs out some starry sunglasses in the play bag).*

With Claire's encouragement, Abdullah does just that. He flies in his imaginary helicopter around the room and some other children clap. In that moment Abdullah tastes expansive life. If Claire hadn't encouraged Abdullah in this rare surge of enthusiasm, this burst of life force, the moment would have been lost.

Some children may need more encouragement and more structure, for example: "*Sounds great, let's pretend this is your helicopter (large cushion) and this is the sky (space above his head).*" So use whatever toys or any available props you have in the room to enrich and support the child to more fully imagine he is in a helicopter, flying round the room.

TECHNIQUE 18: Working with the 'eleventh hour' happening

Sometimes a child will say or do something very important right at the end of a talk-time, at the proverbial 'eleventh hour'. She may, for example, want to change something in a picture she's drawn, or suddenly do something different with a toy she has been playing with. It's important to comment on the change.

Alternatively, you can check for any potential eleventh hour energetic 'charge' so far unexpressed, by saying something like: "*Now we've talked about your story/drawing/play, and we're nearly finished for today, is there anything you would like to do or change?*" Often, at this last minute, the child will say, "*Yes*", and some miniature toy will get thrown out of a sandbox, hugged, put on the adult's knee, shouted at and so on. Or a blob in a painting will get coloured in or torn out of the picture. If this happens, it could be because something has shifted in your talking-about-things-together time.

Whatever happens at this eleventh hour needs acknowledging by the listening adult. It's important to say something like, *"I wonder what you feel, now that you have done that?"* Often the answer is very important, and vital for the healing process of reflection.

> **Aileen:** *Now we have talked about your drawing of the tired Mum, is there anything you would like to do or change in your drawing?*
> **Shaun:** *Yes, throw her in the rubbish.*

This was an important shift at the 'eleventh hour' for Shaun (*see* p.196). He had spent all his time trying to be funny and jolly with his depressed Mum and so this was the first time he has let himself know that he was angry with her.

> **Aileen:** *How do you feel now she is in the rubbish?*
> **Shaun:** *Free as a free thing.*

After this, the adult and Shaun had a really important discussion about how weary he felt trying to play family jester all the time. He also understood, probably for the first time, that his Mum's depression was nothing to do with him and she needed grown-ups to help her get better.

TECHNIQUE 19: When the child keeps repeating the same play story week after week

Repetitive play usually means one or more of the following:

i) Witnessing

The child may need you to witness again and again something awful that has happened in his life.

ii) Working through

The child needs to tell his story a lot, because he feels troubled, confused or disturbed by the emotional theme. He needs to keep trying to process his feelings about a particular person or life experience through this play story. So the repetition of the story is a very important 'working through'.

iii) Rehearsal of the possible

The story includes some important 'rehearsal of a different way of being', which takes time. Children often need to rehearse, for example, a softer, gentler self or a stronger, more assertive self through play, many times, before taking it into reality and integrating it into who they are, and who they are becoming. Watch, however, for repeated rehearsal via story of self-destructive acts, which can occasionally happen. Although it is rare, children can rehearse such self-destructive acts as running away, self-harm, or suicide attempts through their play.

iv) Trying to get through

The child is trying to tell you something via his play, and you are not hearing or receiving his message. So he has to keep telling you, hoping for that moment of understanding: 'message received and understood'. If you are aware, you will sense when this is happening.

Sometimes there is a dull re-playing of a story or playtheme, which comes from a kind of wearisome, *"When are you going to get what I am trying to tell you?"* You can ask the child directly: *"I wonder if I am not hearing something important in your story so that you are needing to tell it again and again?"*

v) **The medium can't convey the message**

Sometimes, the child is stuck because they are using the wrong materials/art medium through which to tell their story. For some children, for example, doing sandplay (placing miniatures in a sandbox) is 'too small' for their big feelings. They may need to tell you their story with percussion instruments or dramatic enactment.

Leon (*see* p.226) for example, got stuck in a repeated wearisome telling about people locked up in the tower of a fort. As an only child, he felt really isolated at home living with his very strict Dad and step-mum. He told his story through miniatures in sandplay. When the adult suggested that they build a fort in the room using big cushions and a table, the story developed dramatically. Leon was able to express some of the rage behind his despondent feeling. As a result he talked to his Dad and successfully negotiated going out with his friends more.

vi) **The need to acknowledge stuckness**

In some circumstances, it is appropriate to comment, *"I think something is stuck here. I think perhaps you have got stuck in what you are doing with me. You do the same thing week after week. I wonder how you feel about that?"* Draw some 'faces' the child might be feeling, so he can just pick one, for example, 'bored', 'need to do it', 'don't know what else to do' faces. Then you have more to work with.

vii) **Repetition as defence**

You may not be helping the child think and feel about something important that he needs help to think and feel about. He's enagaged in repetitive play as a defence against painful underlying feeling, a form of distraction for both of you. So gently guide the child to possible underlying core feelings using the techniques outlined above.

TECHNIQUE 20: Enactments

An enactment is when a child spontaneously acts out an event or story through drama. Sometimes the child wants you to be a character in their fantasy play. Commonly under-tens say something like *"You be the big bad monster and I am the clever princess,"* or, *"You be the horrid teacher and you have to tell me off."* It just comes up naturally in the play of under-tens, and then whoops! How are you going to respond to ensure you are being therapeutic? Before I answer that, here are a few points about the value of enactments:

- Enactments help the child to literally play with ideas.
- Enactment is a way children process their emotional experiences.
- Enactment is a way children feel what it's like to be potent and make things happen.

> Becoming superman for a half hour helps a child overcome the experience of being little and vulnerable, ordered about by parents and teachers. Superman, in play, has a consoling and refuelling function.
>
> Chethik 1989, p.50

- Enactment is also something children use to feel in control, when they have felt helpless in the face of threat:

> Sylvia increasingly demanded that I should act the part of terrifying monsters that pursued her with roars and threatened to eat her up. *"Be a Dalek"*, *"Be a carpet monster"* or *"Be a light-switch monster,"* she said. By making me enact the monsters, I thought she was trying to ... control her terror of being attacked. Barrows 2003, p.158

- Enactment is a way children play with possibility and new ways of being and doing. The ground-breaking child paediatrician and psychoanalyst Donald Winnicott was a key advocate of a child's enactments being supported for this reason:

> If a little girl wants to fly we do not just say, *"Children don't fly"*. Instead of that we pick her up and carry her around above our heads, and put her on top of the cupboard, so that she feels to have flown like a bird to her nest.
> 1949, pp.70-1

What you need in the room in case a child moves into spontaneous enactments

It's good to have a dressing up box. As a child's enactments are usually spontaneous and NOW! - you need things that can be put on or taken off within about ten seconds!

- *A cloak that will fit you*
- *A wizard or witch's hat that will fit you*
- *A few woollen scarves that can be anything*
- *Doctor's bag and stethoscope*
- *A magic wand*
- *Hero cloak for children (some neutral ones and then specific ones such as Batman/Spiderman/Harry Potter)*
- *Animal cloaks for children*
- *Animal heads for children*
- *Monster cloak*
- *Some different masks of benign faces and frightening ones*

Incidentally, *don't use masks for yourself* in this kind of work: they can be far too frightening for children, and they can so easily lose the 'as if' sense of pretend play and enactment, and feel you really are the character of the mask you are wearing!

STRATEGIES & INTERVENTIONS FOR A CHILD'S ENACTMENT
The essential stages

Stage 1 *Child initiates an enactment*
This often involves asking you to join in.

Stage 2 *Get clarification of the role the child wants you to play: consider whether to accept or refuse the role and then prepare*
If the child has asked you to join in - get clarification about the nature of the person they want you to be, and, vitally, whether this person is 'good' or 'bad'. From this you will also be able to decide whether you are going to accept the role or refuse the role (if the latter - *see below*, as to how to make that decision, and what to do then). If you have accepted the role, think whether you are going to grab anything from the dressing up box or not - nothing elaborate - just perhaps a scarf on your head or a shawl.

Stage 3 *The role play commences*
Remember this needs to be child-led play, so don't lead. Let the child take the play where they want to. But play your part for them.

Stage 4 *Decide how and when to end the enactment*
An enactment may end naturally. However, if it seems as if the play is getting stuck, the child is losing energy and engagement or you think the enactment is getting in any way traumatic for the child, call a stop and move into **Stage 5.**

Stage 5 *Reflection time*
This means that after an enactment, when you've both come out of your roles you will then need to sit down with the child and reflect on what has been enacted, focusing on the main emotional and relational themes of the enactment

(and as usual, with a keen eye on how these parallel the emotional and relational themes of the child's life).

If you don't do this, the enactment becomes like an unanalysed dream. In other words - doing the enactment per se is not necessarily of any therapeutic value. The child may have been playing the same enactment regularly *without you*. If there is no processing, with the help of a reflective adult mind, it can be an empty repeating with no learning. What makes it therapeutic is the thinking together about it afterwards, with empathy, enquiry and attunement. As ever, think about whether the child can tolerate direct reference to his life, or do you need to keep your empathy as indirect expression? To further emotionally engage the child in the reflection, the adult can illustrate her thoughts with a spontaneous drawing (*See Big Empathy Drawing as described on* p.79).

How to move from enactment to reflection

It's helpful if at all possible to have a place in the room where you can do enactments, and another place for reflection (I often call the space I set aside for this 'the thinking cushions'). You can let the child know how the process will go by simply saying something like, "*Let's put the clothes back in the box and come and sit on the thinking cushions* (or another place in the room). *Your story has been so important and interesting I would like to think about it more.*"

The putting the clothes away somewhere separate from your thinking cushions is vital. If you think the child is still seeing you in a particular role, or *they* are still in a particular role, spend time 'de-roling' - separating out the enactment self from the real self, and getting the child grounded back in normal reality: "*OK, goodbye monster Munch, goodbye Mrs Peanut*" - then look at the child. "*So back now to being you Melissa, and me, Mary.*"

This is critical, especially for children at a magical thinking age. If there are any signs that a child isn't fully back in the now, repeat the goodbye process or do some ritual like saying " *OK, let's both turn round three times and jump in the air together twice and say welcome back Melissa! You are now no longer the angry dog - bye bye, angry dog! - and hello Melissa.*" Or take the child's hands in your hands and gain eye contact (it's a grounding technique) and say *"Melissa hello, Melissa hello"*, several times. You can then do the *"Hah"* game where you both take turns to say *"Hah"* loudly - it's very funny, and brings the child firmly back into relationship with you.

Tessa (6) had been referred to a counsellor because she was underachieving at school, and was often found sitting on her own in the playground. In their special time together, Tessa wanted Arlene to be the Queen of the Sea Kingdom. She said she would be the baby. Tessa instructed Arlene to take the baby into the bejewelled sea kingdom. She told Arlene to be lovely to the baby and then just 'leave it there' and go 'all angry and cold' on her.

As the story was being enacted, Arlene was thinking hard about the parallels between Tessa's life story and her play story. The parallels were very clear. Tessa had an on-off mum, who was lovely sometimes and then cold and distant at other times, particularly when she drank too much. In Tessa's story, the bejewelled sea kingdom promised everything, but in the end brought nothing but painful isolation. Arlene knew that in order to help Tessa process this, she would benefit from acknowledgement and empathy for having an 'on-off mum'.

Arlene chose indirect expression, as Tessa switched off when Arlene talked about actual events in her life.

Here is what Arlene said at **Stage 5, Reflection time.**

Arlene: *OK Tessa, let's put the dressing up clothes in the box and come and sit on the thinking cushions. Goodbye baby, goodbye queen. So, back to you and me, Tessa. In your story that place of loveliness promised so much, but in fact when the queen went*

> *cold, she left the baby feeling too alone and probably so unloved because of the cold and anger. I'm wondering if that was confusing and painful for the baby, the queen being lovely one minute and then so different the next?"*

Tessa says nothing, so Arelene decides to try deepening the process by asking Tessa to draw the baby and the queen. Tessa draws a baby *"in a fairground with lots of lights and fun"* and then she draws her *"all alone in a dark dead place."* Arelene realises that it's like Tessa in the playground. She is recreating in the playground the experience of feeling too alone.

To ensure that the school staff are not unconsciously colluding in some really unhealthy repetition, at the next staff meeting, Arlene insists on a change. She knows more effort must be shown by school staff to ensure that people initiate contact with Tessa in the playground. She explains that at the moment Tessa is unable to do this herself because of things happening at home. A buddy system (with older children looking after younger children) is set up. Tessa lights up, comes alive at the emotional warmth of her older buddie who helps Tessa make really good contact with her peers.

Responding when the child specifically asks you to enact something traumatic or hurtful

> *"You be the wicked witch and I am the frightened little girl so you have to kill me and spit on my grave ... well, go on then ... "* **Hannah (7)**

So what do you do when, as part of an enactment, the child asks you to hit them, or wants to hit you, or wants you to smash things, or wants to smash things themselves, or poke you in the eye with a stick, or be poked, or drench you with water, or be drenched, or fill your clothes with sand, or enact something sexual, or wants you to enact some frightening aggressor who wees on them?

Sometimes, children will ask you to take part in some deeply disturbing event, which may actually be a re-enactment of some form of trauma or abuse they have experienced. The danger is that we just comply, impulsively and unthinkingly. If we do, we may soon find ourselves colluding in something totally non-therapeutic or even traumatising to the child, such as replaying an inhumane dominance-submission relationship they've known. As a result, we may be simply reinforcing their belief in relationship as being about abject cruelty, lacking in any compassion for human suffering, relationship all about power and control, or power over. So here are some key steps when you think this is what is happening with you and a child.

Step 1: *Reflect on any feelings of shock you have and how they might be a communication of the child's traumatic experience*

When a child has experienced a trauma and not been helped to process it, the raw feelings so easily get projected out, meaning someone else ends up feeling them. They never 'just go away'; instead, as Freud said, 'A thing which has not been understood inevitably reappears; like an unlaid ghost it cannot rest until the mystery has been solved and the spell is broken' (Freud 1909, p. 49). He means until someone has helped the child reflect on and work through the trauma, all manner of painful symptoms and challenging behaviour can ensue.

So when the child's behaviour is an out-of-awareness communication about their trauma, you can end up feeling *shocked as they have been shocked*. You can end up feeling something of what they might have felt when they suffered the trauma. Psychoanalyst Patrick Casement calls this,' communication by impact' (1985, p.97).

And boy, can we feel impacted when working with traumatised children! If, for example, a child has been sexually abused, their wish to enact something sadistic in their play with you can leave you reeling with feelings of repulsion, horror, rage, and disgust. These are likely to be very similar to the feelings the child felt when he was victim to the sexual abuse. So as part of your recovery from the shock and whilst you regain a state of emotional regulation, work to hold in mind play story and life story as I have described earlier.

Step 2: *Follow the stages of empathic listening*

Keep the principles of empathy firmly in your mind (Stages 1 to 3). When you have managed to emotionally regulate yourself, (and during this time, it's fine to pause a little until you do) use enquiry if necessary (Stage 2 of empathy). But if the tie-up between life story and play story is crystal clear, you might go straight into voicing your empathy.

Step 3: *Consider all your options regarding appropriate empathic response and intervention*

a) *Refusing the role option*

You need to think whether to accept or refuse the role the child wants you to play. If you refuse, you need to know how to do this gently, in a totally non-shaming way. Offer empathy and acknowledgement of what the child wants to do, and then offer alternative ways of expression. This is needed because a straight "*No*" can feel so painful to children, particularly to those who have already known so much shame and rejection. Here are some examples of how to do this.

Wajid (10) witnessed horrendous violence before coming to the UK and now gets into awful fights with his brother and other boys at school. He says to Sue his counsellor, in play, "*Hit me*" (in other words, perhaps, "*Hurt me like I've seen my family getting hurt.*" Sue refuses to play - gently and respectfully.

> **Sue:** *I don't want to do that. But I'm thinking, maybe in asking me, that you are letting me know something you have known about hitting and hurting.*

Wren (10) was sexually abused when she was five. She is with Kate her keyworker, who she likes very much.

> **Wren:** *I am going to be a monster and I am going to rip this doll's head off and stick a pencil up her bum and then Kate, you call her a bloody slut.*
>
> **Kate:** *I don't want to do or say that Wren, and we can't do that with the doll, so instead can you show me the feelings and happenings in a story on paper? Here are some pens and pencils - I think it is a story that really does need to be told and for me to really listen well.*
>
> or
>
> **Kate:** *Thank you for telling me this story. I am not going to respond in the way you want, but can you show me all this in the sandplay box instead. Here are the miniatures you can choose from. It's like a little theatre. I think it is a story that really does need to be told and for me to really listen well.*
>
> or
>
> **Kate:** *I don't want to do that but the story of the monster and the doll needs to be told I think, so I'm glad you have. I'll try and draw some of the important feelings in the story you've told me so far (creates a Big Empathy Drawing). Can you tell me if you want to change anything in the picture to be right for you? I may have got some things wrong or not understood something well enough.*

> Kate then empathises with all the horror and terror for the little doll and that no-one was there for her and no grown-up came in to help and say *Stop*!

Ben (7) is frightened of a teacher Mr Thomas, as he has a loud voice and sometimes shouts. Ben has told Penny about this.

> **Ben:** *You be a horrid monster Penny and I am the frightened mouse so you have to shout at me and tell me off and tell me I'm just no good.*
>
> **Penny:** *I don't want to play the monster in your story Ben. So you can show me the story in a drawing instead, I think it will be more useful, and we can see what happens.*

So you can give the child the option of drawing the scene together, or doing a sandplay, where the monster can talk to the mouse and vice versa, or you can play out the scene with puppets. This ensures that the child has more *psychological distance*, whilst still allowing empathy and attunement from the adult. As ever, the enactment needs to be followed by a reflective process. Put the puppets down, away from the thinking cushions, so you can refer to them in your thinking time. The *physical distance* helps give perspective and psychological safety.

b) *Accepting the role option*

If you decide to accept the role of a particular aggressor, there needs to be clear ground rules. These must be followed to ensure you do not re-traumatise the child or strengthen his destructive patterns of behaviour or negative beliefs about himself. Basically, it is vital that in the role-play you still act as the child's advocate. Here is how to do it:

Step 1: Put something on your head - like a garment of clothing (*but never a mask, see above*) or wear something to distinguish you as the sadistic character from you as the child's advocate (no special costume needed for this - you are just you). If you feel some of the words the child wants you to say are just too awful, don't say them, but enact a character of a cruel person in your tone of voice. If the child still insists you say the words, say "*No, I don't want to*", and hold your ground.

Step 2: After the cruel or frightening character has been attacking (you in the role as the aggressor), come out of role, throw off your aggressor clothes and stand next to the child as advocate. Enable the child to take back their power and talk back to the frightening figure (in the form of the aggressor's clothes lying on the floor). If the child is too frightened or immobilised, you can talk to the bully instead, adding appropriate psychological messages as you go.

So Ben asks to play the monster game and wants Penny to be the monster: he says he will be a mouse.

> **Penny:** (in monster disguise): *Ah little mouse, I am coming to get you. I have all the power with my loud voice and frightening ways ...*
> (Ben, squeaking with delight, runs away from Penny. This goes on for some time as Penny sees that the 'mouse' is having fun running away: Ben is clearly not being re-traumatised)
>
> **Penny:** (throwing off monster disguise and standing side by side with Ben) *OK Ben, how shall we deal with this monster with his loud voice and frightening ways?*

If the child doesn't come up with anything, offer some suggestions. Put the monster in a treacle well? Throw him to the four winds? Roll him into a ball and put him in a gigantic canon and fire him off into outer space? And so on. Some people might say, but aren't you encouraging primitive revenge? I would strongly disagree. Very timid children need to go through empowering enactments like this just to feel a sense of strength in their bodies, the physiological sensation of protest, of finding their "*No*" and their "*Stop*" and all the more so with the practitioner as advocate and supporter by their side. It's a first for many children who have 'sold out' to total compliance with a frightening parent, in order to survive.

So this is how it actually continues with Ben and Penny.

> **Ben:** *Make him into sausages.*
>
> **Penny:** *OK, here we go, I'll just prepare the sausage machine but I also want to say something to the monster* (talking to the monster cloak on the floor). *Hey monster, you clearly do not know that mice have a right to be treated gently, and if they need to be told off, to do it in a nice way, not in a frightening way. You had no right to scare mouse like that.*

After this Penny chooses to read the story of *Teenie Weenie* (by the author, 2003) to Ben. It's all about Teenie Weenie who was also doing the far-too-hard things on his own, just like Ben. The psychological message in the book is never do hard things (like taking on bullies) all on your own. Always find some togetherness.

More distancing techniques

Talk directly to the victim in the story the child has been enacting or wanting you to enact with her

Gracie (7) played out a spontaneously violent enactment. She pinned a doll against the wall and shouted *"Shut up, you stupid brat."* Gracie needed to show me this, for me to be her 'vital witness', so to speak, to use my eyes and ears to see and hear what she had seen; to feel the shock and pain that she had felt when witnessing this dreadful event. So I used the technique of speaking directly to the victim in her play. I picked up the doll, held her in my arms and said softly. *"I am so sorry that you have suffered so terribly. That no-one protected you. That no grown-up was there to say, "Stop".*

Move from the performing arts to the visual arts

The performing arts include drama enactments which involve child and adult through bodily participation, whereas the visual arts involve inbuilt *psychological distancing* to support reflecting - through pens, paints and so on. In short, they bring in that vital element of standing back.

Consider moving away from metaphor and enactment into direct conversation about the child's life

I had some sessions with one child who had witnessed repeated domestic violence, after which his mother had to be hospitalised. This child and his mother ended up in a refuge. In one session with me, he said, *"Be a dragon with shining teeth and red hot fire and scare me to death."* Believing by this time in our relationship and that he could tolerate some direct expression, I said quietly *"Perhaps you are remembering your Dad when he was like that."* The child looked at the floor and said, *"He broke my Mummy you know. But she is being mended now."* He no longer needed to do the enactment

What to do if the child's playing or storytelling leaves you unable to think properly

If you are flooded with the images in the child's playing or spontaneous storytelling, or you think you have not been able to hold in mind some of the emotional themes from the story, take time after the talk-time with the child to reflect again, without the child being present. Divide your page into two columns, one with the heading, *Child's life story* and the other with the heading *Child's play story*. Then write down the emotional themes common to both. Then during the following talk-time, you can say to the child, "*I have been thinking about your very important story in the week. I want to show you my picture reply to it.*" I've described how to do this kind of 'picture reply' on p.79 (*The Big Empathy Drawing*).

Some people suggest that if you bring the enactment up again on another occasion for the child, it could be potentially intrusive, as the child may have moved on from there. I disagree. *Whilst timing is important*, these powerful key themes in a child's life, such as feelings of abandonment, horror and desolation, are not something you quickly move on from or get over. They live on to haunt the child and derail healthy development emotionally, socially and academically, until they are addressed by a mature adult mind capable of mentalising and providing validating empathy.

What to do with what the child has made

With sandplay pictures, ask the child whether they would like you to take a photo of what they have made. I have never met a child who said no. One teenager said, "*When you take a photo of what I made, it makes it not not worth it.*"

Make sure you have two copies of the photos as the child may lose his. If the child has done a series of sandplay pictures, which show a clear continuation or development of a theme or themes over time, it can be very powerful to lay them all out on the floor in one session, side by side, and talk them through with the child.

In terms of things that are made like paintings or clay objects, if you are working in a school setting, it is best to store them in a safe place. Then the child can take them home if they like at the end of all your sessions together. However, there should be no hard and fast rule here. An image may be hugely powerful to a child who is then desperate to take it home. If so, let him, and photograph it first so that if it gets broken at home, or loses its magic because it is no longer in the context of your time together, it can be re-made or remembered. By caring so well for the child's images, the child can get a strong sense of *"I care about you."*

Chapter 11: Talking about feelings through story

If you want your children to be brilliant, tell them fairy tales. If you want them to be very brilliant, tell them even more fairy tales.

Albert Einstein

Introduction

Stories! I really want to share with you why stories are an essential and often profoundly moving resource for anyone who wants to connect at a deeper level with a child. You can convey empathy for their particular life circumstances and troubles, along with vital knowledge about the human condition; hope, and ways forward, and all without once referring to the child's actual life.

This keeps the most defended of children feeling psychologically safe and protected against shame. So many children feel acknowledged in their particular plight by an appropriately chosen therapeutic story. They are like a kind of soul food for them. Hence they ask for that story to be read again and again and again.

So this chapter is designed to empower you to use story as a therapeutic tool with children and young people. I'll look at what makes particular stories therapeutic, referring both to the brain science as well as psychology. Then I'll explore how to choose a published therapeutic story relevant to the emotional issues of the child you're working with. Finally, I'll give you some vital information about how to make up your own therapeutic story, including useful lists of emotional themes and psychological messages to support you. I'll use an actual therapeutic story as an illustration throughout this section.

Overall, my hope is that this chapter will inspire you to dare to engage your imagination in healing conversations with children; to take the plunge to compose your own stories, and see how potent they can be in moving the child or teenager into more positive thinking or action, enabling them to feel deeply seen, and often serving as a highly respectful 'jolt' out of stuck and negative ways of feeling and thinking into new ways of being in the world.

What is a therapeutic story?

A therapeutic story is a story designed to help children reflect on their emotional states and relationships, in a way that enables them to live their lives in a better, more creative and more thoughtful way. In a therapeutic story, the psychological processes of the central characters and their adventures are packed with meaning. There is frequent comment on the central character's mental and emotional states. The characters suffer; they get stuck, and they often make bad decisions.

But then things change. The central character finds themselves on a transformative journey. This is because, at some point in the story, someone or something appears who helps the character to make different choices and so find a far more creative way of dealing with what life has thrown at them. As a result, the main character successfully adopts -

- A new behaviour
- A new way of being
- A new way of thinking
- A new way of feeling
- A new way of seeing things

Therapeutic stories can touch children on the deepest level. They can also teach children to empathise with the plight of others. Therapeutic story is a vehicle through which to teach children key psychological and scientific research findings about the human condition that will help them to live their lives well.

Therapeutic stories always include:

✔ empathy for the child's situation

✔ important knowledge about emotions, relationships, and the human condition

✔ important psychological messages and permissions, for example: *You can ask for help; You have a right to protest about unkindness; Children have rights* (see Appendix V, *Key Psychological Messages*)

The key reasons why therapeutic stories can be so healing

- Therapeutic stories can be used as a vehicle to convey to children profound, evidence-based insights, in a palatable way.

- Therapeutic stories can enable a child to dare to reflect on their painful life experiences, instead of running away from them or feeling overwhelmed by them, because the story brings safe distance.

- Therapeutic stories can give the child a sense of being profoundly understood. This can bring the child a sense of relief, a knowing that feelings can change and transform, that feelings do not simply have to be endured or repressed.

- Therapeutic stories offer a child new ways of seeing their problems, thinking about their thoughts and feeling their feelings.

- Therapeutic stories can enable children to reflect on more creative possibilities of how to live their lives and deal with their problems.

What makes therapeutic story such a safe conversational tool?

As therapeutic story uses the disguise of metaphorical images, and a different context, it enables the child to look at his powerful feelings from a 'safe distance', particularly when straight talking is just not working. Therapeutic stories offer protection through the use of metaphorical disguise, so the child can retreat to the safe position of *'This story is not about me'* whenever they like. This is particularly important for the child who easily feels shamed or exposed.

Therapeutic stories can avoid the child's resistance, defensiveness, blocking their ears: *"I hate it when you talk to me about feelings/Don't talk to me like that! /Blah blah blah."* This is because therapeutic story offers indirect as opposed to direct expression, as in the saying, 'One tells something to the door, so that the wall will hear it' (Rowshan 1997, p.50). In other words the child can go along with identifying with the plight and the joys of the main character but with none of the shame that might be triggered if a grown-up were to talk to him directly about the issue.

Whereas many children refuse to listen to an adult talking to them directly about their feelings, they will listen to a story about 'someone else' experiencing something similar to what they have experienced.

How therapeutic stories help children to feel and think differently about their painful life experiences

All sorrows can be borne if you put them in a story.   Isak Dinesen 1957

In a good therapeutic story, the child is likely to identify with the story's central character, the one who is grappling with the very same difficult feelings/life issues as he is. In so doing, the child is likely to go on the same journey as the main character in the story. He will probably understand the central character's defeats and obstacles intimately, because they resonate with his own defeats and obstacles.

And because of all this, the child may no longer feel so alone with his problems and feelings: because hey presto, look, *this* character in *this* book is having them too! The child is then likely to feel something of the character's relief in coming through a very painful and/or difficult time to a place of empowerment, creative possibility and/or resolution. So he will be in a very different place in his mind post-story to pre-story. Pre-story he was on his own, with none of the empathy, psychological messages (mature reflection) or creative possibilities he now has post-story.

The science of therapeutic story listening

When you listen to a boring Powerpoint presentation, the language processing centres (Broca's area and Wernicke's areas) light up in the brain. But brain research (Mar et al 2011) shows that it's very different when we're listening to fascinating stories. Here so many other parts of our brains light up as well as those involved in language processing. That's why listening to stories can so entrance and emotionally engage both children and us adults.

a) *The sensory cortex lights up with a good story*

Researchers (Mar et al 2011) found that the part of the brain activated in story-listening is the sensory cortex, meaning that the person experiences events in the story *as if* the events were actually taking place around her in reality. The more engaging the story, the more engaged the listener, the more activation in the sensory cortex. In other words, the listener is seeing, hearing and sometimes even physically reacting (in her head) to everything she hears.

So if you have some very important psychological messages for a child, conveying these through story can be hugely impactful as the child can get emotionally and sensorially involved. What's more, research shows that children experience marked physiological reactions to stories (strong visceral reactions: Rall & Harris, 2000) so don't be surprised if they shiver, cuddle close, or get very animated when listening (Bar-Haimet al, 2004).

Hasson (2013) also looked at listening comprehension. He found that the more the listeners understood the story, the more their brain activity dovetailed with the person telling the story. When the adult is storyteller and the child is story listener the more they will both experience being in synch and togetherness.

b) *The insula lights up with a good story*

When a story is really gripping, the listener identifies so much with what is going on, and empathises with central characters, that in effect the story becomes *her* story, from the brain's point of view. Her insula lights up. The insula is the part of the brain vital for self-awareness, body awareness, and here-and-now perceiving (Craig 2009). As University of Princeton's Uri Hasson (2013) says, 'A story is the only way to activate parts in the brain so that a listener turns the story into their own … experience … storytelling is the only way to plant ideas into other people's minds'. This research informs one of our key decisions to use so many short 'stories' about children in this book, to help you as reader to really engage in the ideas I've been presenting.

c) *Brain networks used to listen to story are the same as those activated in socially intelligent thinking*

In 2009, Raymond Mar (York University, Canada) carried out a meta-analysis (86 fMRI studies) of what happens to people when engaged in the act of listening to stories. He found that the brain networks used to listen to stories were the same as those we use in our capacity for *mentalising*. This is the ability to skillfully manage our transactions with other people by both reflecting on what we are thinking and feeling in the moment, and imagining into what the other person may be thinking and feeling, and why. We know from Hauser's (2006) research that the more psychologically-minded teenagers are, (that is, the more their capacity for mentalisation is developed), the more they are likely to thrive socially and emotionally in life.

So it is deeply significant that therapeutic story can develop mentalising skills as well as social understanding around such central human themes as loss, betrayal, longing, outrage, the desolation of aloneness and the uplifting, energising experience of togetherness. In fact Mar et al (2009) found that pre-schoolers who had lots of stories read to them were better 'mentalisers', more reflective about their social world, than those who had not had lots of stories read to them. Interestingly, but not unexpectedly, television watching didn't have this same effect.

d) *Choosing and talking about the stories affects the capacity for empathy*

Finally, it's worth remembering that Aram & Aviram (2009) found that when mothers carefully chose stories for their children which spoke about emotional situations and relationships, their children rated higher than other children in terms of social understanding and level of empathy, even after the level of maternal education was taken into account.

Mothers' preferences for such books may also be related to the nature of their conversations with their children during storybook reading. A good therapeutic story will invite a deeper level of discussion about relationships and emotional situations. In fact, Bhavnagri & Samuels (1996) found that stories focusing on relationships promote preschoolers' social adjustment and the understanding of the 'other' more than stories which lack this element.

So whenever you're reading or telling a child a therapeutic story, discussion during or afterwards is likely to support the development of his empathy and social intelligence. As the International Reading Association (IRA) states: 'It is the talk that surrounds the storybook reading that gives it power, helping children to bridge both what is in the story and in their own lives' (*IRA & National Association for the Education of Young Children* (NAEYC) 1998, p.199).

Choosing published children's therapeutic stories

The first big decision is whether you choose a published therapeutic story for the child you're wanting to help, or whether you make one up. Both of these are of value, particularly if you find a therapeutic story that makes important comment and attunes empathically with what the child is going through. If you can't find a published story that speaks of emotional issues and themes relevant to the child's life, then it's definitely time to make one up. But as there are many out there, I'll first talk about published stories and what to look for.

Published storybooks usually won't say on them that they are a therapeutic story. It's only by reading them that that you will know that that's what they are. To get you started, I have included a list of potent therapeutic stories in Appendix VII.

If you have chosen a published therapeutic story make sure you read it to the child, as opposed to the child reading it on her own. This way you can monitor the child's reactions throughout, leaving enough time at the end of the story for reflection together. Reading the story aloud to the child also means you are using your voice to add lot to the rich quality of what the story conveys.

Even with teenagers, if they'll let you, still read the story aloud to them as your tone of voice is such a key factor in optimising the therapeutic potential of the story (this is as opposed to the teenager taking the book and reading it on their own in their bedroom or saying they have but they haven't!). Some teenagers really like being read to again such a long time after their childhood years, and others have never been read to, so for some it can be really fun and novel. But you might have to use a bit of techno-savvy. Put the story into a powerpoint for example, project it on a wall and give them a beanbag to chill out on whilst you read it!

The therapeutic potential of published children's stories: Tips on what to look out for

i. When you read a published story, are you moved, emotionally engaged, satisfied? If *you* aren't, the child probably won't be either. If you are bored with too many words or dull bits - the child probably will be too.

ii. Is the central character in the story facing a problem? And then do they manage to overcome it through relationship and reflection, rather than quick fixes? Lots of children's 'emotional' stories offer quick fixes. That's not how change happens in real life.

iii. Are the central character's emotional states and painful feelings central to the story?

iv. Choose picture books which grab the child's attention and will engage them from the start. This is the same for teenagers (but sadly there are all too few therapeutic picture books or manga style animation books for teenagers. I have written one for teenagers called *Smasher* (2008): you could also use this to inspire your own stories for teenagers).

v. The fewer words the better - one to six lines per picture is ideal. This means the story will be more like a powerful poem where every word matters. Remember, grab the child's attention and keep it. Additionally with children who have poor concentration, you have limited time. Also psychological messages can get lost with too many words.

vi. Avoid stories with just too much detail, too many sub-plots. There needs to be one or two key psychological messages ringing out loud.

vii. Choose stories with sufficient disguise and no moralising. Some are so heavy-handed, with a sense of *"Now I'm going to tell you, child, a worthy story that you will relate to."* With such stories, any self-respecting child I've ever met would quickly realise that the adult is intent on him or her 'getting the message', and totally lose interest, and any respect for you.

viii. With a child who can't yet read, or has limited attention span, you can summarise the content for each picture, if reading every word is going to lose his interest.

How to make up your own therapeutic story

This section will address all you need to know about how to make up and deliver your own therapeutic story to a child. I will help you in the transformative process of how you get from the child's actual life situation (for example, a child witnessing domestic violence) to a fantasy realm communicated in such a way as to make the story therapeutic for the child.

Choosing the main character

For disguise and indirect expression, which as I've said will provide protection for the child, think of a character who is sufficiently different from the girl or boy with whom you are working. Choose a fantasy character, or choose a child of the opposite sex, different age and so on. Give the character a name very different from the child's actual name. Once I told a child called Celia her life story using unicorns. She was totally gripped. At the end of the story, I said, *"And the unicorn's name was Celia."* She ran out of the room. It was one of the best moments of supervision in my life. I realised just how important disguise is as a mechanism of protection for the child.

Make sure that the character is of age-appropriate interest to the child - for example, dinosaurs and fairies might work with four or five year olds but not with most older children. Teenagers may find superheroes or real characters more acceptable. That said, the 'emotional age' of some teenagers is much younger than their chronological age, so stories about how animals or fantasy creatures cope and deal with feelings may still be appropriate. Where this is the case, introducing the story to the teenager with an explicit comment such as - *"I use this story with younger children, but I wondered what you thought about it?"* can help avoid the teenager feeling patronised or humiliated.

Choosing an imaginary landscape to provide the context for the character's psychological journey

The imaginary landscape again supports the transforming of the child's actual life situation into the realm of the symbolic. For example, the situation of a child who has seen his mother repeatedly snorting cocaine may be transformed symbolically into lands of volcanoes, swirling swamps and deathly deserts.

All dreams happen in a landscape and portray feeling states so well. Here are some landscapes you might like to consider for your story. Choose which best portrays the emotional world of the child you are working with, or the emotional world they have known which is still causing them emotional pain.

Desolate	Nightmarish
Frightening	Chaotic
Bleak	Overwhelming
Topsy-turvy	Unsafe
Barren	Harsh, hostile

Of course use settings and landscapes of cultural relevance for a child - an orderly supermarket scene for example, would not be appropriate for a child in a North African orphanage.

Choosing the story's emotional themes

Have a look at the chart on p.382, *Common Emotional Themes for Troubled Children*. From the list there, think of the emotional themes central to this child's life story. These may be the themes that are coming up in his play too. In making up your story, these themes will be the ones experienced in the story by the central character.

At this point I want to introduce a therapeutic story to illustrate all of the above points and those which follow.

The Day After the Worst Day Ever

This is a therapeutic story to help children who have suffered trauma and shock. Too many children have had something shocking happen to them, which has left them reeling with anxiety, depression, anger or full blown Post-Traumatic Stress Disorder (PTSD). They often feel that life, as they have known it, has ended. This story acknowledges just how painful and frightening things can feel when good things in a child's life, often expected to continue forever, suddenly change into something bad. Here are some examples of shocking events:

- Parents announcing that they are no longer going to live together
- Coming home from school and finding mother drunk and unconscious on the floor
- Being told Dad/Mum has moved out.
- Being told that your parent or sibling is terminally ill
- Seeing Dad hit Mum/Mum hit Dad for the first time
- Being taken into care
- The day the child is sexually abused by their parent/relative/friend of the family
- Being told that it's not safe to live in your country anymore, feeling like you've lost everything that matters when you suddenly move to a strange country

One Chinese client I shall never forget described the day when he was caned on his hand by his mother, for the first time. He was just four years old. Before that he remembered being really happy. Then that day when he was four his mother beat him as he was not practising his piano enough. *"You will thank me later because your piano playing will be so envied,"* his mother said. My client remembered just crying and crying from utter shock for days, and reported being deeply depressed for a very long eight years after this. He said part of him was grateful to his mother, as he was now very good at playing the piano. *"And the cost?"* I asked. *"The cost was dreadful,"* he said.

Here is the story, for a child who has experienced trauma ...

The Day After the Worst Day Ever ...

Aysha pretended the horrid thing hadn't happened.
But of course it had happened.
"Don't think about it," Aysha said to herself.
"Just get on with life."

So the day after the worst day ever
Aysha went to school as she always did.
She ate her school lunch as she always did.
She walked home from school with Anton and Steph as she always did.

"What a beautiful day" said Anton.
Aysha only saw grey clouds.

"What a beautiful yellow-winged butterfly" said Steph.

Aysha only saw a squashed fly in a dirty gutter.

"Yummy ice cream" said Anton.

But Aysha only felt a sharp biting cold on her tongue.

That night Aysha had horrid dreams of broken bottles, pooey loos,

Spikey worlds and thunderstorms.

Then falling and falling into a dark dark nothing.

The next day was the same, but worse.

"Don't frown at me, Steph" said Aysha.

"You're bonkers, Aysha," said Steph,

"I was smiling at you."

"Let's play camping," said Anton.

Camping was Aysha's bestest game.

But today it felt so stupid and dull.

"You're no fun anymore Aysha," said Anton.

At school Aysha felt too much.

Sometimes her body felt like it was on fire,

Sometimes like a frozen rock.

One minute she screamed and frightened other children.

The next, she hid under her desk.

"What's happening to me?" thought Aysha.

"Sometimes I'm like a mouthy monster and then a fearful ferret."

So she tried to feel nothing, but that didn't work either.

At lunchtime Aysha felt so bad she just ran and ran
To the woody bit at the far end of the playground.
"It's like I don't know which way up the world is anymore," she thought.

"You called?" said a voice from behind a big oak tree
Aysha saw a man watering some withering flowers
"Who are you?"
"The school gardener. My name is Mr Elfin"
"That's an unusual name," said Aysha.
"It's because my other work is as a woodland elf" said Mr Elfin.
*"I help plants, animals and children who are struggling, too much
with life."*

Aysha looked down at her shoes.
"Sounds a bit like me actually Mr Elfin," she said.
*"Something's just happened in my life and now the world's gone bad
Like a nightmare's got stuck in my brain."*

"Hmm," said Mr Elfin.
*"I wonder if it feels like everything good is somewhere else.
And you try to forgot, to get on with things
But yucky feelings follow you everywhere
And you want to know how you can get your happiness back?"*

"Goodness Mr Elfin." said Aysha,
"You really DO know."
Mr Elfin looked sad and said,
*"Sorry to tell you this Aysha, but the past can't go into the past
Until someone helps you with it now.*

So why don't we travel together to what you've known?
But this time I'll be with you."

Suddenly Mr Elfin started to look far more like a woodland elf
than a gardener.
And then to Aysha's surprise he magicked up a large Flip-Flop-Bird
And invited Aysha to hop on its back.

Together Aysha and Mr Elfin soared up up into the dark sky
Then through Storms of Sadness and Shouts of Shock
Through Great Clouds of Cruelty to Heartless Hills
Then through Blaming Bog, to Lonely Lake.

"What are these terrible places?" asked Aysha
Feeling horrible dread in her tummy.
"They are the places you've known, Aysha" said Mr Elfin
"You've suffered them all, with no help, all alone.
But not any more. I'm with you now, to see, to hear, to know."

Aysha started to cry,
"The bad thing was too hard.
It was too hard, just too hard."
"I know," said Mr Elfin softly,
"And worse, was that no-one helped you with it
And no-one knew how much you were hurting.
And no-one helped you to know that none of it was your fault."
They travelled on to more 'mind-places.'
But as Aysha felt the warmth of Mr Elfin's being there
And saw his knowing eyes and heard his voice

And knew that he knew

Aysha felt stronger, and as she did

The terrible shock started to leave her.

After that day, Aysha often sat talking with Mr Elfin

In playground time, whilst he did the gardening.

Many times Aysha spoke of her rage and fear and deep deep sad.

Many times Mr Elfin listened to the trillion changes the bad thing

had brought to Aysha's life.

Then one day, Mr Elfin said, *"Aysha, I'm needed as a gardener in another*

school now. The time is right.

You're wise and strong now, from your own knowing.

But know too that my elfin self is always close by."

Aysha was comforted to know that.

Soon after Aysha, Anton and Steph were walking back from school.

"What a beautiful day." said Anton

"Yes", said Aysha, *"What a beautiful day."*

"What a beautiful butterfly with yellow wings" said Steph.

"Yes," said Aysha *"Such shiny wings."*

"Yummy ice cream," said Anton.

It was the best Aysha had ever tasted.

"Let's play camping," said Steph

They cooked pretend sausages on a pretend fire

And sang songs in the long long grass.

"Ah life is good," said Aysha.

To her delight, she suddenly felt the flutter of elfin wings

> Like a gentle breeze above her head.
>
> *"Ah you know that now!"* said that familiar voice.
>
> *"Yes I do,"* said Aysha, and then she paused,
>
> *"Perhaps the … most important thing of all to know!"*

Choosing evidence-based psychology/neuroscience about the human condition to include in your therapeutic story

A therapeutic story, by and large, will inform children about vital psychology concerning the human condition which is specific to the emotional pain they are experiencing. Leaving a child without this knowledge is, in my opinion, a form of neglect. After a painful life event, for example, too many children end up thinking that they are mad or bad, rather than realising that what they are feeling and thinking may be totally appropriate to the situation and, as in Aysha's case in the story, represents a totally understandable response to awful shock.

For example, feeling depressed and powerless after your parents split up is natural. After such a shocking event, some children feel deeply negative about themselves, the self-referencing: *"It was my fault Mum and Dad split up"*. This can continue for years, even a lifetime. Not informing a child of crucial facts about the human condition, or about human emotionality, can be extremely harmful to their emotional well-being.

So in our story - *The Day After the Worst Day Ever,* there are lots of psychological facts about PTSD and the effects of trauma on body and mind. By hearing the story, the child suffering in this way should feel that what is specific to their pain and its various manifestations, in their behaviour and symptoms, is being truly acknowledged and understood. Or let me put it another way: the story indirectly helps the child to understand a lot about traumatic shock and what it does to mind and body. Here are some examples:

Fact about the human condition **(i)**

We know that in PTSD the high levels of stress hormones colour perception. Danger and threat can be seen everywhere - even in utterly benign environments. As Van der Kolk, leading neuroscientist and psychologist on PTSD says: 'The world increasingly becomes an unsafe place: innocuous sounds provoke an alerting startle response; trivial cues are perceived as indicators of danger' (1999, p.13). 'Traumatised children tend to communicate what has happened to them not in words, but by responding to the world as a dangerous place' (Van der Kolk 2003, p.20).

> *"Don't frown at me, Steph"* said Aysha.
>
> *"You're bonkers, Aysha,"* said Steph,
>
> *"I was smiling at you."*
>
> ***
>
> *"Yummy ice cream"* said Anton.
>
> But Aysha only felt a sharp biting cold on her tongue.

Pertinent to the story and to the biochemistry and bodily states of PTSD is also John Milton's (1608-1674) statement in Paradise Lost: 'The mind is its own place, and in itself can make a heaven of hell, or a hell of heaven'.

Fact about the human condition **(ii)**

Traumatic shock and the failure to properly process what has happened commonly leads to states of hyper-arousal, problems with attention and concentration, and physical symptoms. As a result, the child or teenager may make attempts at emotional numbing, trying to feel nothing, to stop the pain. As Van der Kolk (1999) goes on to say: 'The person's own physiology becomes a source of fear' (p.13). Also, responses to strong emotions are often reduced to flight/flight reactions, rather than emotions being seen as useful information for what you want/don't want, and signals for positive action. But then what the child experiences all too often is an awful to-ing and fro-ing between hyper-arousal to emotional numbing and back again. This rollercoaster in itself can feel deeply disturbing to the child.

> At school Aysha felt too much.
> Sometimes her body felt like it was on fire, sometimes like a frozen rock.
> One minute she screamed and frightened other children.
> The next, she hid under her desk.
> *"What's happening to me?"* thought Aysha.
> *"Sometimes I'm like a mouthy monster and then a fearful ferret."*
> So she tried to feel nothing, but that didn't work either.

Fact about the human condition (iii)

It is important for all of us to have someone help us process traumatic events. It is impossible to heal oneself from the pain and shock of traumatic experiences. It is only possible in the presence of a person whose reflective, thoughtful, non-judgmental mind enables us to process the extreme psychological assaults we have suffered. But we know that just thinking about the trauma or talking about it with someone who is not good at listening, and who is not empathic, can re-traumatise.

In contrast, when traumas are shared with someone who can offer emotional regulation, empathy and compassion, memories can be transformed and integrated into something manageable. The 'affect labelling' studies bear this out, in showing that talking about a trauma (to someone who can truly listen) is far more effective in lowering arousal levels than distraction, cognitive reappraisal or just bearing the pain (*see affect labelling studies*, Kircanski et al, 2012).

Aysha started to cry.

"The bad thing was too hard. It was too hard, just too hard."

"I know," said Mr Elfin softly,

"And worse, was that no-one helped you with it

 And no-one knew how much you were hurting

 And no-one helped you to know that none of it was your fault."

They travelled on to more 'mind-places.'

But as Aysha felt the warmth of Mr Elfin's being there,

And saw his knowing eyes and heard his voice

And knew that he knew.

Aysha felt stronger, and as she did

The terrible shock started to leave her.

Choosing key psychological messages to include in your story

As well as including some key psychological *evidence* specific to the pain of the child, a therapeutic story should include other kinds of psychological messages. These are the ones you think the child needs to hear. By and large psychological messages will be communicated to the central character, by one of the other characters/beings in the story. Some messages are designed to challenge and replace the child's current negative, life-limiting or often grossly inaccurate beliefs about themselves, others, or even life in general. Other messages will empower the child, leading them to take positive action in their lives.

Once again, psychological messages used in a therapeutic story should always be evidence-based in the sense that their validity can be entirely backed by psychological and/or neuroscientific research studies. So if people accuse you of just putting ideas in a child's head, or say it's 'just indoctrination' - they'll be wrong! That is, of course, if you ensure all the time that the messages you choose are never your personal opinion but can stand up to evidence-based scrutiny!

By way of example, my published story, *The Day The Sea Went Out …* (2003) is about the 'art' of grieving. The main character - Eric the Sanddragon, is doing what a lot of children do when hit by some awful loss, just trying to get on with things (Eric's loss is his beloved sea, that one day goes out and never comes back). But this coping mechanism can lead to a debilitating depression, as happens to Eric.

One key psychological message in the story is taken from the work of John Bowlby: 'It is not possible to grieve without the presence of another' (Bowlby 1973). So Eric finds someone to do his mourning with! This theory is then reinforced by the neuroscientific evidence that emotional and physiological regulation comes from crying out one's grief with someone who can offer solace, and not by bottling it up (Rottenberg, et al, 2003). The story also offers insights taken from Freud's 1917 paper, *Mourning and Melancholia*, in which he speaks about the pain of grieving an attachment figure. Again, this is backed by the science of grief, which shows that 'coming off a loved person' is as painful as 'coming off heroin'. This is because the opioids triggered by loving an attachment figure and taking heroin are both highly addictive. (Panksepp 1998).

Let's look at the psychological messages in the story *The Day after the Worst Day Ever*. In the story, Aysha, who has suffered traumatic shock, thinks that the best thing is just to carry on as normal. She soon realises that there is no normal, and that her mind and body have been hugely affected by the shock she has experienced. So the key psychological message in the story is that when experiencing a terrible shock, it's vital to get help from someone who can offer you empathy, emotional regulation and help you feel all the feelings about the trauma that you may have blocked at the time.

"Hmm," said Mr Elfin.
"I wonder if it feels like everything good is somewhere else.
And you try to forgot, to get on with things

But yucky feelings follow you everywhere

And you want to know how you can get your happiness back?"

"Goodness Mr Elfin" said Aysha,

"You really DO know."

Mr Elfin looked sad and said,

"Sorry to tell you this Aysha, but the past can't go into the past

Until someone helps you with it now.

So why don't we travel together to what you've known?

But this time I'll be with you."

***

"What are these terrible places?" asked Aysha

Feeling horrible dread in her tummy.

"They are the places you've known Aysha" said Mr Elfin

"You've suffered them all, with no help, all alone.

But not any more. I'm with you now, to see, to hear, to know."

***

After that day, Aysha often sat talking with Mr Elfin

In playground time, whilst he did the gardening.

Many times Aysha spoke of her rage and fear and deep deep sad.

Many times Mr Elfin listened to the trillion changes the bad thing

had brought to Aysha's life.

How to convey the psychological message through your therapeutic story

a. *Keep psychological messages no longer than two lines. Any more and you will be verging on lecturing and in danger of the child switching off, losing concentration.*

b. *Don't make one of your characters communicate two psychological messages in one sentence. It's too much to take in and both messages will lose their power and impact.*

c. *The way these messages are expressed to the child will need to be adapted and given in developmental age-appropriate language, and disguised in a way that makes them a part of the story.*

d. *Ensure against a character conveying a message in a patronising or 'teachy' way.*

e. *As you will see from the list on p.405 some of the Key Psychological Messages begin 'Sometimes children feel ...' and others are more personalised comments, for example, "If you don't like yourself, it could be that ..." Beginning your sentence with "Sometimes children feel ..." is appropriate for children who may find sentences with 'you' in them too direct.*

The development of plot and the four stages of a good therapeutic story

So finally, let's think of the therapeutic story as a journey from a painful place A, to an empowering place B. But getting to place B is never a quick fix (for example, aliens come in and make it all better). It is only reached as a result of a combination of *relationship, reflection, and positive action* on the part of the central character. I'll illustrate the stages by reference to the story in this chapter.

Stage 1: Empathy

In your story, describe the emotional pain of the main character or what he or she is struggling with (the emotional pain and struggles of the child you are working with, and disguised, of course). If you can, have the main character use coping strategies similar to those coping mechanisms used by the child. Show how these chosen coping mechanisms are leading them to deeper troubled waters, or down a road that is self-destructive and/or destructive to others. That said, try to convey empathy for why these paths have been chosen, when it seems to the character in the story that there was no other way. They were doing the best they could. The story should never convey any blame for their choices, so your child listener should never be left feeling shame through identifying with the main character.

In our sample story, *The Day After the Worst Day Ever*, Aysha is suffering from PTSD. She attempts to cope with it by trying not to feel anything, and then moves from implosion to an explosion of feelings in desperate and failed attempts to manage the difficult feelings and often unbearable physiological hyper-arousal which result from her PTSD.

Stage 2: Stuck points, crisis and the cost of defence mechanisms

In your story, have the main character reach a stuck point, or crisis. Show the too-high emotional cost to the character in terms of the coping strategy he or she is using In our sample story, Aysha is becoming more and more troubled. Her friendships are suffering. She is behaving in challenging ways at school. She has nightmares and physical symptoms.

Stage 3: Relationship and reflection

The relationship and reflection stage is the opposite of stories with a quick fix. Quick fixes are not therapeutic (the problem is magicked away, the child wakes up and realises it has been a dream, the child moves house so doesn't need to suffer the bully anymore, and so on). People do not change their lives for the better with quick fixes. They change through relationship and reflection, important conversations or time with emotionally healthy adults. Without relationship and reflection, the story becomes unbelievable and not like real life at all. So this is the stage of your therapeutic story to include key psychological messages which will be conveyed through one of the characters. These messages are part of what the child needs to hear to feel empowered.

Stage 4: Empowerment

Through relationship and reflection the character is able to move into some form of positive action. So the empowerment stage is not about happy endings, but rather about using options, emotional resources, permissions, insights, and far more creative ways of dealing with the situation than the character was using at the start of the story. In the story, after the empowerment stage, the character's experience of himself/others/life will be altered, affording him a far more positive view of himself and finding that the world is a far better place to be.

In our sample story, Mr Elfin provides Aysha with empathy, helping her to reflect on and make sense of what happened to her, as she re-visits her painful memories *(I've already covered which messages Mr Elfin gave Aysha above)*. Aysha cries and rages, until she finds her own strength and 'knowing', and is no longer afraid of her painful story. As a result, from a neurophysiological perspective, the stress hormones in her brain will no longer be colouring her perception; she begins to find life 'good' once again.

How to know if your story has been effective

To conclude, you will know if your story has been effective because of the child's response. A positive response is one where the child's level of absorption and concentration is tangible. This is often followed by *"Can you read/tell the story again?"* Or even *"Can you read that bit of the story/page again?"* A negative response is where their attention wanders early on or later on. This 'supervision' will enable you to question: is the story too wordy? Patronising? Not disguised enough? Too long? Not presented in a really appealing way, say in a sandplay box with little figures? Remember, when you get feedback from a child, you can always modify your story!

Chapter 12: What to do when a child doesn't want to talk - bringing it all together

Introduction

This chapter is all about the child who doesn't want to talk about his feelings. When a child is clearly troubled but reluctant to talk about his feelings, it's a pointless task to try and 'prise his feelings out of him', and also potentially damaging, psychologically. The child is likely to feel pushed, invaded and want to withdraw even further. He may not open up again. So in this chapter we will look at what we can do instead.

Before we do so however, it's important to acknowledge that it can be hurtful for any adult when a child rejects our attempts to listen, to try to understand, or to offer her a compassionate response. What can really help when this happens is to know why. So the chapter will open with an understanding of just how hard it is for children who have been let down or hurt by adults to dare to trust us again.

Following on from this, I will summarise many of the resources I've discussed throughout the book to help you to move forward. Then I'll focus on the importance of looking at ourselves: in other words, when the work seems to be stuck, whose defences are in play? Is it really the child's defensiveness or our own defences getting in the way of the conversational flow? This section will also explore various pitfalls in our way of 'being and doing' with a child which could leave a child feeling too psychologically unsafe to want to talk to us.

But my overall aim with this chapter is to enable you to become interested, curious and resourced with all the options I've already covered when you hit that wall of "*I don't want to talk about it*". So instead of feeling so defeated that you turn away from the child, you persevere with different ways of engagement; always taking into account of course, the importance of the right place and right time for conversation with this particular child!

> The success of [a therapeutic conversation] depends on the [child's] capacity to trust another person with their helplessness and pain.
>
> Van der Kolk 1999, p.538

Let's not underestimate the time it takes for some children who have been very let down or hurt by adults to trust and dare to open up. First and foremost, I suggest you keep in mind the relational needs of the defended child who is resistant to talk-time.

The relational needs of the defended child who doesn't want to talk about his feelings

- To help me feel and talk about my painful feelings in my own time, at my own pace, in the presence of an emotionally regulating adult
- To have someone find the words to speak about what I have felt when I can't find words because my painful feelings have never been transformed into thinkable thoughts
- To have someone understand why I have needed to build walls to keep people from knowing my feelings
- To have someone help me understand what has made me not trust people with my feelings
- To be helped to discover that talking about painful feelings with a warm, compassionate adult can bring huge comfort and relief

- To have someone understand that to dare to feel painful feelings can be very frightening to me
- To have an adult empathise with what it feels like to be me
- To have someone understand that empathy, if offered to me in a too direct way, might be painful too, as it makes me feel what I am trying not to feel
- To have someone know what it is like for me to feel that I am utterly bad/worthless and to explain why children come to think like this through no fault of their own.

Recognising how hard it can be for some children to trust

Your kindness, non-judgmental stance and concern can be experienced as dangerous

To a child, care and warmth can touch their heart so much that they start to feel what they don't want to feel, because it doesn't feel safe to do so. Some children are frightened of this kind of 'melting', as your kindness may erode the very defences that have helped them to manage their life up to now. They feel they need a hardened heart to survive a too-hard life.

Your kindness can also be painful to fully feel, because it is in such stark contrast to what the child has known before. As a result, the child may feel pain at what he has been missing out on for so long. Kindness can also awaken the child or young person's attachment needs, when for so long they told themselves they really didn't need anyone, or they were better off with self-help. Such children and young people needs to be given time to feel psychologically safe enough with you to dare to feel again.

Just more of the same?

If the child has had too many interactions with adults which have left him feeling dominated, controlled, told off, lectured at, and shamed, it may be really difficult for him to get out of the mindset of '*just another grown-up's lectures*' when we try to offer him a therapeutic conversation in talk-time.

Reaching out didn't work before ...

If he has reached out (verbally or non-verbally) to an adult in the past with emotional distress, either as a baby, or child, and he has ended up feeling worse not better, you are going to need to work hard to change his perception, or strongly-held belief, that self-help is better than seeking comfort from a grown-up.

Non-verbal stress triggers

There could be something non-verbal in your communication, perhaps your tone of voice, a hand gesture, look on your face or even your hair colour or clothing that somehow reminds the child of a painful experience he had with another grown-up in the past, which raises his anxiety level with you now.

So how to go forward from here? Let's now look at what you can do to engender a sense of psychological safety in your talk-time.

Acknowledge and respect the child's need *not* to speak about their feelings

Find a way to convey to the child that you understand that he doesn't want to speak about his life or life events with you right now.

> **Harry:** (burying himself under a pile of cushions) *Don't talk to me about feelings.*
>
> **Adult:** *Perhaps it just doesn't feel right or safe enough for you to want to speak to me right now about important things in your life.*
>
> *or*
>
> **Adult:** *Perhaps it's too hard to feel and think about this right now.*

It's important that these comments are said gently, with no big deal being made, otherwise the child can feel shamed and exposed and even less likely to communicate or listen.

When appropriate for a specific child, understand and empathise with his need to keep people out and his experiences private. Start from where the child is. You can use validating empathy with a comment such as:

> **Adult:** *No wonder you don't want to speak to me, when so many grown-ups have let you down. How do you know that I am any different?*
>
> *or*
>
> **Adult:** *I know life has been too hard for you at times, so maybe you've had to build a kind of fortress around you. Why should you trust me yet? Too many grown-ups in your life haven't been trustworthy.*

Or we can talk through a puppet (if this is age appropriate for the child), empathising with why perhaps the child doesn't want to talk. Below is how you could use what I said to Harry by talking to Mr Bear puppet:

> **Margot:** *You know Mr Bear, I think perhaps Harry has had just too many grown-ups telling him things, bossing him about, not listening to him, not understanding what Harry needs. No wonder he doesn't want to listen to Mrs X (use your name here) - just another annoying grown-up! (Mr Bear whispers in your ear) What's that Mr Bear? Oh you don't like being bossed about either (Mr Bear whispers again) so you can really understand what Harry might be feeling if that has happened to him!*

We can also tell the child that it is very understandable to try to cut off from painful feelings. At the same time, we can reassure him that such feelings can be thought about in ways that might help him feel better, particularly if he is with a kind, understanding adult who can help with the thinking. Most children and teenagers understand the concept of 'emotional baggage' from the past spoiling your life now. From this starting point you can talk about how the 'baggage' can be worked through in conversation with you so that it no longer blights life. Of course a child or teenager may rubbish what you say for the moment, but that's OK: he may still have taken in your comment at some level.

Work towards helping the child feel as psychologically safe with you as possible - a summary of some of the techniques

> Being right next to the person ... so tenderly, so closely with so much feeling, melts resistance. The [child] finds himself wanting to speak, wanting to share ... naturally coming upon essential parts of [who he is] previously hidden from the world as well as from himself.   Fosha 2000, p.30

The child will only be motivated to share his feelings with you if he is pretty confident that he will feel better (more emotionally regulated) afterwards, rather than worse (more emotionally dysregulated). In other words, if there is no sense of a lifeboat, children will very sensibly not want to jump into the stormy sea!

If the child is telling you very clearly by his actions and words that he doesn't feel safe to speak about his feelings with you, then it's up to you to improve the level of psychological safety in the room. You are far more likely to achieve this if you're warm, empathic and playful. This approach is often referred to as establishing a *therapeutic alliance*. So, do some safe, ice-breaking, fun things together, using humour, and enable the child to find you warm, playful and genuinely curious about and accepting of all aspects of what makes him, him.

Additionally, in order to give him a sense of the likelihood of you offering empathy not shame or disapproval, you can tell him stories about other children (actual or fictitious) who have done something similar and how you met this with compassion and the wish to understand, rather than criticism or a bland non-response (failed attunement). For example: *"I once knew a girl who stole things, but no-one knew that the reason she did this was because she was very unhappy. She gave what she stole to other children to get them to like her. But do you know what? Actually, she just wanted her Mum to like her. It was that which was making her so unhappy."*

Also remember to consider whether the child will feel psychologically safer with direct or indirect expression, therapeutic story, sandplay, or a drawing with which to convey empathy with no direct reference to the child's life. All these methods give the child the option to take the safe position I've discussed, that of *"This story is not about me, it's about the character in the story."*

> The younger child may focus on 'the angry crocodile' or the abusive doll and explore the emotions in the activities of the toys before rage can be personally owned. Horne 1999, p.66

As we saw in Chapter 4, working *indirectly* often works best with children who are defending themselves from feeling painful feeling from their past, such as despair, hopelessness, fear or anger. If we try to talk *directly* with them about actual events and people in their life, it can strengthen their defensiveness, and they may never let us in. Then you are back in the realm of *"Don't talk to me about feelings"*, making you just one more person in the child's world who they want to shut out as they return to the safe known of self-help. One child said to me, *"Stop trying to get into my brain"* which tells us a lot! For him, my adult's understanding clearly felt dangerous rather than relieving (*see* p.343).

As well as the stories '… *about a child who* …', you can also create a story of a creature who is going through some of the same things that happened to this child. That way the child can listen to what you say without feeling shamed, scared, or emotionally dysregulated. Indirect expression respects the child's defences. The child can take or leave the empathy/psychological messages in the indirect expression of a story (*see* p.289).

Emotion worksheets can also increase psychological safety. The pictures in the exercises can be viewed by the child from a standing-back position. In this way, they act as containers for feelings which could otherwise be experienced as overwhelming, chaotic or unthinkable (*see* p.180).

Asking the child to "*Show me*" through a drawing rather than "*Tell me*" can help to make the child feel less exposed and less demanded of. Once the feelings are organised into an image on a piece of paper, they can be thought about in a clear, non-threatening way. This in itself can bring real relief from having put onto paper (externalised) what has previously been experienced only as disturbing inner states (private worries, thoughts and feelings swirling around in the child's mind and body). The sequence is as follows: from troubling feeling, to image, to thought-about-feeling (*see* p.173).

Furthermore, because of the use of drawings, the actual relationship between the adult and child can be experienced as far less threatening than if the feelings were being talked about directly, without the use of "*Show me*". There is literally something between you and the child, the drawing, providing a safe 'third' focus through which you can build your relationship.

> To show oneself only through … a picture … is to protect oneself, whilst at the same time enjoying the gratification of self-revelation. In other words, safety comes from a sense of being once removed: "*I am not showing you me, I am showing you my drawing.*"   Storr 1972, p.28

In other words, in healing conversations, children will often 'do' rather than 'say'. One of the children I worked with, **Tanya (13)**, didn't talk to me for 18 months apart from a few sentences. She would, however, do amazing sandplays. I would say, "*What would happen next?*" She would 'show me' what would happen next in the sand. That way we worked together over time to establish such psychological safety that she could eventually talk freely, fluently and directly about her very painful experiences.

I would always look at Tanya's sandplay and hold in mind Tanya's life story (*Holding in mind both the child's life story and play story*, p.48, on how to do this). Her life story concerned being sexually abused by her father and then abandoned by him. Her mother physically abused her and then also abandoned her. Her life themes of invasion and abandonment were very clear from her pictures, and I was able to comment - all in metaphor of course - about the powerlessness of the little children and creatures in her story in the face of the cruel men and monsters.

I said, "*The little ones, they known too much pain, too much aloneness. No-one was helping them.*" Over time in our sessions, some of the little creatures in Tanya's story started to gain power, and from time to time, Tanya even started to enjoy fun and humour in our time together.

And finally, always remember that with *most* children, empathy will lower defences and increase psychological safety.

Respect and empathise with the child's defences

Defences always need to be treated with great respect as they may
be the only way that the [child] can hold him or herself together.

Oaklander 1978, p.62

For some children, reality is just too abhorrent. For example, a child may have a Mum who is terrifying when she gets angry: but the child may need to tell herself that she has a wonderful Mum. For the moment, you need to leave this defence in place. This Mum is the only Mum the child has!

We must never speak directly against a parent whom a child is idealising, or needing to keep 'good'. The child had to live with that Mum or Dad for years, and may continue to do so. The child may need to think that her Mum is OK because her Mum is the most important person in her world. It would be completely inappropriate for us to challenge that position with judgmental comments such as *"Your Mum was very bad to do that. She is cruel to you."* A lot can be said indirectly through metaphor. For example, you can tell the child a therapeutic story about cruelty and how to manage it if you are just a little person or ficticious animal. The story's important psychological messages will get through on a subliminal level.

Another example of respecting a child's defence around a parent was the grieving boy **Mahmud (9)** He said, *"My Daddy was killed by a car."* Mahmud needed to defend himself from feeling the shock and agony of the fact that his father had hung himself. He needed the listening adult with him to allow him this fantasy for a while.

Our work is to be respectful of all feelings, but to be sensitive as to when a feeling may be used as a defence. As a rule of thumb, a defensive feeling will not move us in the same way that an underlying core feeling will. As the listening adult, you are unlikely to feel moved:

- ◆ If the child's feeling has a repetitive, unchanging quality about it
- ◆ When the child gets stuck in the same negative thought patterns that accompany the defensive feeling
- ◆ When something in their tone of voice or body language feels inauthentic

Don't make the child feel bad about being non-communicative

Instead of saying, "*You seem to be having difficulty talking today,*" you might just acknowledge what's happening by saying something like, "*Some days you seem to be able to talk to me about what you are feeling more easily than on other days.*" (Watchel 2008, p.288).

Don't keep a child in painful feelings for too long

Allow the child to take breaks when talking about difficult things. Respect the fact that, in contrast to adults, children (defended or not) often stay for far shorter periods of time in painful emotional states. They tend to move quickly on to something else and return when they're ready. As Hughes (2007) says, 'Children often have a greater need for taking breaks in the dialogue because of their greater difficulty with maintaining attention, regulating emotion, or maintaining motivation.' (p.176)

So don't keep the child talking about their painful feelings when it's clear that he needs to move away for a while in order to come back to the subject later. If he's talking about painful feelings, let him move away to lighter, more playful contact with you, if he wants. This will enable him to feel safe enough to move back into feelings talk when he is ready. If you keep responding sensitively in this way, he will trust you to be a good 'safety barometer'.

Things to do to help a child think about the costs and benefits of bottling up their feelings

If the child is willing, you can invite her to explore what she fears might happen if she spoke about her feelings instead of bottling them up. On the following pages are some things you can do to support you and the child in this task.

Option I

Over the next few pages are exercises to enable children and young people to reflect on their fundamental stance of self-help, and think about daring to share! *(you are welcome to photocopy the charts on the next three pages)*.

Ask the child to look at pp.328-329 and draw or write in the box what they fear would happen if they did talk about their feelings with you. Basically this is the thing that is putting him or her off from doing so.

Respond to how the child completes the chart with empathy and possibly psycho-education where appropriate. So you might say, *"No wonder you feel scared to trust me with your feelings and talk about what is happening in your life ... so many people you have trusted have let you down."* In addition, you might add some simple psycho-education about how when people speak about their feelings, or express feelings such as crying or angry protest, with an empathic person, they can actually feel better physically and emotionally (*see affect labelling studies*, Lieberman et al 2011, Pennebaker & Chung, 2011, *and see above*, p.308).

You could also tell children the story of *A Nifflenoo Called Nevermind* (Sunderland 2001). This is a story about a child who says *"Never mind"* to all sorts of horrid things that happen to him. He actually *does* mind, but he's afraid of his feelings and letting himself know about them. But when he does have his real feelings, it's actually fine - there is a bit of a flood and thunder and stuff but basically that's OK too. Because he has stopped bottling up feelings, he can get on with things feeling far, far better about himself and his life. The story directly addresses the child's fear of fully feeling or expressing his true feelings.

TOO BIG FEELINGS

Tick/mark (☑ ☒ ☺ ☹ ☹) any of the
following feelings that feel too big inside you.

- ☐ Too much hate
- ☐ Too much hurt
- ☐ Too much love
- ☐ Too much fear
- ☐ Too much worry
- ☐ Too much jealousy
- ☐ Too much shock
- ☐ Too much sadness
- ☐ Too much anger
- ☐ Too much yucky feeling
- ☐ Too much heart-break
- ☐ Too many bad memories
- ☐ Too much messy feeling
- ☐ Too much feeling I'm bad
- ☐ Too much not liking myself
- ☐ Too much muddled up feeling
- ☐ Too much *"What's the point of this life?"*
- ☐ Too many horrid, frightening thoughts
- ☐ Too much hating and loving someone at the same time
- ☐ Too much wanting something to happen which isn't happening

**If you have a too-big feeling that is not on the list,
then write or draw it in this box instead.**

© 2015 Worth Publishing

What might happen if I let you or another grown-up help me with my painful feelings?

I might get really sad

I might get really angry

I might get really scared

I might cry

... or something else might happen

If I tell someone how I feel, instead of keeping my feelings to myself: (*circle any below*)

I might not stop crying

I might get very angry

I will drive them away

They'll think I'm mad

They'll think I'm bad

They'll think I'm rubbish

They might laugh at me

I'd lose my street cred

They won't like me anymore

They might think I am sissy and weak

. . . .

or write your own worries here –

Option 2

Have some clear glass or plastic jugs and fill one up with red water (using cochineal or paint), another with blue, another with green, another with yellow and another with brown. To be very clear you could also label the jugs. Have one large empty jug with the child's name on it. Then you can say to the child:

> *OK, can you decide which colour water you'd like for each of your feelings? For example, which colour do you want for sadness? Which for anger, which for happy, which for fed-up? Here's a jug with your name on it. Pour in how much of each of these feelings you have.*

Encourage the child's spontaneous response. It's just a rough gauge but you'll usually get a sense of which feelings are predominant for the child.

Ways to explain to a child what it means to defend against painful feelings

a) *The tangled string explanation:*

> **Adult:** *Sometimes painful feelings are like tangled string. They can get all mixed up inside you. One part of you may want to sort out the tangle, to tell someone about your feelings, whilst another part of you may definitely not want to, and so you carry on trying to deal with the painful feelings tangle all on your own. That's too hard, and it keeps spoiling your life.*

You could then play this out in sandplay to help engage the child. Use actual tangled string and a little miniature toy figure getting all tangled up in it.

b) *The heaviest suitcase explanation*

> **Adult:** *When you find someone you can really trust and you tell them about the difficult things that have happened to you, or are happening to you, it can feel such a relief. It can feel like laying down the heaviest suitcase you've been carrying all by yourself, for far too long. It can be like saying to that person "You do some of the worrying now. I'm too tired to do it on my own anymore."*

c) *The Pandora's Box explanation*

You might also use the story of Pandora's Box to help you:

> The jar was almost empty; everything that was cruel, violent or swift had left it. All that was left, right at the bottom, was a little thing … calm and assured. It was hope. Comte 1994, p.158

How what you're doing and how you're being might be getting in the way

I've looked at this from many angles throughout the book, but this section is designed to consolidate the different possibilities and ways forward.

The child may be feeling psychologically unsafe with you

Ask yourself, am I being warm enough, calm enough, emotionally strong enough with the child? Am I being respectful enough of the child's need to move away from painful feelings for a while in order to return to them when ready? Alternately, is the child perhaps not ready yet to take in my empathy, so I need to establish a better working alliance first through child-led play or Theraplay games? (*see* Booth & Jerberg, 2010). In other words, do I need to think about how *I* am being and behaving, and do I need to become more adept at opening our time together with play, fun and curiosity? All these things will put the child at ease.

You may be over-questioning

Lots of questioning can be experienced as a kind of interrogation. This is particularly the case if after the child has answered your questions you give nothing back, no empathy, no understanding. Again, the child may not want to open up to you afterwards. Why would they? Speaking is not of value, if nothing comes back; the over-questioning may have made them feel worse, not better (*see* p.142).

You may be being too silent, too still, too voiceless or even faceless!

Research into the neuroscience of a 'still face', (blank expressionless face) shows that children and infants find the blank face of an adult highly disturbing, causing elevated stress hormones (Rosenblum et al., 2002; Field, 1994).

As I mentioned on p.156, prolonged exposure to high levels of cortisol is damaging to the developing brain and can cause cell death in systems key for memory and social and emotional intelligence (McEwen, 1999; Bremner & Narayan, 1998). Other research has found that when infants repeatedly fail to meet a lit-up face in their parents, later on they may be unable to use social contact well (Lier, 1998). For some children, the 'blank screen face' in the adult trying to engage them in talk-time is not neutral at all, but rather a painful memory-trigger of a depressed, angry or emotionally cold adult in their lives. Wachtel (2008) makes the point well:

> A refusal to interact ... [may be experienced] not as a corrective emotional experience, but as a repetitive emotional experience; that is as an enactment of earlier [disturbing] interactions with the parent. p. 229

I offer the following passage to show how some adults are unable to offer the child a sufficiently enlivened response. As a result, they can only provide the child with limited relational experiences. These can be insufficient to motivate the child to want to open up and talk about his feelings.

> How many rich forms of human connectedness does the adult offer in how she is relating to the child? How many different colours, hues, tones and qualities of energy state does she have available for engagement? So in the end, does the child enjoy some of the richest vistas of human relating possible, and so is profoundly moved by that relationship, or does she meet something deadening? Does the adult flatten the emotional energies the child already has, by emotionally bland responses? Does she leave unborn the very aspects of humanness that are undrawn in the child, and so remain undrawn in their times together?
>
> Whether the relationship is to be a rich or bleak experience depends so much on the inner world of the adult. Is this an expansive place, offering a whole range of emotional landscapes, from the deepest tenderness to the fullest passion? Or is it a tight, choked place, only offering relationship from a place of depletion? If so, the child may well protect her own expansiveness, becoming increasingly tight and closed herself. And if there are 'gardens' in the adult's inner world, are they withheld in the name of properness, in the name of boundaries? Metaphorically speaking, does the child end up getting the 'sterile scrubbed clean room' aspects of her adult's inner world?
>
> And the language the adult offers, is it a dead language devoid of metaphor, image, colour? So is there only impoverished connection with empty words - no music of tones, or timings - linguistic poverty? How can the adult help the child to become undefended if she herself is fending off the child with concrete little words, which make no call on the riches of the human imagination?   (The Author)

Perhaps Jean Magagna, who was Head of the Child Psychotherapy Department, Great Ormond Street Hospital for many years, says it most succinctly in the statement: *'Do we heal together or defend together?'* (2005)

You may need to increase your warmth, expansiveness, creativity, playfulness and self-awareness

In light of the above, as part of offering the richest possible connection with a child, making your voice, playful, musical and soothing can have a very positive effect. Seth Pollak found that a soothing adult voice activates oxytocin in the child, an anti-anxiety chemical (*see* p.60) This of course will really put the child at their ease (Seltzer, Ziegler, & Pollak, 2010). Find a means of communicating what you are saying that really engages this particular child. One of the best ways is to switch mode of communication. Most children don't have negative associations with an adult playing in a sandbox - so try conveying your empathic response through a story in this medium. Or use crayons and paper (*see* Big Empathy Drawing).

Importantly, whether we are able to offer the richest possible connection with a child or not depends a lot on our own level of self-awareness and whether we ourselves are carrying lots of 'emotional baggage' (*see below*). In other words, have we had enough 'therapeutic conversations' in our own life and enough lovely relational play? An adult's emotional baggage gets in the way of warm, empathic, playful therapeutic conversation with a child. Flat affect, and somewhat colourless play (dulled voices and blank faces) in adults often come from cutting off their own painful feelings, and can also be indicative of insufficient joy-inducing interactions in their own childhood!

The good news is that it is never too late to support your work with sessions of personal therapy or counselling (being particularly careful to find a warm empathic therapist who can laugh and engage you playfully as well as being deeply empathic in response to your painful life experience). So, if you are feeling a bit lacking in being able to offer the child a rich range of relational play responses, think of buying some sessions for yourself with a play therapist, child therapist, or Theraplay practitioner and ask them to play with you! (*contact The Institute for Arts in Therapy and Education, London for a list of practitioners who can provide sessions for this purpose, see Appendix VIII*).

You may be inadvertently assuming what a child is feeling instead of asking the child what they are feeling

One particular adult assumed that all children miss their counsellors in the holidays. She didn't check up whether this was actually true for **Mel (7)**.

> **Mel:** (hits a toy car especially hard on the table)
>
> **Adult:** *Mel, I think you are telling me that you are feeling angry about the holidays coming up.*
>
> **Mel:** (looks perplexed) *I was just trying to get a little shell out that's got stuck under the steering wheel. You're weird.* (looks mistrustful and turns away from the adult)

As Fonagy (2005) says, 'It is a huge leap to assume that just because your child needs you to help him with his painful feelings, that he has attachment needs and feelings towards you.' (p.143)

You may be misattuning

Perhaps you and the child started well in the sense of an enlivened and engaged exchange. But then, the child starts to close down with you and the conversation loses its flow. It may well be that you have done something inadvertently or said something misattuned. So the best way forward is to quickly think through the issues I've been looking at:

◆ Have I not set up a safe relationship base before starting to talk about feelings?

◆ Have I been too direct?

◆ Have I been using too many questions?

◆ Have I got the child to stay in negative feeling for too long?

◆ Have I come in with my own agenda about what I want the child to talk about?

Then, if it doesn't seem to be any of these things, think about this question:

◆ Might I be defending myself from feeling some of the painful emotions in the child's life story and/or play story, such as despair, hopelessness, fear or anger? (*see* p.108)

I'll address this last point in the next section.

Whose defences are they anyway: the child's or ours?

We are blind to our own blind spots! If we haven't worked through our own emotional baggage, we can be out of awareness, cut off from the child's feelings. This means we may simply not be able to hear certain forms of emotional pain. This can lead to us unintentionally block the child's stories of distress, and/or unintentionally invite a stiff upper lip. This is why child counsellors and therapists are required to undergo their own in-depth counselling or therapy.

When adults can't feel the child's pain, the child often senses that the adult will not be emotionally available in important ways. Their right brains pick up in milliseconds what it is safe to feel and not feel with this adult. As a result, they are often unwilling to engage in important talk-time. This can throw an uncomfortable spotlight on an adult's lack of one of the following: warmth, empathy, or the capacity to listen to specific feelings (someone might be very good, for example, if a child talks about anger, but emotionally unresponsive if the child talks about grief).

Tara was a child counsellor, who had never really grieved the death of her grandmother, or the fact that her much loved father walked out on the family when she was fifteen. Tara worked with **Alex (6)** whose schoolwork had gone downhill since his father had left the family home to live with another woman. Through sandplay, Alex repeatedly played out themes of loss and leaving. He also did sandplays of scary monsters eating up all the good people in the world. Tara repeatedly asked Alex to tell her about his scary monsters. She never picked upon the themes of loss and leaving. Tara was literally blind to them as she was blind to such feelings in herself. Alex's behaviour and learning did not improve from his talk-time with Tara.

The child may sense that you are too busy trying to manage your own feelings, to be able to help them with theirs. This may be especially true for a child who has been acutely aware of the emotional state of a troubled parent. They will be hyper-alert to what you are feeling or what they think you are feeling.

Lizzie (13) remembered an occasion when, as a little girl out with her mother, she had badly hurt her arm. Her first thought was *"Where is the nearest loo, so I can get away from my mother and cry on my own?"* Lizzie was aware that her own sadness always seemed to trigger her mother's sadness and so she had to cope not only with her own distress, but also with that of her mother. She often felt flooded by her mother's feelings, which felt far more distressing than her own. Lizzie was given counselling at school as she constantly came over as very anxious. It didn't work. Lizzie sensed that her counsellor was dysregulated herself. So she stopped going for talk-time. Lizzie was right. Her counsellor was struggling emotionally. Her house had just been repossessed by the mortgage company. Lizzie never knew this, of course but as Eleanor Armstrong-Perlman said, (2010, personal communication): *"We can keep the child from the verbalisation of the truth but not the truth itself."*

What to do if you think your emotional baggage is getting in the way of you being fully emotionally available for the child

As adults, the best gift we can give a child we are working with - or living with - is to go into counselling or therapy to deal with our own childhood pain. Having your own counselling will also help you separate out what belongs to the child and what to you. Without this, you can over-react or under-react to what the child is telling you. If this is your experience and counselling is out of your reach for some reason (although it is free via GP surgeries in the UK, albeit often with long waiting lists) then do find someone you trust and can confide in to talk with. The process will start with you.

Troubleshooting

"What do I do when a child only talks about happy feelings when I know they are troubled?"

This is a common syndrome in children who have learnt that to have any feelings other than nice ones is too dangerous for a number of reasons.

i. It makes a volatile parent erupt in some way (for example, weaken, cry, or get angry)

ii. It loses their parent's approval, love, affection and so on

iii. The parent or the family as a whole gives the child the message (verbal or non-verbal) to stop having the feeling he is having: the child unconsciously internalises this message as a prohibition against expression or even experience of the forbidden feeling

The trouble is that, if we don't do anything, the child may go into adult life cut off from their anger, fear or grief. But as Freud knew, and his knowledge gained from observation has been ratified by many neuroscientists and other psychologists today, such feelings do not just go away. Rather they are pushed underground, often resulting in debilitating symptoms such as phobias, obsessions or self-harm. Moreover, cutting off on anger often means cutting off on passion, spontaneity and joie de vivre. In other words, "*I don't feel very much pain, but then I don't feel very much life either.*" Either way, the cost of just having 'nice feelings' is great.

Looked at from another angle, aiming to enable a child to develop the capacity to enjoy enriching relationships, the child professional may be deluding herself that she is doing some very good work when the child stays over-long with positive feelings. Of course if the child is to be enabled to trust us, enjoyable times together are essential. If, however, the child is as sweet as pie in a talk-time, and then goes out and hits someone in the playground, then something is amiss, and we have most likely colluded in the child's need to keep our time together all happy and nice.

So if all the problematic feelings are happening outside the talk-time, it's likely that core painful feelings are not being addressed with the child professional. If this happens, ask yourself how you might be blocking the child. Could the child perceive you as too vulnerable to want to show his real feelings? Does he perceive you as invested in keeping everything nice? Or is the child worried that if he really shows his true feelings of rage and hate, impotence or humiliation, or talks about some traumatic incident, that you will judge him, punish him or reject him? With such a child, the best thing is to say something like this:

Adult: *I notice that you only bring your nice feelings here. I wonder what stops you bringing other feelings, such as anger or worry or fear or feelings about painful things that have happened to you? Some children only bring nice feelings because* ... (drawing on a big piece of paper some of the following, using age appropriate language)... *they are frightened I will think badly of them if they*

show me what they really feel, or tell me about the hurtful things they did to someone else. But that's not right. No child is born bad. If children do things to hurt others, it's always because at some point they have been hurt in some way.

or

Some children think they will feel horrid if they talk about bad things that have happened to them. But actually often they feel a lot better. By talking about the bad stuff with adults like me who don't blame or punish, but try to understand, they often feel a real sense of relief.

"What do I do when a child just wants to play football in talk-time?"

Child: *Let's just play football.*
Adult: *I don't want to play football for all our time together today, because it's not what we are here to do. But I will play football for ten minutes.*

If you feel wary about being this assertive, ask yourself whether it is because you imagine a negative reaction from the child, for example that they won't like you, or they might sulk or get angry. If that's the case, well, that can be useful. These are real feelings: your response to them can show your capacity to empathise and understand.

> **Adult:** *You seem angry about me saying that and, I guess, disappointed. Perhaps it feels like I have spoilt our time together.*

If the child acknowledges this:

> **Adult:** *I can understand that.* (then reiterate your original explanation about the purpose of talk-time) *Our time together is about helping you with what's stopping you enjoy your life.*

"What do I say if a child's been in trouble? Do I talk about it, or pretend I don't know?"

Use your discretion. If it's something very significant - such as setting off the school's fire alarm, it's best to bring it up. If you don't talk about the incident the child was involved in, they may have fantasies that you know, and are not talking about it because it is too awful or that you secretly dislike them for what they did. So it's often best to put the cards on the table. This way you can talk about the incident whilst at the same time conveying empathy. This dispels the child's myth of: "*If I tell her, she will think I am a monster and hate me like everyone else. Her liking of me is too precious. I can't risk losing that, so I'll not talk about what happened.*"

But make sure you bring the subject up not in a lecturing way with a telling off (you can be sure other people are doing that!!) - but with an approach more like "*I heard that you set off the fire alarm. Would you help me understand what made you do that?*" And follow it with empathy. "*My guess is that you must have been feeling really stressed or feeling too much inside to do that.*"

I once heard a talk-time session where the adult started off, "*Now we need to talk about your bedwetting problem.*" It was hugely humiliating for the child. She left the room and never returned to the sessions. So tone, choice of language and timing is everything, and lots of thinking is needed before any talk-time about how you are going to raise the issue in a way that the child will feel empathised with, not judged or criticised. If the child feels the latter, you just become another adult in the long line of those who have already punished their behaviour without understanding that in many cases, 'A child's language for feelings is their behaviour' (Jay Vaughan, personal communication, 2010). In other words if the challenging behaviour is to stop, we need to enable the child to speak about the feelings underneath.

"What do I do if the child keeps asking to go to the toilet?"

Name it, in a "*I'm wondering if ... ?*" way:

> **Adult:** *What I notice is that if we ever start to talk about your Mum being in hospital, you want to go to the toilet. I am thinking perhaps I am not making it safe enough for you to talk about such a painful thing? And if I am right, how clever of you to find a way to tell me that I am not making it safe.*
>
> *or*
>
> **Adult:** *When you are with me, I notice that you want to leave the room to go to the toilet a lot. Maybe it's because you are finding if difficult to be with me, or I am not helping you feel safe enough with me?*

"What do I do if the child attacks my kindness and just rebuffs all the positive things I say to her?"

As I described on p.317 sometimes being with a warm, kind, empathic adult is painful for a child as it brings him right up against the realisation of what he has been missing out on, often for years - for example, an adult who listens, really listens; or an adult who shows compassion and empathy rather than blame and criticism; or an adult who lights up when they see him.

Now one might imagine that having those things at last is just a lovely experience for every child. But for some the contrast with what life has brought them so far is too awful, so they have to spoil what you offer. One way is to dismiss it, or smash it up in some way (getting angry, saying the time with you has been rubbish, saying you are rubbish) as it really doesn't fit in with their internal working model of how they see themselves. This is so beautifully expressed by the famous psychoanalyst, Bion:

> The [child] feels he is being allowed an opportunity of which he had hitherto been cheated. The poignancy of the deprivation is thereby rendered the more acute and so are the feelings of resentment at the deprivation.   1959, p.115

Talk about this with those gentle 'wonderings into the air' that we have talked about throughout the book, which demand no response from the child whatsoever. You might say something like:

> **Adult:** *I notice when we have a fun time together, you kind of want to smash it up at the end. Perhaps a part of you loves the fun times we have but another part is hurting inside because it is so different to what you have known before in your life.*

For other children, if you praise them, they do not hear it. This can be because their self-image is so bad, that your words seem wrong and don't fit how they see themselves.

> **Child:** *She's only saying that, because she wants something - she doesn't really mean it - she's just saying it because she gets paid.*
>
> or
>
> **Child:** *I don't deserve it. She wouldn't think that if she really knew me, knew all the horrid things I've done to people.*

All you can do is be aware when you think this is happening and say to the child:

> **Adult:** *I guess my praise and liking of you is not getting through to you. What a shame. I wonder if it is a bit like this for you? (Big Empathy Drawing, p.79)*
>
> or
>
> **Adult:** *You see yourself like this - not likeable, not OK and I come along and see you like this - lovely and delightful and very thoughtful - and somehow what you think and I think don't fit? Will you change the picture to be right for you? (then you can add psycho-education) When some grown-ups haven't been good at seeing the lovely things about you, it's easy to think you're not OK.*

"But is talking about painful feelings with children who don't want to talk about them really a good thing?"

Sometimes when a child has bottled up feelings for years, there is an explosion of feelings once they eventually come out. Some adults may be frightened by the intensity of these feelings, but we need to ensure that we've done enough personal work on our own feelings so that we are comfortable to facilitate any intensity from the child. For many children, the sheer pressure of having held in their feelings for so long and trying to manage them all on their own can mean that when they do eventually express them, it's a huge relief and especially so when they are met with an empathic response.

After several talk-times with a trusted adult **Charlie (9)** dared to let go of his defence of anger and coldness and let himself feel the pain of his parents splitting up. At one point he asked, *"How do I put the mountains back when the snow has melted?"* It was a plea for compassion towards his uncertainty.

Jodie (14) had learning difficulties. For most of the time she was silent and passive. Then, suddenly, she would half-scream, for no apparent reason, before going back to being a 'too-good' child. After two years of this, she was given one-to-one time each week with someone trained to help children talk about feelings. With this teaching assistant, she would let herself really scream and shake with fear. She did this facing the adult, who held her hands. Jodie had been too frightened by the intensity of her own fear to really feel it on her own, yet it had been leaking out in those half-screams and making it impossible for her to concentrate on her schoolwork.

The adult then found out from social workers, that, at one time, Jodie had been sent to a children's home. As punishment on several occasions, she had been locked in a cupboard. She had been too frightened to cry out. She had stifled her natural need to scream with fear. Once she had screamed out her pain with the psychological safety provided by the teaching assistant, she no longer screamed and her schoolwork and friendships improved dramatically.

When children have defended against intense feelings like this for years, it often comes as a real surprise and great relief to them to let go of often years of emotional baggage, realising that nothing and no-one has been damaged or destroyed in the process.

Here are some of the things that children who used to bottle up their feelings have said about not bottling them up anymore:

Ann (11): *There were my sad feelings and then there was the telling about my sad feelings, and the one helped the other very much.*

Bea (12): *I'm used to feeling bad all on my own. But after talking to Mr Terry, our maths teacher I realised that all alone was worse than feeling bad.*

Henny (4): *I've got too many scary jangly feelings in my mind. When I talk to you they go away.*

Simon (12): (having released years of anger in talk-time): *It's funny you know, for the first time today I really enjoyed my drama group, I had a laugh with my mates.*

How best to support yourself in having healing conversations with children

When you are offering children this wonderful gift of conversations that can change their lives, it may at times cost you emotionally. Being with such distressing stories, and often raw, intense and unprocessed feelings, repeatedly meeting mistrust and strongly held defences, coupled with the anxiety that you may encounter a child protection issue, can all leave you feeling emotionally drained and dysregulated yourself.

This is why the best thing you can do for yourself and for the child is ensure that you, as an emotional regulator, get emotional regulation! This can be in the form of consultation with people who have been having healing conversations with children for many years. It's often known as supervision. The best consultation comes from people who have a qualification in healing conversations with children (for example, child psychotherapy, child clinical psychology, child counselling). There are supervisors' lists available and I've included some sources at the end of the book.

It is also important to bear in mind that in the end, however skilled, resourced and empathic you are, YOU might not be the person that this child wants to confide in. But if you've done the kind of work I've been describing in this book, you will most likely have planted some very precious little seeds in the child's mind. These seeds are called:

- interest in psychological thinking
- interest in how my past experiences colour my present
- interest in how relationships work and how some can cause so much pain and others cause so much pleasure
- desire to seek out close warm, empathic relationships because of how good the child or teenager is now feeling

These are seeds of hope, because together they are key to a child thriving and being able to use their short time on this amazing place called earth really well. One day the seeds will grow, resulting in the child finding another warm, empathic adult out there, whether it be someone like their grandfather, a teacher, their brother's friend, a counsellor …

So let go of the need for every child you meet to talk to you, and celebrate the ones who do. Having *Conversations That Matter* with a child is one of the greatest gifts you can offer to him or her, and one which may well change you forever as well!

APPENDIX 1

MENTAL HEALTH IN THE UK, AND THE LINKS TO PROBLEMS IN CHILDHOOD

In this section I'll give you some key and shocking statistics showing how much suffering there is in our population in the UK. Much of this would be preventable if far more adults were able to offer children and teenagers meaningful talk-time. All too many children suffer multiple shocks, losses, traumas, which are then carried as emotional baggage through their teenage and adult years. As discussed in this book, talk-time frees us from baggage so we can get the most out of life rather than being held back all the time by the pain of the past.

To put the following shocking statistics into context, there are 13 million children in the UK.

GENERAL

- Half the people with mental health problems in the UK had their first symptoms by the age of 14 (HMG/DoH, 2011).
- 80% of children with behaviour problems at age 5 will go on to some form of anti-social behaviour in later life (DoH, 2004).
- 80% of people who commit a crime had a conduct disorder as a child (Sainsbury Centre for Mental Health, 2011).
- There are over 700,000 children with problem behaviours, anxiety or depression, three quarters of whom are not getting treatment (The Centre for Economic Performance's Mental Health Policy Group and the London School of Economics, 2012).

DEPRESSION

- The number of young people aged 15-16 with depression nearly doubled between the 1980's and the 2000's (Nuffield Foundation, 2013).
- Doctors are being forced to prescribe anti-depressants to children and young people, against National Institute for Clinical Excellence (NICE) guidelines, because so many children and young people are being referred for help with emotional issues and waiting lists for psychological therapies are so long (BMA, 2006).
- Over 46 million prescriptions for antidepressants were dispensed in 2011 (Health and Social Care Information Centre, 2012). Even taking into account repeat prescriptions, this is a huge number as there are only 60 million people in the country.

SELF HARM

- 10% of 15-16 year olds self-harm (DoH, 2012).
- Over the last ten years, the number of teenagers admitted to hospital for self-harm has increased by 68% (YoungMinds, 2011).

FAMILY BREAKDOWN

- By the age of 15, almost half of all children in the UK are no longer living with both their parents. A million children have no meaningful contact with their fathers (Centre for Social Justice, Westminster 2013).
- Half of all children will experience family breakdown (The Bristol Community Family Trust and the Centre for Social Justice, 2011).
- Almost one in two children experience family breakdown before they finish school (Benson, 2013).
- When a child has experienced family breakdown (with no help to talk about feelings) they are 75% more likely to fail at school and 50% more likely to become addicted to alcohol (Centre for Social Justice, 2006).

- Between 50,000 and more than 2 million children experience parental mental ill-health (NSPCC 2014, p.14).
- Between 920,000 and up to 3.5 million children are subjected to parental alcohol abuse (*ibid*).
- Between 250,000 and up to 978,000 children are subjected to parental drug abuse (*ibid*).

BULLYING

- Almost half (46%) of children and young people say they have been bullied at school at some point in their lives (Chamberlain et al, 2010).
- 38% of young people have been affected by cyber-bullying (*ibid*).
- In 2011/12, over 30,000 children called ChildLine about bullying (*ibid*).
- 18% of children and young people who worried about bullying said they would not talk to their parents about it (*ibid*).

DOMESTIC VIOLENCE (children exposed to this)

- As many as 1 in 6 children are exposed to violence in the home (NSPCC 2014, p.4).
- 1,796,244 children are subjected to parental violence (NSPCC 2014, p.14).
- The total cost of domestic abuse for the state, employers and victims is estimated at around £16 billion per year (Walby, 2009).

DISCIPLINE

- Physical punishment of children continues to be widespread.
- Over 40% of children/young people report being smacked, on the bottom, leg, arm or hand (Radford et al 2011, p.111).
- 50% have been threatened with smacking (*ibid*).
- 19% have had parents who threaten to send them away (*ibid*).
- 35% have had parents call them stupid or lazy (*ibid*).

- Over 66 % have been regularly shouted or screamed at (*ibid*).

ABUSE and NEGLECT

- In 2013, there were 179,000 children in need, due to abuse or neglect (NSPCC 2014, p.56).
- In 2013, 73,999 children under the age of 16 reported that they had experienced sexual abuse (*ibid,* p.32).
- 1 in 20 children in the UK have been sexually abused* (*ibid* p.33)
- I in 12 young adults experienced physical violence at the hands of a parent or guardian during childhood (*ibid*).
- 1 in 5 young people aged 11-17 years have experienced severe maltreatment (*ibid*).
- All forms of abuse in childhood were associated with poorer mental health and elevated delinquent behaviour (Radford, 2011).
- 1 in 6 young adults were neglected at some point during childhood (based on interviews with 1,761 young adults, aged 18-24 years) (Radford et al, 2011).
- There were over 21,000 children in the UK on child protection registers or the subject of child protection plans under a category that included neglect in 2012 (Department for Education, 2012).

* A recent report found that 31% of local safeguarding children's boards reported no specialised therapeutic services for victims of child sexual abuse in their area and therapy provision for children who have suffered sexual abuse as patchy throughout the U.K., leaving all too many children having no access to conversations that matter (Berelowitz 2013, p.23).

APPENDIX II

CONVERSATIONS THAT MATTER BETWEEN PARENTS AND CHILDREN

Delivering difficult news

We sometimes need to deliver difficult news to our children or teenagers or talk about a change to family life that will have significant impact for them and us. When we have to deal with the really big topics such as the ones below, I believe it would really help if we all had skills in how to have helpful and healing conversations with our children and teenagers:

- A family member or other loved one who is ill, dying or suffering from an addiction
- Transitions (for example, moving house/moving schools/moving country, family member leaving home, someone going to prison and so on)
- Bullying or other problems with peers/friends, falling out, not able to make friends
- Conflict in the family, family hardship, on-going arguments, separation or divorce
- Being hurt by a family member/seeing someone you love get hurt (emotionally or physically)

I can imagine this list looks daunting and it would be easy to assume that you need a different knowledge base and skill set to address each of these separate issues. But my experience (both as a parent and as someone who has worked with many parents and children over the years), is that if you can engage a child in a meaningful conversation about one of these issues, *you can actually engage the child in all of them.* This is because the key underlying principle involved is to *empathise* with the full range of feelings your child is likely to be having, checking out with the child of course to see if you are right.

Integral to this is the fact that children in painful life circumstances are desperately in need of someone who is not afraid of talking about their feelings and can stay with their pain, rather than trying to get them to just feel 'happier'. By way of a simple example: in the hugely multi-tasking life of a parent, when your child complains that their brother has called them an unkind name, it's totally understandable to give them a *"come on, get past it"* type of message whilst chastising the brother. But it can make all the difference in the world to the child if you start the conversation by saying, *"Wow that really hurt your feelings when your brother said that."*

So now let's look at the kind of things we can do, to have successful *conversations that matter* with our children. Here are three key stages:

Stage 1: Deliver the difficult news or talk about the significant change to family life, with empathy

Stage 2: Having given your child the time to take in the news, raise the subject again, supporting them to voice all their feelings about it. Acknowledge and empathise.

Stage 3: Help your child to grieve and find their empowered anger (which we know is key to positive change, see p. 368 and below)

Stage 1: Deliver the difficult news or news of significant change, with empathy

Make sure you are in an emotionally strong enough state to deliver the news. Practise what you are going to say. Get to the point, without excuses or long explanations (however tempting this might be sometimes). Pick a time which is not going to be rushed or interrupted: so after school, not before, and not when you need to be somewhere.

Start with a short preamble such as *"Sally, can we talk a minute? I have something to tell you."*

Here are some examples of things we might need to tell our children:

> **Parent:** I am sorry to tell you that your Dad and I have decided not to live together anymore.
>
> **Parent:** I am so sorry to tell you that Mum is very ill. Her body is not working as it should be. At the moment we don't know how bad it is and whether her body can be mended or not.
>
> **Parent:** Because of Dad's work we are going to need to move house and live in a different part of the country.

Once you've delivered the news in a simple and clear way, empathise with the fact that your news is likely to have been a shock for your child. On some deep level, most children, teenagers and adults who have never previously experienced trauma expect that life will continue in the same vein as it has always done. Here are examples of the sorts of things you can say.

Empathising with the probable shock

> **Parent:** *I guess this news comes as a real shock and it will probably take time for you to feel and think about what I have said, so I promise we'll keep talking about it together. Also as soon as I have any more news of course I will tell you.*

Then answer any of your child's questions in an age appropriate way. If the child doesn't naturally ask questions on hearing the news, you could add,

> **Parent:** *Is there anything you want to ask or need to know about what I have said?*

Children will not necessarily voice their feelings at this stage. Feelings about such a big event can take time to become aware of, let alone to be felt or thought about. The child may need your help to do that (*see* Stage 2).

In contrast, some children will have strong feelings immediately. They might cry or run off or look terrified or get very angry. Our role is to empathise with all and any of these feelings. The key is to simply allow our children to have the feelings they are having. So much failed connection between parents and children results from us trying to persuade them to have a different feeling to the one they are having, or from *talking at* them rather than *listening to* them. So, to avoid a major misconnection, please look at p. 378, *Adult to Child Responsiveness* checklist.

Misconnections often happen because it's all too easy for us to be with our children's feelings in the same way our parents were with our feelings. Many of us did not get enough or perhaps even any empathy as children, when we were at a time of real need. So be kind to yourself if you find it's a bit like learning a new skill, like learning to riding a bike. It can take time before the whole 'empathic response thing' flows easily. But it is really worth it, to support our own children in ways that are far more likely to help.

Stage 2: Having given your child the time to take in the news, raise the subject again, supporting them to voice all their feelings about it. Acknowledge and empathise

This vital next step will ensure that your child is supported in his feelings and thinking after having heard the news, instead of being left alone to try to come to terms with it in his own way. It is also a key time to check whether he has misunderstood something or descended into self-blaming fantasies *("If I hadn't been so naughty/demanding Dad would not have that awful illness now")*. Before you set off, you'll need to sense the right moment to re-open the topic, when your child has had some time to let the news sink in. It could be later that day, the following morning or the next evening, for example. Then you can try approaching the subject again, like this:

> **Parent:** *I wonder if you have felt or thought anymore about what I told you yesterday about ... (the issue)?*

If the conversation flows with feelings and questions, great. It shows your child is starting to process, and trusts you to respond to their questions respectfully. Where the child doesn't ask questions or talk about the impact of the news in any meaningful way, it can point to the fact that they might need your help to actually have their feelings about it in the first place. In other words, they may be stuck in raw sensation, in response to the news, unable to symbolise their feelings into thoughts and words. Other children may be feeling emotionally numb. So let's have a look at how to help our children become aware of what they are feeling.

How to help your child to be aware of the feelings they are having
Children and teenagers who are struggling to know what they feel about painful news, often reach for words they are familiar with, like *"It's not fair,"* *"It's all rubbish"* or *"I hate you"* (*see* p.120) which fail to accurately represent the feeling states they are grappling with. At times like this, as Dan Hughes (2014) so beautifully puts it, we sometimes need to -

> ...take the lead in speaking for the child or speaking about him ... Such initiatives are presented as guesses rather than interpretations or facts and the child determines whether or not they reflect her inner life. It is about gently initiating exploration of difficult themes and respectfully moving away from these themes when the child signals 'enough'.
>
> Dyadic Developmental Psychotherapy: *Toward a Comprehensive, Trauma-Informed Treatment for Developmental Trauma Disorder*

One way we can do this as parents is to suggest feeling words and emotional themes, using images or drawings. So you could start by saying this *"I can imagine you might be feeling something like this ..."* - and then write or draw the feelings you can imagine your child might be having. You might even want to try using a Big Empathy Drawing (*see* pp. 79-95, *for detailed discussion of this technique*). But the aim is 'co-created empathy' *(see* p.222*)* so say something like this to your child:

> **Parent:** *But sometimes grown-ups get things wrong - so would you tick or colour in the feelings that feel right for you and cross out the ones that aren't right, and add any I've left out?*

Once the child has done this, you can empathise with what he has changed or amended.

> **Parent:** *Thank you letting me know that you actually feel very let down by me over this.*

But before choosing the words for your drawing, it's important to think carefully. Hold in mind a full range of emotional responses that your child might be having to the news. To help in this process, please do have a look at *Common Themes for Painful Childhood Experiences,* in Appendix III (p.382). By checking through each category of feelings on the table, it should help you to think about different aspects of what your child might be feeling, rather than just homing in on one or two specific feelings.

We need to do this because, just like adults, the child's reaction to painful or shocking news will be complex and multi-levelled. So please avoid thinking only in terms of 'sad 'and 'cross' which used alone could fail to address the probably deeper levels of fear, powerlessness, self-blame, anxiety or confusion. The trouble is that if we only address the simpler perhaps less painful feelings, our children may not feel fully connected with us or understood, and so may decide that talking with us doesn't help.

To see how *Common Themes for Painful Childhood Experiences* can be a support for you, let's look at an example of a parent, Janet, who tells her child Matty that she is going to separate from Matty's father. She tries to talk to Matty again the next day after her initial announcement of the 'bad news'. But Matty says hardly anything. She just shrugs her shoulders and says that it is OK that Janet and Ed are separating.

A few weeks later, the school contacts Janet to say that Matty is often seen staring blanking out of the window for much of the school day, and Janet finds out by chance from a neighbour that Matty has been seen wandering the streets after school instead of coming home. So she decides to have another go at a conversation, this time using empathy and acknowledging the feelings that Matty is likely to be having. Janet uses the table *Common Themes* to choose what she imagines might be appropriate feelings and emotional themes.

Without knowing that what she's doing is called this, Janet uses a technique called ' indirect expression' (*see* p.69). This means that instead of saying *"I can imagine you might be feeling ..."* which can be too intrusive for some children after they've received painful news, she says, *"When parents separate, I've heard that some children feel xxxx"* – and she shows Matty a drawing she's done (*see opposite*). The conversation goes like this.

> **Janet:** I can imagine you might be feeling a whole host of painful things about what I said about me and your Dad separating.
>
> **Matty:** No not really Mum. It's whatever you want.
>
> **Janet:** When their parents split up, I've heard that some children feel some of these things ... (shows Matty her Big Empathy Drawing).

Janet's Big Empathy Drawing

Janet can now talk while she points to the relevant parts of the picture - not using all these words, of course! - but just some of the things that seem right at the time depending on the child and the situation.

- Shock - Some children feel shock. They wanted the arguing to stop but not for one of their parents to move out

- Fear/worry - Some children feel worried or frightened. They think, *What will happen to me now? Is everything going to change now? Is anything going to be the same anymore? I hate this...*

- Pain of loss - Some children hurt a lot inside, thinking that they will never be the family they were

- Let down and angry - Some children feel angry with one or both of their parents. *Why didn't Mum and Dad work harder at trying to stay together, or why wasn't I consulted over this?*

- Self-blaming - Some children feel it's their fault. If they hadn't done x or y, their parents wouldn't be splitting up. But it is never their fault.

> **Janet:** *Matty will you tick or circle any of the feelings in the picture that you might feel too? And if things are missing, will you write or draw them on the picture?*

Matty ticks all the feelings Janet has written/drawn except for pain of loss. Perhaps Janet's choice of words, weren't right for Matty here? Matty then writes on the picture in big red writing 'Cry forever' and 'Hate you forever'.

> **Janet:** *Thank you for letting me know that you really hate me over this. I can see that. It wasn't your choice, any of this, I can totally understand that you really hate me right now for bringing so much unwanted change into your life. And cry forever, I am so so sorry that you feel so hugely sad about it … and when you want to actually cry will you let me be there for you and hold you?*
>
> **Matty:** (nods slightly) *Maybe*

After this conversation, the two of them have many more conversations. Matty starts engaging a bit more with her schoolwork and comes straight home after school. She is still often very angry with Janet. Janet keeps empathising and validating: *"No wonder you feel angry with me."* Eventually the traumatic loss is processed in a healing way, and the new family unit becomes close again.

You might be thinking, *"Using a drawing? That feels so strange and unnatural."* But many parents I have worked with are pleasantly surprised by how easily the drawing flows once they get out pen and paper in preparation for an important conversation. Children and teenagers I've worked with often say how they prefer 'drawing talk' to face to face which can feel too embarrassing, too much.

Before looking at Stage 3, I think it will be useful to look at another example of what a parent can say regarding the delivering of painful news, this time looking at when a family member is seriously ill or dying.

Stage 1: *Deliver the difficult news or talk about the significant change to family life, with empathy*

If you have just received news about a life-threatening illness, it's essential to wait to tell your children *after* you yourself, or you and your partner or relevant other adult family members have had time to feel and think and emotionally work through the shock, so that you can tell your children in the least frightening or overwhelming way possible. Once again, make a space and a time, say you'd like to speak about something important, and then deliver the news simply and clearly, with short sentences.

Stage 2: *Having given your child the time to take in the news, raise the subject again supporting them to voice all their feelings about it. Acknowledge and empathise*

Once again I'll illustrate what a parent might say, using the resource as before of *Common Themes for Painful Childhood Experiences*. I'll look at how a parent can then talk more effectively with their child with the help of a Big Empathy Drawing drawn prior to the conversation (*see* p.367). With such a conversation about a family member being seriously ill or dying, the child will need both empathy and reassurance about how they will continue to be cared for in a very loving way: that the other key people in their world will take over and ensure they will continue to feel very safe and very loved in the world.

Shock

The well parent's response:

> **Parent:** *I am so sorry for what must feel like a terrible shock for you. I know Mum is your world, your safety, your rock, and you love her so so much. So I will always be here for you when you want to talk, or ask questions, or to cry or shout. And we have time now for you to be with her in very special ways and to do the things you need to do with her and to say the things you need to say with her and we will both help you with that.*

Frightened or terrified

Either parent or another significant adult:

> **Parent:** *I can imagine you may be feeling so frightened for you at times and so frightened for your Mum.*
>
> *or*
>
> **Parent:** *Perhaps part of you is really frightened. You might be asking yourself questions like "What happens if Mum dies? How would I manage? What if I (the other parent) died?"*
>
> *or*
>
> **Parent:** *A lot of children who have this happen worry something bad will happen to their other parent or other people they love, or even to themselves. But I promise you, the rest of us, me, your gran, your aunts and uncles will be there for you and make sure you continue to feel really really safe in the world and really loved and really looked after.*

Anger

Ill parent's response:

> **Parent:** (pointing to the drawing) *Perhaps a part of you is furious for me getting so ill or for not getting well. It's not what Mums should do. They should be big and strong and well. They shouldn't die. Perhaps a part of you wants to scream at me, "How dare you get so ill, Mum!"?*
>
> Alternatively you could try:
>
> **Parent:** *Perhaps a part of you is angry that now you have an ill Mum who can no longer do the things that well Mums can do. Or perhaps you are angry with the people who can't mend me, or can't make me well again?*

The pain of loss

Either parent:

> **Parent:** *I can imagine that you sometimes feel in pain at Mum's pain. Like "What hurts my mum hurts me."*
>
> or
>
> **Parent:** *I know it can be so painful for any child to watch their parent get worse and worse not better and better.*
>
> **Parent:** *If I can help you with that in any way, I am right here for you. In fact I have some ideas for things we can do together.*

or

> **Parent:** *Also I guess you know this, but you can go on loving your Mum forever. What she has given you and the lovely times you shared together will continue to warm you and make you feel loved and strong inside for the rest of your life. No one can ever take those lovely memories of you and your Mum away*

Powerless

Well parent's response:

> **Parent:** *And I guess you would long to make your Mum better, to mend her and it's so painful that you can't.*

A note on soothing the pain when a parent is seriously ill or dying

There is a real place here for reminiscing together. When we bring to mind a loved one, even if they are no longer alive, it activates opioids (well-being chemicals in the mind - *see* p.81). A child who has lost a parent has not been left with nothing: they have been left with all the lovely memories of the special times they had with their Mum (hence the importance of creating a memory box - full of photos of Mum, things that remind the child of Mum, things owned by Mum, taped messages from her, talking photo books and so on). Also it can be helpful to provide an image: a death in the family can feel like the world has ended, but actually of course it is not the whole world, but a part of the world. Some parents like to say something like this *'Wherever you see light, like a star in the sky, that's*

me looking down and sending all my love to you' (*see* Winston's Wish 2012).
In fact I thoroughly recommend using the very many superb resources of
Winston's Wish (a charity for bereaved children) *www.winstonswish.org.uk*.

Angry

*How dare you
leave me.
Why didn't
you look after
yourself?
I hate the people
for not mending
you!*

Shock

*My safe world
ended just now*

Fear/ Terrified

*Mum might die.
What about Dad?
Might I be an
orphan?
How will I
manage without
her?*

Pain of Loss

*Watching her get
worse.
Her pain is my
pain.*

Worried

*In case I damage
Mum more by
crying / behaving
badly.*

Powerless

*I can't mend my
Mum.*

Responses to grief

We will now move on to **Stage 3**.

Stage 3: Help your child to grieve and find their empowered anger

In his research, the eminent psychologist Leslie Greenberg found that people recover well after painful life events if and when they are enabled to grieve and to express what he called 'empowered anger' (Lane et al 2014) in the presence of an empathic listener. So our Stage 3 is about us as parents supporting our children to be able to do these things.

Parent-child conversations which enable our children to express empowered anger

Empowered anger is anger that we own - *"I feel ... "*, rather than gamey, blaming anger *"You are ...*(rubbish)"*, for example). Empowered anger is about finding a strong place within yourself that is not a put down of the other person but rather a protest, felt on a deep embodied level.

So this part of emotionally healing conversation between us and our children involves gently modelling the difference for them in our own interactions, and then gradually and equally gently correcting them over time if they continue to use, *"You are"* rather than *"I feel"*. Incidentally, this is a vital skill for any conversation that matters, including those between adult partners. In his very extensive research on failed adult relationships, John Gottman found that angry *"You are ... "* statements were highly predictive of early divorce (Gottman 2007). So we can model the healthy expression of empowered anger for our children at any time, in how we behave ourselves in our own dealings with other adults.

As a hard-pressed parent, it's so easy to be defensive in the face of a child's anger, and to come up with facts, corrections and explanations. But this will bring about misconnection. Children need their angry feelings towards us as their parents to be heard and acknowledged. So in the face of your child's anger it's really helpful if you can remember to use this technique borrowed from psychotherapy. Just begin your response with *"So you are seeing me as someone who ..."* Or, *"So you're experiencing me as ..."*

For example, *"You are seeing me as someone who really doesn't understand how difficult things are right now for you ..."* Even if you think your child's perception of you is unfair or even off the wall, it's their perception. You are not saying *"You see me that way, so I am that way."* Instead, you are simply acknowledging their perception - *"So you are seeing me as ..."*

In summary, the key thing is, *don't argue back*: instead, *reflect back,* so the child can see that you have understood what they are feeling. All too many of our children think that we will either punish them or cry if they express their angry feelings towards us, so they keep such feelings to themselves or get angry with someone else instead (like a sibling, for example). Of course this won't support the healing process they need to go through after a painful life event.

In addition, you can actively support your child in finding their voice of empowered anger with you by using the 'unfinished sentence' technique (*see* p. 175). This technique can enable your child to move from *behaving* their angry feelings in anti-social ways to make their point, to *thinking about* and *voicing* their feelings in sophisticated ways. This technique can be used on an on-going basis when there is some kind of broken connection, or rupture between you, or after an argument.

With my little girl from the age of four, when I confronted her about something, she would often leave the room in a huff, hurting or cross. I would follow her, sit next to her and say, *"Would you finish the sentence, I'm angry with you Mummy because...."* She would often respond so well to this. I would re-iterate why I felt I needed to confront her with whatever had been happening, but then would empathise and acknowledge her anger. The break in our connection was mended very quickly, with her emotional literacy enhanced. In fact on one occasion when her sister was cross about something and sitting under the table sulking, my little girl went under the table and said, *"Would you finish the sentence, I'm angry with you because..."* I thought her sister might hit her, but she just politely ignored her!

It is the empathic responses we give our children at times of conflict and intense feeling that result in their being able to do far better emotionally, socially and academically; and it actually positively impacts their physiology long term too, resulting in calmer bodies and calmer minds - something we could all do with !

Unfinished sentences you can use to help your child voice empowered anger

> *I hate it when you*
> *I am so cross with you that ....*
> *I hate you for ....*
> *I need you to know that ...*
> *The worst thing for me has been ...*
> *What I wanted from you was ...*
>
> *I really resent it when you ...*
> *I don't want to talk to you about ...*
> *I want you to know that ...*
> *I resent the fact that ...*
> *The worst thing for me has been ....*

When you are faced with a child's anger as a result of you giving them painful news, you can either write down these unfinished sentences on separate pieces of paper (half page of A4 for each) and give them to the child to fill in by drawing or writing, or you can simply open up the subject like this:

Parent: *I can imagine that you must have some angry feelings about me and Dad splitting up/moving house/being too ill to play with you and so on. It would really help me to understand, if you finished some of these sentences for me. Is it OK if I read them out? Fine to pass on any. I promise you, that I will just listen and try to understand. I won't get angry back or cry or anything.*

After this - just listen. Remember, no defensive response or factual correction. Then if you can, come up with an empathic response. But if that feels one step too hard to begin with, just acknowledge what they have said, praise their courage for letting you know and say you will really think about what they said and get back to them later.

Here is examples of using unfinished sentences to enhance children's empowered anger about hearing that their parents are going to separate.

Child: *I hate it when you ...* keep crying, cos Dad's moving out. I hate it. I thought parents were supposed to be the big strong ones - now it's like I have to be that for you.

Parent: Thank you for letting me know that. I thought it was bothering you. Yes I have arranged to see a counsellor so that I don't leave you feeling my feelings as well as yours.

*****

Child: *I hate it when you ...* argue with Dad over the smallest thing. I hate feeling like I'm living in someone else's war.

Parent: It must feel like we are bringing our pain into the house and then it gets right into your life. I'm sorry we have put you in this position.

*****

Child: *I hate you for ...* putting yourself before us. I knew you were miserable with Dad, Mum, but aren't Mums supposed to put their children first, because we weren't miserable with Dad?

Parent: So you are seeing me as selfish. You would have preferred that I put up with my feelings so you could keep your Dad living in the same house.

Child: ***I'm so cross with you that*** … *I asked you to stay Mum, not to go, but I soon realised what I think doesn't come into it. My opinion is nothing, is it?*

Parent: *You really resent not being consulted about this, as part of this family.*

*****

Child: ***I really hate it when*** *… you and Mum want us to take sides, like I'm being torn in two.*

Parent: *Wow I didn't realise that you felt that. I can only apologise. I'll talk to Mum and we'll find a way of making sure that doesn't happen again.*

*****

Child: ***I need you to know that …*** *I hate you calling me your son. I don't feel like your son anymore now you are living abroad.*

Parent: *So you're saying that having a too far away Dad, feels like not having a Dad at all. As if the distance wipes out the connection we have. If you feel that, no wonder you feel so angry and hurt by my moving out and not just down the road.*

*****

Child: ***The worst thing for me has been …*** *the shouting. It made me sick in my stomach.*

Parent: *I am so sorry it hurt you so much. How brave for telling me just how dreadful it has been for you.*

*****

Child: ***What I wanted from you was …*** *for the rows to stop, not for you and Dad to split up*

Parent: *I guess that was an awful shock when you found out that was going to happen*

As part of helping our children find their voice of empowered anger, helping them know they have rights can be important as well, for example some of the following:

- A right to get the help with this that you need
- A right to have a childhood
- A right not to worry about your parents so much
- A right to feel carefree, a right to do things other children do
- A right to be happy again after this painful event and hopefully strong and wiser as a result.

Parent-child conversations which enable children to grieve

With [the loss] of a loved one, we find ourselves plunged into one of the deepest and most troubling emotional pains of which we as social creatures are capable ... (Panksepp 1998, p. 260)

So now I will move on to look at using conversations that matter to help children grieve from a painful life event.

Unfinished sentences you can use to help your child voice grief

Here are some example of unfinished sentences which can be used by children to express their grief and pain of loss:

I long to be ...	I'm hurting so much because ...
I feel gutted because ...	Sometimes I feel like ...
I have lost so much because ...	The worst pain of all about this is ...
What I want more than anything else is ...	

Child: ***I long to be*** … *in an unbroken family, like everyone else in my class.*

Parent: *You so want things to be just as they were with us being a together family. You so wanted me to stay, not to go.*

*****

Child: ***I feel gutted because ...*** *by leaving mum, Dad, you've left me too (the pull for most parents here would be to get defensive and say "You are wrong, I haven't left you, I love you so much," rather than sticking with empathy) …*

Parent: *Although I absolutely love you, cherish you and adore you, nevertheless right now you feel left by me. That must really hurt and I guess there are other feelings you have towards me too about that - anger, rage, and a "How dare you go Dad?" perhaps?*

*****

Child: ***I'm hurting so much because ...*** *Daddy is never going to live with us anymore*

Parent: *I can see your heart is breaking about that … Such a painful thing to let yourself know that and so brave to really know it so strongly*

or

Parent: *I am so sorry our separating is breaking your heart*

*****

Child: ***The worst pain of all about this ...*** *is that I lost you Dad, then because of losing you I lost my home because we couldn't afford to stay in the house anymore and so I lost my school and so then I lost my friends.*

Parent: *Dreadful. You have lost too much - I am so so sorry for all the pain I have caused you.*

*****

> **Child:**   ***Sometimes I feel like*** *… crying forever - sometimes I feel nothing*
>
> **Parent:**   *So your too sad feelings come and go. They come and go*
>
> or
>
> **Parent:**   *It's too hard for anyone to keep feeling such big feelings all the time. No wonder you need to numb the pain sometimes too.*

Is it OK for a parent who is also grieving to cry in front of the child?

In some situations it may be a relief for our children if they see us cry, or if we cry together. They may feel reassured that crying is normal, and safe. But there is a huge difference between tears rolling down your face, and loud distress. A parent's loud distress can frighten children, and sometimes it may be better if we allow our children to know we are really sad, but cry in private or with another adult. That said, authenticity is such a gift for a child: *"I feel really sad about this"*: *"I feel angry about what you did just now"* (the latter in a voice that is not in any way frightening or angry).

Of course, navigating our own emotions at the same time as those of our children is a big ask for any parent. Remember, you may need support for yourself as well.

Empathising with the child who does not want to feel

Here are examples of what to say when a child is not ready to voice their anger or grieve. As I mention throughout the book, and above (p.360) one excellent way is to address issues indirectly: *"When this happens, some children feel …"*. And proceed with a Big Empathy Drawing, as I've looked at earlier. This allows emotional distance for a child who is more defended.

Here are some examples of other things you can say to empathise with the not wanting to talk about their feelings - as ever, not everything at once!

Parent's responses:

- *You haven't really said what you feel about me and your Dad splitting up*
- *Perhaps it hurts too much to feel right now about what's happening in the family*
- *Maybe it's too hard to feel your feelings at the moment*
- *Perhaps you can't feel sad, because of all the other feelings you are having*
- *Perhaps it sometimes feels that there is no space for you to be hurt or sad, because of all the other things you are feeling about what's happening*
- *Maybe you're trying to keep an "Everything's OK" face to stop the sad and cross feelings coming through*
- *Maybe you're trying to keep an "Everything's OK" face because you don't trust that I will listen or understand your feelings well enough*
- *How can I help you find the courage to talk about what's happening with us at home?*
- *I guess sometimes it's hard for you to feel all the painful feelings about all this. Perhaps it sometimes feels just too much, too awful, too big*
- *Sometimes people get angry because they are fighting off all the hurt inside*
- *Sometimes children are only able to ever feel their sadness after someone's really heard their anger*

But sometimes it is just about giving the child time, and in that time, making sure home is safe, secure, there are predictable routines, warmth, food, enough good people around, ongoing empathic responses for other things that happen in the day to day life of your child, and discipline with empathy not with anger (see in particular three really supportive books for this: *How to Talk So Kids Will listen and Listen So Kids Will Talk, How to Talk so Teens will Listen and Listen so Teens Will Talk*, both by Adele Faber and Elaine Mazlish (Piccadilly Press) and *Principles of Attachment Focused Parenting* by Dan Hughes (WWNorton). Also ensure that you are having enough support and empathy yourself, and that you have conversations about other things.

So I hope that this section of the book will both support and inspire you to have healing conversations with your child during and after those inevitable difficult and challenging times of major transition in the child's life. In a way I think all parents have to be like therapists at times, whether we like it or not. When we are effective in that task by taking the time to really imagine into the emotional pain of our children, and we find the words to say it, it is such a gift for our children and for the relationship we have with them.

ADULT TO CHILD RESPONSIVENESS CHECKLIST

Failed Response	Spoken or underlying unspoken message	Attuned response	Spoken or underlying unspoken message
Disapproving	Don't cry (meaning your feelings are making me uncomfortable). Non-verbal messages of 'We don't have feelings like that in this family - stop having that feeling you are having	Accepting	Child cries. Wow you are hurting so much. Let it out, that's just fine, let it all out (in gentle soothing voice) I'm here now, I'm right here for you.
Dismissing	You'll get over it (smiling at the distressed child) Come on now do try to cheer up! You're making me sad just looking at you (underlying message is, 'Don't have the feeling you are having, have an easier one instead' (for me)	Empathic	So you are feeling pretty miserable right now. So much pain and hurt about X
Defensive	Don't you be cross with me now Don't blame me How can you feel like this after all I've done for you? (guilt inducing)	Open	You are letting me know just how angry you are with me. How let down you feel by me. So you are seeing me as someone who just doesn't understand what you are going through. So you are seeing me as someone who is not seeing how important this is for you.
Deflecting (changing the subject)	Changing the subject (unspoken message: 'I can't handle what you are feeling right now, so I am going to try to get you to focus on something else.')	Acknowledging	So let me see if I have understood what you are saying. You are furious with me about Dad and me splitting up. You hate me for not staying together for you. Is that right?
Diminishing	You're not hurting as much as you say you are. You're over-reacting. You're making a mountain out of a mole hill.	Accurate	Will you help me to understand what you are feeling about this?

ADULT TO CHILD RESPONSIVENESS CHECKLIST

Failed Response	Spoken or underlying unspoken message	Attuned response	Spoken or underlying unspoken message
Defining (theorising)	I'll tell you why you are feeling what you are feeling, for example – You are just over-tired dear.	Curious	Will you help me to understand what you are feeling about this?
Talking at the child (advice, little lectures)	What you need to do is just put all this behind you and get on with your life. No point dwelling on it, what's happened has happened.	Connecting with the child	So right now this is really spoiling your life/bugging you. It's hard for you to think about other things, enjoy the things you usually do at the moment.
Competing	I am feeling worse than you, so I can't give attention to what you are feeling…. In fact I need you to pay attention to what I am feeling. (usually unspoken, but conveyed)	Prioritising the child	Wow, I can see you are really angry about this …. let's sit down and talk about it. You have my full attention.
Clichés	Life's hard/Be a man/Get over it /Don't cry/ Be Mummy's little soldier. / No-one said life was going to be easy / Welcome to the real world.	Language specific to the pain of this particular child	You have had so much loss in your life and some people let you down badly, so of course its hard to trust again
Ignoring	No response or minimal response, as if the child's feelings are not really an event at all	Attentive	Thank you so much for letting me know what you are feeling about that. Because now we can think together about what to do about it
Questioning (as avoidance of child's pain)	Why do you feel that? / What's the point of feeling that? / How long have you been feeling that? So what do you intend to do about it?	Imagining in	I can imagine when he said that, it must have really hurt your feelings
Overwhelming (invasive, over-involved)	Oh my poor baby, Oh this is dreadful, awful See now you've got me crying too.	Attuning	So you're really worried about what might happen and you've been holding those worries all on your own until now

© Worth Publishing 2015

Dealing with lying and stealing

Here are two Big Empathy Drawings to show how you can have safe conversations with children about such difficult issues as lying or stealing. Please ensure that you 'shame-proof' such conversations by saying something like this: *"Can we think together about why sometimes you take things that aren't yours? Some children do it because of X (point to relevant section of the picture). Other children do it because of Y. If any of these things are something you feel, just colour them in. If you do it for another reason just write or draw that too."* You'll find guidance on how to use drawings like this throughout the book.

Talking about stealing

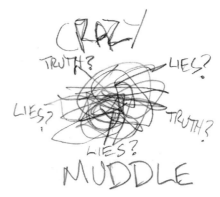

Talking about lying

APPENDIX III

COMMON THEMES FOR PAINFUL CHILDHOOD EXPERIENCES

1. CUT OFF FROM FEELINGS

- Too painful to keep feeling some things
- Bottling it all up
- Closed down
- Emotionally numb
- Frozen
- Cut off

2. FEELING POWERLESS/HOPELESS

- Helpless/powerless to change things
- People act on me, and I can't act on the world
- Can't find my "no"
- Without a voice
- Can't get him/her/them to stop
- Living a life of lost battles
- Wide open to being attacked
- Keeping on letting in what I want to keep out
- Feeling like I'm a nothing
- Hardly there at all
- Overlooked
- Unnoticed

3. WANTING TO ATTACK/DESTROY

- Like I've got a war inside me
- Like I've known too much war
- Wanting to smash up the whole world
- Fear of harming the person I love the most
- Fighting to keep the pain away.
- Fighting to keep the sadness away
- Fighting to feel powerful because I have no power
- Fighting in case the bad thing happens again
- Fighting off the hurt that never leaves me
- So tired from all the fighting but not safe enough to stop

4. LOW SELF-ESTEEM/SELF-HATE

- I'm rubbish
- Never happy with myself or what I do
- My own worst enemy
- Spoiling the good things that happen to me
- Feeling ugly/stupid/unlovable
- Feeling like I'm a nobody
- Full of critical voices in my head
- Wanting to get away from myself
- The pull to hurt myself

5. WORRIED/ANXIOUS

- Always worrying
- Worried about something bad happening to me
- Worried about something bad happening to people I love
- Often fearing the worst
- My worries spoil my happiness

6. FRIGHTENED/TERRIFIED

- Frightened of losing everything
- Dreading the bad thing happening again
- Desperate to make her/him happy/ well again
- Full of silent screams
- Fear of destroying what's important to me
- When Mum wobbles, the whole world wobbles
- A Mummy who got broken and didn't get mended
- Trying to mend my Mum/Dad but never managing
- Our family can't seem to save each other

7. FEELING OF NOT BELONGING

- On the outside
- Looking in from the outside
- Round peg in square hole
- Shut out/left out
- Living in a world of closed doors
- Unwanted
- Brushed aside
- Not feeling special to the people I need the most
- Like a stranger in my own world

8. FEELING ALONE/LOST/LONELY

- Wandering/aimless
- Unable to reach anyone
- No-one to make the hurting stop
- And no-one knows
- And no-one knew
- No-one to catch me if I fall
- No-one to help me
- Not able to get them to understand

9. THE PAIN OF LOSS/LONGING/ YEARNING

- Heart broken
- The hurting goes so deep
- Like a terrible wound that no-one sees
- Like my world ended that day
- Shattered
- In bits
- Like living in a world where it's always winter
- Longing for things to be how they were before

10. FEELING HURT/ LET DOWN/ BETRAYED

- People/person lacking in empathy
- People/person lacking in concern
- Someone could have helped but they didn't
- Falsely accused
- Misunderstood
- Rejected
- Left out
- Broken promises
- Hurt to the core

11. FEAR OF DISAPPROVAL/SHAME

- Watching my every step
- Not daring to really feel
- Not daring to be me
- Not daring to do, in case its wrong
- Scared I'll be too much.
- Never free to say what I really feel
- What I do is wrong/Who I am is wrong
- Just waiting for the next telling off

12. FEELING GUILTY OR THAT "I AM BAD"

- Full of guilt
- Feeling the bad part of me could destroy the good
- I did this bad thing
- Feeling rotten inside
- A criminal
- Evil

- The cause of other people's unhappiness
- Keep hurting/attacking the person I love the most

13. FEELING THAT LIFE'S JUST TOO HARD/TOO MUCH STRUGGLE

- It's all too difficult/too much
- Maddened with the all too much
- Stop the world I want to get off
- Very, very old.
- Seen too much, heard too much, thought too much
- Wanting it all to stop
- Living in an upside down world
- Like living in a crazy play/chaos
- Like living in a world that make no sense

14. IN SHOCK

- Everything falling out of everything
- All smashed up
- Too full of scream
- Living hell
- Seeing what I don't want to see
- Hearing what I don't want to hear
- Like a nightmare got stuck in my brain
- Living in a world of broken people
- The world ended that day
- Like someone shot me full of holes

15. FEELING WOUNDED/DAMAGED

- Too bruised by life
- Emotionally battered
- Walking wounded
- Just too many knocks
- No-one cares for me, so I care for no-one
- Steal, lie, hurt, survive
- A world without kindness
- Wanting to spoil
- Wanting revenge

16. FEELING RUBBISHED/ USED

- I'm a doormat
- Dumped on
- Used
- Taken for granted
- Discarded
- Spat out
- Filled with other people's rubbish
- Humiliated
- Brushed aside

17. FEELING ANGER/RAGE/HATE

- Ready to snap
- Full of bottled-up feelings
- Feeling like a volcano
- Wanting to scream and scream
- So deep in cross that sad won't come out
- Like a walking bomb
- Cold hard hate
- Hate like ice
- Wanting to hurt as I've been hurt

18. FEELING MISTRUSTFUL /UNSAFE

- As if the only person I can trust is me
- Can't trust after that happened
- Unable to be off guard, even for a minute
- Keeping everyone out
- Making sure no-one gets close
- Not feeling safe anywhere with anyone
- Living in a world that's out to get me

19 . FEELING JEALOUS

- Using my eyes to drink in someone else's Garden of Eden
- Wanting what they have for me
- Watching her love go to him not me
- In torment
- Too much pain because of them
- Keeping on fighting to stop the hurting

© Worth Publishing 2015

385

APPENDIX IV

CONVERSATIONS THAT MATTER IN THE CLASSROOM

As Petrash (2003, p.32) says: 'It is imperative that education directly touches the hearts of children'. We spend over 10,000 hours teaching children in school. How many hours do we spend listening to them speak from their hearts about what life really means for them?

The current situation

There is now far greater awareness in schools of emotional and social intelligence than there was some years ago. Government and policy makers understand that schools should be about far more than just academic attainment. Despite departmental emphasis on discipline and behavior management, there is now wide recognition amongst the educational workforce that a child's capacity to achieve academically is often dependent on their emotional well-being. As a child's social and emotional intelligence is now understood as being as important as IQ, emotional literacy is seen as increasingly important in schools.

PSHE is part of all OFSTED inspections. However, because there is still far greater emphasis in schools on academic results than on personal development, we are in danger of teaching subjects rather than children. If we are to ensure that more schools prepare children for life, not just exams, then what we provide for children in their 10,000-12,000 hours of school life needs to go further, and deeper.

But the question is, how can we best support teachers in talking about what really matters to children? As Sharples (2008) says, 'There had been many policies put out as a knee-jerk reaction, for example, the SEAL Programme. Teachers are not supported well enough. They are [now] meant to be doing things that psychologists are trained to do'.

How do we support teachers to have therapeutic conversations?

The 2013 OFSTED report on PSHE entitled *Not Yet Good Enough: Personal, social, health and economic education in schools* comments that:

> Learning in PSHE education required improvement or was inadequate in 40% of schools. Relationships education required improvement in over a third of schools … Approximately one third of respondents to the online survey wanted to learn how to deal with mental health issues such as coping with stress, bereavement and eating disorders. Too many teachers lacked expertise in teaching sensitive and controversial issues, which resulted in some topics such as mental health and domestic violence being omitted from the curriculum. In 20% of schools, staff had received little or no training to teach PSHE education. Teaching was not good in any of these schools. p.7

Despite all the advancements in EHWB, PSHE, and SEAL, I argue that we are still not teaching children the most fascinating subjects of all: what it means to be a human being, how to live life well, how people change people for better or worse, and so on. PSHE and the SEAL materials offer children lots of tips on how to handle stress well but not on how to handle life well. In short, at present, schools don't teach children how to be able to flourish in the difficult, painful, messy, confusing, overwhelming, challenging, grief-ridden, awesome, frightening, at times hellish, amazing circumstances of life.

And with the sorts of statistics I mentioned in Appendix I, PSHE in schools is so needed. Let's look at some key stats relating to education. Half of all children will experience family breakdown. One in five children see their parents separate before the end of their first year at school. Almost one in two children experience family breakdown before they finish school (Benson 2013). When a child has experienced family breakdown (with no help to talk about feelings) they are 75% more likely to fail at school and 50% more likely to become addicted to alcohol (Centre for Social Justice, 2006).

I ran a thinktank at the Centre for Child Mental Health in London (2009) for adults who had experienced family breakdown in childhood. The overriding theme of the group was that decades later, they were still experiencing the psychological scars. They all said, *"If only someone had helped us as children. No-one talked to us about it."*

Why therapeutic conversations are needed in the classroom

In one PSHE lesson I observed, each member of the Year 5 class was asked to bring in a family photo. They were asked to talk in pairs to one another about what the photo meant to them. There were four adults in the room, the teacher, two learning mentors and myself. The children were queuing up, desperate to speak to the four of us and show their photos. This was not the instruction. Nevertheless the children had all made the wise decision that if you need really good listening you are more likely to get it from a mature adult than from another eight year old. Some powerful and vital conversations ensued.

The lesson exemplified how desperate children are to talk about what really matters to them to someone who can really hear. One little girl sought me out and then was in raptures for five minutes whilst she talked about the happy looking couple in the photo, herself and her brother. The latter had recently been taken into care. She needed me to listen so well for those five minutes. When the children were asked to sit down again, she couldn't take her eyes off me.

These children needed the respect and dignity of sufficient time, with an adult who could really listen. The time constraints of the lesson did not allow this for most of the children. Again, if we are to really take EHWB in schools on board fully, surely we must find a way for all children to benefit from such quality listening on a regular basis.

What we can do to make things more therapeutic for children in the classroom

Having thoroughly audited the personal and social aspects of PSHE resources for the National Children's Bureau, I found the words 'manage' and 'strategy' (in terms of what to do with intense emotions) grossly over-used. All of us have to 'manage' our feelings, we have no choice! Such words as used repeatedly in the DfES documentation may result in a child dulling, cutting off from or controlling their negative feelings, rather than embracing all that energetic force and channelling it into some really worthwhile venture.

At the moment we have the situation where teachers are teaching PSHE and SEAL with little or no training, little knowledge of how to formulate an empathic response, or how to deepen and develop a reflective process in a large group of children. Many teachers feel very unconfident. As PSHE involves working directly with children's feelings, teachers need specific training in how to respond. As Armstrong-Perlman (2007) says, *'If we don't support teachers with training in what to say and how to respond to children's feelings, we are asking them to experience profound emotional impact in the classroom without the tools to manage it.'*

Without training, teachers may not know how to respond to the kind of statements that I witnessed in a PSHE class recently. A child said, *"My mum drinks so much, I worry each day that I will go home from school and find her dead"*. This is really not an easy comment to respond to. Without training, many teachers will also be unaware of their own blocks and defence mechanisms, which can prevent them from being open to being fully impacted by what the child is telling them.

Moreover, a lack of response, or failed response from a teacher, is potentially dangerous for the child. With an inadequate or failed response, the child may feel shamed or exposed. As a result, the child may conclude that speaking about feelings makes him feel worse not better, so he won't do it again.

Geddes (2006) states, 'Teachers are not expected to become therapists. But teachers can work therapeutically with greater insight into and understanding of pupils'... experiences.' (p.2). Arguably the most empowering vehicle for change in terms of a child's personal development is not the content of the PSHE curriculum, but the PSHE teacher herself. Her ability to be in relationship with her pupils, to facilitate meaningful dialogue between them, to empathise, inspire, and demonstrate personal awareness, can do so much to enable the child to feel psychologically safe in the classroom, valued and understood; and so enabled to learn.

If teachers were supported with supervision and basic counselling skills (as outlined in this book), they could hold invaluable therapeutic conversations with children or young people, without, as Geddes says above, being therapists. I would argue that all PSHE policies and list of goals, however admirable, will be limited in their effect, until there is consideration of which aspects of emotional health and well-being can be *taught* didactically and which need to be *experienced* relationally.

In short, people change in the most profound and positive ways: not through cognitive understanding of emotion but through emotional arousal in the context of relationship. This can happen in the context of *Conversations That Matter* in the classroom.

From Teacher and Child

I have come to a frightening conclusion.

I am the decisive element in the classroom.

It is my personal approach that creates the climate.

It is my daily mood that makes the weather.

As a teacher I possess tremendous power to make a child's

life miserable or joyous.

I can be a tool of torture or an instrument of inspiration.

I can humiliate or humor, hurt or heal.

In all situations,

it is my response that decides whether ... a child is

humanised or de-humanised.

(Haim Ginott 1975)

Keyrelevantsectionsinthisbookforteachers

The 3 Stages of Empathy	43
How to convey empathy	69
Psycho-education	97
How to say it	119
Mentalising in the healing process	78
Talking about feelings through story	289
Reflective summaries	182
Talking about feelings through drawing, play and sandplay	211
"Show Me"	173
Emotion worksheets	180 / 326
What to do when children don't want to talk	315

CLASS INTERVENTIONS USING THE ARTS THERAPEUTICALLY

The 'puppet's got a problem' intervention

This is a great intervention for a whole class or group of children. Choose a big puppet and give him or her a name. Then gather the group of children around you whilst you sit on a chair and hold the puppet. Start by saying, *"Elly (*the puppet*) has got a problem and wonders whether you can help."* You'll have in mind a problem that probably lots of children in the class are experiencing or have experienced. Say what the problem is and ask the children to put up their hands and talk to Elly suggesting what she should do. Then enact the suggestions in a puppet theatre or in relation to other puppets, if you have less space.

> **Adult:** *Elly has a problem and wonders if you could help her. Well, you see, when she gets home at night, her dad and her mum keep arguing. Do you think you know how that might make her feel?*
>
> **(audience responds)**
>
> **Adult:** *Very good, yes… she says you are right. It makes her feel sad and frightened and angry. She so wishes she could stop it but she thinks she can't. Elly says she hides under her bed but that makes her feel worse. She doesn't understand why. Will you help her? Why do you think it makes her feel worse, not better?*
>
> **(audience responds)**
>
> **Adult:** *Molly says thank you. She thinks she understands now why it makes her feel worse not better. So how should she deal with the problem?'*
>
> **(audience responds)**
>
> **Adult:** *Thanks for the brilliant suggestions. Shall we see now what Molly does?*

Using some of the best suggestions, Molly tells her Aunty; they go to see Mum and Dad. They tell Mum and Dad that the arguing is making Molly sad and scared and ask if can they find another way of talking to each other, or to go and get someone to help them with their problems. Mum and Dad say sorry and go off to see a couple therapist or another kind adult who can help them.

Using puppet plays in the classroom for pupils to explore common and troubling emotional issues (for children age 6 upwards)

One of the most powerful ways of helping children to begin to think psychologically is to perform plays on key emotional themes, which many of them are likely to have to address in their lives at some point, or are already addressing. Give the children a list of 'plays' to choose from. Here is a good list to start with, but make sure it is age appropriate.

Difficult things in the life of a child

- A child is being bullied
- Being worried about a parent and their stress or unhappiness
- A child with a grown-up who says "*Don't tell*" about something
- Parents fighting
- A brother or sister being repeatedly unkind
- A pet dies or a child is frightened they will do
- A grown-up doesn't believe something the child says that is true
- A child is feeling lonely at playtime
- A child is feeling he isn't like anyone else in his class, a not-belonging feeling
- A child is frightened of the dark
- A child is missing their parent but thinks it's too babyish to tell anyone
- A child is worried that someone in their family might die or leave

In an ideal world, you would have a puppet troupe bought in for this task (say once a month or at least once a term) who would enact the themes most popular for the children. But if not, you yourself could enact a scene (using say four puppets) or get a teaching assistant to help you. If you have no puppet theatre (they are worth investing in and are relatively inexpensive) you could use a desk edge as a place to hide characters behind, or a cupboard.

After you have done the play you can ask the child audience what the troubled puppet in the story should do. You can enact their answers. Alternatively you can do the whole play with the resolution and key psycho-education built in.

Make sure you have left enough time for the children to fully reflect on what they have watched. You might like to ask the children to draw their responses. Then proceed with group reflection time, and include further psycho-education about the topic as appropriate.

Children making up their own puppet plays (for children age six upwards) Here, children in a classroom setting start by looking at the list of troubling emotional issues for children of their age (*see above*). Again you can ask the class to add to the list if you like.

Then divide the class into small groups, no more than five to a group. Each group is asked to pick one of the themes on the list. They themselves make up a short play using puppets, which they will enact to the class using a puppet theatre. Tell them that the play can be with or without a resolution. If they don't come up with a resolution, you can ask the audience of children for various options of how the painful situation might be resolved.

A note on using puppets with teenagers in a classroom setting When using puppets with teenagers, choose mostly sophisticated people puppets. Leave out that cuddly lamb puppet that toddlers like, or have it around for those moments when the teen actually lets you see the emotionally younger self he or she has been hiding. Using puppets with groups of teenagers is again a great way to introduce them to this way of reflecting on the issues troubling them. You might play out or get them to play out (*see above*) some of the following themes:

Difficult events in the life of a teenager

- Teenager finds out they are pregnant and tells Mum
- Controlling boyfriend won't let a girl see anyone or text anyone and needs to know where she is all the time
- A depressed teenager feels worthless and unattractive
- Parents tell the teenager that they are splitting up
- A teenager is a victim of cyberbullying
- A teenager is coerced into taking drugs just to keep her boyfriend
- A group bully another teenager but one person in the group feels really bad about it
- A teenager gets drunk, is taken to a police cell and then lies to their parents about what has happened

Group discussion and then coming up with different ways of finishing the story which you or they can play out are again very powerful with this age group.

Reading therapeutic stories to a school class

Some critics may argue that it is irresponsible to read (or show, with pictures on a powerpoint) therapeutic stories for the whole class. They may be concerned that it will disturb some children. Such criticism reveals unrealistic notions of 'happy childhood'. As I mentioned on p.25, two of the bestselling children's authors, Jacqueline Wilson and J.K. Rowling, include some of the most awful emotional pain imaginable in their narratives (dread, terror, hopelessness, catastrophic aloneness, abandonment, futility and so on). And as we know, so many children cannot get enough of these stories. I would argue that this is because the books speak to them about what they themselves have felt from time to time.

So the stories are deeply affirming whilst at the same time offering the protection of emotional distancing. So it could be argued that children in the class situation need *more* books on painful situations, to mitigate any sense of being left alone with their pain, particularly if the story listening is followed by pupil and teacher reflection time.

It's not difficult to make up a psychologically-based story, relevant to the key emotional themes of children in the class (*see also* Chapter 11, *and* Sunderland 2004). Ten minutes before the end of a PSHE class I visited (*see* p.389), the teacher asked each child in turn to say one feeling they had about their life at the moment. Going round the circle, 90% of the children talked of sadness or loss. One boy stood up and said, *"I need you to know that I am sad all the time."*

In the busy life of a school, it is all too likely that such profound and poignant statements by children are not followed up by teaching staff. Things can be very different in terms of ensuring children get the empathic responses they both need and deserve, if the teacher picks up on the emotional themes shared by many of the pupils and uses therapeutic stories. Then she can build in whole class story listening sessions (preferably presented visually) with time to reflect together post-story.

In the case of this particular class, with so many children struggling with loss, the story should offer empathy, acknowledgement and something on the psychology and brain science of loss. Through the story, children can learn about how loss feels and how normal it is to feel this way, as well as the psychological messages on how to be with grief in ways that can enrich their lives rather than de-rail their emotional well-being and development.

What to do after the class has listened to a story

Using the following model, you can ask each child to draw a picture in response to the story or the bit of the story that he or she related to most. Some may want to share their pictures and then it's vital that the teacher provides empathic listening in response (as opposed to saying nothing!). Through discussion, the teacher can also help the children draw out the emotional themes in the story and then she herself can underline some of the psychological messages and the psychology involved.

Working model for the teacher-led therapeutic conversations in a school setting

This model is inspired by a Year 6 PSHE lesson taught by Julie Fellows, currently Head of a CofE Primary School. The stages, set out below, are not designed to be fixed or inflexible. Inflexibility might interrupt the flow of the reflective process. So teachers are advised to hold them in mind, whilst working with what happens in the lesson, in their own way.

Stage 1: *Choosing an emotionally charged topic/stimulus relevant to many of the lives of the children/young people in the group/class*

Stage 2: *Questions to the class about the stimulus*

Stage 3: *Acknowledging and empathising: developing the reflective process*

Stage 4: *Definitions, elaborations and teacher's psycho-education*

Stage 1: Choosing an emotionally charged topic/stimulus

The teacher offers an emotionally charged stimulus, such as puppet play, role-play or they tell a story with visual props. Where possible, the choice of theme is based on emotional issues pertinent to many of the children in their class. The teacher is also vigilant as to which particular emotional issues are interfering with the pupils' learning. When there is the luxury of small mentor-led groups, theme-based learning can be even more powerful. For example, schools could provide a 'Family Issues' group for pupils who have experienced family breakdown. The small group setting with the trained adult leader provides the psychological safety to speak more freely. This would not be as costly as, say, Nurture Groups, as it would be a time-limited intervention.

Stage 2: Questions to the class about the stimulus

The teacher asks the children to 'imagine in' to what has been presented. For example: *"How would you feel if you were the gardener in the story?"* Alternatively, she may ask the children to draw or make an image in response to the stimulus. She might then do a 'Show and Tell', using a Circle Time model.

Stage 3: Acknowledging and empathising

The teacher then picks up on the emotional themes raised by the children in Stage 2, in response to the stimulus. She reflects back what they say, so they feel heard and understood. If a child speaks about some personal pain, he needs an empathic response from the teacher.

Stage 4: Definitions, elaborations and teacher's psycho-education

The teacher opens up a wider discussion, and questions the class about the meanings of the emotional themes and the more complex mental states being explored in the group for example: *"Has anyone else felt so angry, like Ben, that it was hard to forgive?"* *"What does betrayal mean? What does 'too hurt to forgive' feel like? How would you show these feelings using images?"*

The teacher then brings in illustrations from history, literature, art or film about the emotional themes the children have been discussing and provides statements/quotations from psychology and even neuroscience (if possible) on the themes being explored.

Here's an example of this simple model in action.

Stage 1: Choosing an emotionally charged topic/stimulus

The children are all age ten or eleven. The end of term show they were working on was Peter Pan. The teacher was also aware of its relevance for several members of the class in terms of loss and separation, feelings of rejection and complex feelings of sibling arrival. The teacher took this passage from Peter Pan as her initial stimulus.

"It isn't that kind of pain", Peter replied darkly.

"Then what kind is it?"

"Wendy, you are wrong about mothers."

They all gathered round him in affright, so alarming was his agitation; and with a fine candour he told them what he had hitherto concealed.

"Long ago," he said, *"I thought like you that my mother would always keep the window open for me, so I stayed away for moons and moons and moons, and then flew back; but the window was barred, for mother had forgotten all about me, and there was another little boy sleeping in my bed."*

I am not sure that this was true, but Peter thought it was true; and it scared them.

"Are you sure mothers are like that?"

"Yes."

Stage 2: Questions to the class about the topic/stimulus

Teacher: *What do you think Peter Pan might have felt at the window when it was closed and someone else was sleeping in his bed?*

Sam: *Not loved anymore, shocked.*

Teacher: *Well done Sam. So the rest of you, if you were Peter Pan, shut out of the window and your Mum didn't let you back in, what would you feel?*

Billy: *Furiosity!*

Teacher: (smiles in an appreciative way)

Gemma: *I would feel abandoned, if you know what I mean, excluded from everyone.*

Teacher: *So alone. No-one coming to help or comfort you.*

Gemma: *Yes.*

Stage 3: Acknowledging and empathising - developing the reflective process

Sam: *I would not be able to forgive my Mum if she did that to me. I would feel betrayed.*

Teacher: *So you would feel so betrayed and angry, it would be hard to forgive.*

Sam: *That's right.*

Teacher: *Have any of you ever felt like Sam, that someone did something that hurt you so much, you felt you couldn't forgive them?*

Nathan: *I did once. A fox took my rabbit. I can never forgive.*

Teacher: *Dreadful. I can really appreciate your strength of feeling over that.*

Polly: *If I was Peter Pan and I said to my Mum I was hurt, and she said sorry, I would forgive her.*

Teacher: *Yes, if someone offered me forgiveness, personally I'd find it hard to turn it down. Can any of you think of a time when you have forgiven someone?*

Ravi: *Steve called me really foul names and then Mrs Smith (learning mentor) helped us work it out and Steve said sorry, so I forgave him.*

Teacher: *Brilliant. Well done.*

Peter: *I just can't imagine my Mum ever doing that to me. She loves me too much.*

Teacher: *Did you know, that some children don't feel like you? They don't feel loved or they are not sure of that love. Sometimes when a new baby is born in the family the older children get worried about how much their Mum loves them, even when she loves them very, very much.*

Ned: *Yes I felt that.*

Teacher: *Yes Ned, you had a new baby in your family didn't you? Sibling rivalry can feel very painful. Some children feel they are not loved when their Mum pays more attention to their brother or sister than them. But is it often their fear colouring reality. Sometimes the smartest thing to do is to say something like, "Mum, when you pay attention to the baby, I think you don't love me anymore. Is that true?" Then she can help the pain to go away.*

Teacher: *Sam I want to pick up on your word 'shock' now. Shock can sometimes feel like being hit with some awful truth. In shock, some people say it feels as if is their world stops or stands still. Have any of you ever felt like that with shock?*

Sarah: *When my Gran died it felt like that.*
(This leads on to the other children talking about when their animals died. Another boy said he felt shock when his Dad said he would visit, and then he didn't turn up).

Teacher: *You have all shown great courage in sharing these things with the group. Thank you. When we suffer shock the best thing is o find someone and tell them. I wonder if any of you have done that, chosen to share a feeling with someone in your life and you felt better because of it?*

Toby: *When I tell other people what I am feeling, I feel better because it means I don't have to think about the worry, over and over again.*

Teacher: *Clever you. Have any of you managed to say something that made someone else feel better when they were upset?*

Sally: *My friend said she was not a good friend. I said you are a good friend to me.*

Teacher: *Do you think she believed you? Did she feel better?*

Sally: *Yes she did.*

Stage 4: Definitions, elaborations and teacher's psycho-education

The teacher then moves into a more cognitive mode, once again working with the emotional states, which the children themselves have raised.

Examples of questions:

When we say we feel betrayed by someone, what does that mean?

When someone says "I need time to heal", what does it mean?

When we say we can't trust someone, what does that mean?

How can you support someone who is unhappy because they have lost something or someone?

The children eagerly put up their hands to answer the questions.

Teacher: (chooses envy - a feeling that has not been picked up and discussed so far, but the teacher knows that several children in her class have recently felt the pain of envy particularly with who was chosen for the best parts in the school show and who got what marks in the exams) *And perhaps Peter also felt envious of the new boy in his bed. Do any of you know what envy feels like? Have any of you felt that?*

Ned: *Yes - when my baby brother was born.*

Teacher: *And I can see several of you nodding your head. Envy hurts a lot. There are three sorts of envy* (she writes them on the board) *- malign envy, benign envy, and emulative envy. With malign envy, it means that you feel so much pain because the other person has what you so want and don't have, so you spoil it - like spilling orange juice on someone's brand new trainers. Benign envy is when you just feel pain at what the other person has. But you don't want to spoil it. You may also wish them well. Emulative envy is when you say to yourself, "Stuff this, I will do x or y in my life, for example, work harder, dare to take a risk and so on, so I can enjoy something similar to what they have/are/ do, in my own life". And so you find in yourself a strength and passion to make something good happen in your life. Malign envy is about being destructive, whereas emulative envy is about being creative. Have any of you felt any of these types of envy?*

The conversation continued with further explorations, discussion and personal experiences about betrayal, trust and envy. There was a particularly poignant moment when a girl was grappling with a very complex issue, namely that of how difficult it is when you tell someone they are your very best friend and what it does to your other friends when you do that. A real issue. The class also discussed the difficulties of how to tell someone something in confidence and then not know whether they will betray you or not

I walked out of that lesson, very moved. There is something beautiful about human beings reflecting on such a deep level, and even more so when the people who are doing it are all aged 11. The teacher had pitched the lesson just right: an excellent integration of cognition, feeling and personal experience. These children had PSHE every week. Just imagine how much their capacities for self-awareness, mentalisation and reflection were developing as a result. This is school as preparation for life, not just work.

APPENDIX V

KEY PSYCHOLOGICAL MESSAGES

Child Rights

◆ All children have a right to have a voice that is heard and respected.

◆ All children have a right to feel safe in the world.

◆ All children have a right to feel loved.

◆ All children have a right to feel special.

◆ All children have a right to say "*No*" or "*I do mind*" and to be heard and respected.

◆ All children have a right to be different and still be loved.

◆ All children have a right to disagree and still be loved.

Children for whom issues of trust/mistrust are focal

◆ It can be really hard to trust people if grown-ups have let you down, misunderstood you, not listened to you, not realised that you were unhappy, hurt your feelings or your body.

◆ You might feel that nobody will ever understand you, but it's probably that you haven't yet found people who will.

◆ There ARE people in the world who are safe and trustworthy.

◆ There are people in the world who are kind and whose kindness will never turn into cruelty.

Children who think that the bad thing that happened is their fault

◆ Sometimes children think it is their fault that their parent is suffering (*fill in as appropriate* - illness/divorce/depression, for example) but they are wrong. These things are out of their control.

◆ Sometimes children get muddled and think that when someone hurts their body or does bad touch, that they deserve it or have asked for it in some way. They're wrong. It is never the child's fault.

◆ It's never OK to hurt children's bodies because it hurts their minds and brains too.

◆ Some children get muddled and think they're unlovable, but they're wrong. Often it's just that someone in their life isn't good at loving or showing their love, because in their childhood someone wasn't good at loving them either.

◆ When parents blame children for a horrid thing that happens, it's often because they are passing their own pain/guilt onto the child.

◆ Sometimes a child thinks that just thinking angry or hating thoughts about someone can actually make a bad thing happen to them. It can't. It's called magical thinking.

Children who cause hurting

◆ If you hurt someone's body or feelings, it's never OK, but it can help to know that when children cause hurting, it's often because someone hurt them in some way (their feelings or their body).

◆ A child who keeps hurting other people is not bad or evil. Their unkindness or cruelty usually comes from being treated unkindly or cruelly by someone else.

◆ A child who keeps hurting other people needs help from grown-ups who know how things that have happened to a child in the past can make them cause hurting in the present.

◆ If a grown-up sees a child who causes hurting as all bad, it's because they are not thinking about the painful things that have happened to that child.

◆ No-one is ever born bad. People can behave in a cruel way because someone has been cruel to them or because very painful things have happened in their life in another way.

Children who are hurting (normalising responses to emotional pain)

- If someone in your life is making you feel miserable, trying to manage it all on your own is far too lonely. It's really smart to tell a kind grown-up who can then help it stop.

- If someone in your life is frightening you, being quiet and saying nothing about it often makes things get worse, not better. Ask for help from a kind grown-up because they can make it stop.

- If you have an unhappy grown-up in your life, (*fill in as appropriate* - for example, one who drinks too much or takes drugs, is very ill) it's very understandable that you feel frightened/alone/very unhappy yourself/miserable/it's all too much some of the time.

- If you have an unhappy grown-up in your life, it's so smart to tell a kind grown-up because then they can help you and the grown-up. Or they can call on other kind grown-ups to help too.

- It's normal to feel jealous of your brother or sister from time to time, or the new baby. The smart thing is to let someone who is good at listening know that you are hurting about it.

Children who don't want to ask for help

- When something in your life feels just too difficult or awful, it's such a smart thing to ask a safe, kind grown-up for help.

- Life is an amazing gift, but people can use the gift badly or well. There are grown-ups who can help you to use it well when you think you are using it badly.

- It's so brave to tell your feelings and fears to a grown-up you trust. It's like daring to come out of a lonely, dark cave.

- Broken hearts get mended far quicker if you get help from a safe kind grown-up to mend them.

◆ When you dare to start to trust a kind grown-up, your world will get warmer and safer. It's fine to take your time to really trust a grown up before you talk about the painful stuff in your life.

About crying

◆ Crying is a natural thing. It's what our bodies and minds want to do when we are sad or disappointed.

◆ Scientists have found that crying with a kind grown-up (instead of on your own) is really good for the body and helps your body, your brain and you of course, feel better again.

◆ It's a really brave thing - not a weak thing - to cry with a kind understanding adult who can be there for you whilst you do.

Children who feel isolated/too alone

◆ No child should have to manage something really scary/horrid/just too sad (use as appropriate) on their own.

◆ People and animals feel unhappy/dull and grey inside when they have too much time on their own. Like it or not, our brains are wired to need people.

◆ Doing the too hard stuff in your life with a grown-up helping you is so smart. It's too miserable and lonely to try on your own.

◆ When children have not felt helped by grown-ups in a time of need, they sometimes think it's best to manage things all on their own. But usually this makes them get more unhappy and more in a mess.

◆ It's never a good thing to take on bullies on your own.

Children who've had an awful shock

- When a horrid thing happens, it's can feel like your world is ending, and you'll never be happy again. There's often a far better 'around the corner' that you just can't see yet.
- Broken hearts get mended far quicker if you get help from a kind understanding grown-up to mend them.
- The past can't go in the past until someone really kind helps you feel and think about it in the present.

Children who fight a lot

- When people can't control what happens to them, fighting can make them feel like they can.
- When people fight a lot, it's sometimes because they are fighting off the hurt inside their heart.
- When people fight a lot, it's sometimes because the world feels too frightening.
- When a child has felt powerless, it's not surprising that they never want to feel like that again, so they may move into being tough and fighting instead.
- Being powerful through fighting or hurting can never make you happy. Happiness comes through being powerful with kindness.
- Sometimes a child feels the world is out to get them, because at some time, someone in their life was out to get them.
- When grown-ups have all the power and you feel you have none, being tough and hard can feel like getting power back. But real power is 'power with someone' (to help people), not power over someone (to hurt).

Children with dreams for their life

- If you have a dream for what you want to do with your life, you can find someone who understands you and your dream, and who will help you find ways to follow your dream.
- You can follow your dream, even if people say to you that you will never make it. Look for people who will help you follow your dream.
- Dreams can come true, but they often come true in different ways to the one you expect.

Children with low self-esteem

- If you think you are rubbish, it's often because people haven't told you about all the lovely things you are.
- If you think you are rubbish, it can be because someone in your life hasn't been good at loving (usually because of how they were parented when they were little).
- When children don't like themselves it's often because grown-ups haven't done a good enough job of making those children feel special.

Children who have built walls around their heart to keep people out

- If you've been really hurt, it's understandable that you build walls round your heart. But that can leave you feeling lonely and empty.
- If you've been too hurt, it is understandable that you build walls round your heart. But then lovely people can't reach you either.

Children who fear failure and making mistakes

- Mistakes can be really useful when we learn from them.
- If you aren't good at something, that's OK because you can always be good at something else.
- If you aren't good at something, it can be because fear of not being

good at it is making it hard for you to learn.

◆ Too much fear of not doing well means your brain can't work well, so tell a kind grown-up that you're frightened of not doing well, so they can help.

◆ If a grown-up wants you to be perfect, that is not OK. Try saying, *"I will not be perfect for you."*

Children who bottle up feelings

◆ Bottling up painful feelings does not mean they go away. In fact, they tend to get bigger and stronger, because of all the pressure of being bottled up.

◆ Trying to manage feelings that really hurt all by yourself is often lonely, frightening and doesn't work. In not telling someone, they tend to hurt more.

◆ If you tell someone kind and understanding about your painful feelings, it can take the scariness and the pain out of them.

◆ You can ask for help with your feelings from someone who can understand. You do not have to 'soldier on' with them alone.

◆ Why carry around emotional baggage, when telling someone means not carrying it anymore and so having a better life?

Permissions - A therapeutic story often contains important permissions, for example:

◆ You have every right to say *"No"* or *"I do mind."*

◆ You can be different.

◆ You can change the way you feel.

◆ You can let go.

◆ You can live the life you want rather than the life your parent wants you to want.

◆ You can ask for a cuddle when you need one.

The Warm, Tender, Feeling Safe Room •

- Tenderness
- Compassion
- Gentleness
- Empathy
- Hope
- Kindness
- Secure attachment
- Capacity for friendship

FEELI
ROO

The Relationship Skills & Repair Room •

- Capacity to de-escalate
- Capacity to listen
- Capacity to negotiate
- Focuses on resolution, not blame
- Capacity for give and take
- Capacity to consider different viewpoints

Too

U
N
L
I
V
E
D

The Sensory & Savouring Room •

- Appreciates being alive
- Love of nature
- Love of culture/the arts
- Capacity for awe and wonder
- Appreciates beauty in the world
- Moments of meeting
- Capacity to savour

The Adventure Room •

- Spontanteity
- Searches for knowledge
- Excitement
- Drive
- Explorative urge
- Sense of adventure
- Welcomes new experiences and opportunities

clos

APPENDIX VI

many

L
I
F
E
○

Capacity for emotional regulation ◆

Handles stress well ◆

Ability to be still and at ease ◆

Reflects rather than discharges or defends ◆

Curiosity in own inner world and that of others ◆

The Calm & Reflective Room

●

Capacity for shared delight ◆

Capacity for joy ◆

Creativity - plays with ideas ◆

Rich imagination ◆

Humour ◆

Capacity for excitement ◆

Capacity for fun ◆

The Fun & Play Room

●

Capacity to follow through ◆

Spontaneity ◆ Flow ◆

Perserverance ◆ Vision ◆

Drive and will ◆ Courage ◆

Life force ◆ Passion ◆

The Drive & Alive Room

●

ors

Capacity to seek comfort and solace ◆

Ability to 'suffer well' ◆

Capacity to grieve ◆

Motivated to address emotional baggage ◆

Understands how painful past experience ◆
colours perception of the present

The Emotional Pain Processing Room

●

APPENDIX VII

SOME RECOMMENDED PUBLISHED THERAPEUTIC STORIES

Hope after awful loss

Empson, J. (2012) *Rabbityness* Child's Play International

For children feeling lost and alone

Donaldson, J. & Scheffler, A. (2009) *Stick Man* Alison Green Books

Working together as a team in the face of adversity

Donaldson, J. & Scheffler, A. (2002) *Room on a Broom* Macmillan Children's Books

Donaldson, J. & Scheffler, A. (2013) *Superworm* Alison Green Books

For children who are, or who have known despair/depression

Tan, S. (2010) *The Red Tree* Hodder Children's Books

For children who have known tragic loss

Rosen, M. (2011) *Michael Rosen's SAD Book* Walker

Sunderland, M. (2003) *The Day the Sea Went Out and Never Came Back* Speechmark Publishing Ltd

Sibling rivalry

Bright, R. (2011) *Mine!* Puffin

Clarke, G. (1998) *Along Came Eric* Andersen Press

For children whose anger covers up painful feelings

Sunderland, M. (2008) *Smasher* (for adolescents) Hinton House Publishers

Sunderland, M. (2003) *How Hattie Hated Kindness* Speechmark Publishing

For children who suffer from fear/anxiety

Ross, T. (2008) *I'm Coming To Get You* Andersen

Sunderland, M. (2003) *Teenie Weenie in a Too Big World* Speechmark Publishing

Sunderland, M. (2001) *Willie and the Wobbly House* Speechmark Publishing

Young carers/children with troubled parents/witnessed domestic violence

Sunderland, M. (2010) *Monica Plum's Horrid Problem* Speechmark Publishing

For children who are being/have been bullied

Ross, T. (2007) *I Want a Friend* Harper Collins Children's Books

Sunderland, M. (2003) *Ruby and the Rubbish Bin* Speechmark Publishing

Sunderland, M. (2001) *A Nifflenoo Called Nevermind* Speechmark Publishing

Sunderland, M. (2001) *A Wibble Called Bipley and a Few Honks* Speechmark Publishing

Sunderland, M. (2008) *Smasher* (for adolescents) Hinton House Publishers

For children who feel alone

Ross, T. (2007) *I Want a Friend* Harper Collins Children's Books

For children who yearn for someone to love them who isn't good at loving

Sunderland, M. (2001) *The Frog Who Yearned for the Moon to Smile* Speechmark Publishing

APPENDIX VIII

USEFUL CONTACT DETAILS & ADDRESSES

How to find a counsellor or therapist for yourself

BACP (British Association of Counselling and Psychotherapy)
Mailing address:

British Association for Counselling and Psychotherapy

BACP House, 15 St John's Business Park, Lutterworth, Leicestershire LE17 4HB

Tel: 01455 883300 Monday-Friday, from 9.00am until 5pm

Fax: 01455 550243

Email: bacp@bacp.co.uk

Website: www.bacp.co.uk

Find a therapist: http://www.itsgoodtotalk.org.uk/therapists/

UKCP (United Kingdom Council of Psychotherapy)

Address: 2nd Floor, Edward House, 2 Wakley Street, London EC1V 7LT

Tel: 020 7014 9955

Email: info@ukcp.org.uk

Find a therapist: http://members.psychotherapy.org.uk/findATherapist

The Institute for Arts In Therapy and Education

Address: 2-18 Britannia Row, Islington, London, N2 8PA

Tel: 020 7704 2534

Email: info@artspsychotherapy.org

Website: www.artspsychotherapy.org

Finding an Arts Psychotherapist or Counsellor:

http://www.artspsychotherapy.org/find-a-therapist

Who to contact if you are worried about the safety of a child and want to talk to someone

NSPCC
Head Office address:

NSPCC, Weston House, 42 Curtain Road, London EC2A 3NH

Tel: 020 7825 2500

For help, advice and support: 0808 800 5000

Email: help@nspcc.org.uk

Family Lives (ParentLine Plus)

Address: CAN Mezzanine, 49-51 East Road, London N1 6AH

Tel: 0808 800 2222

Email form: http://www.familylives.org.uk/how-we-can-help/email-support/

Who to contact if you are looking for a counsellor for your child or teenager

The Institute for Arts In Therapy and Education

Address: 2-18 Britannia Row, Islington, London, N2 8PA

Tel: 020 7704 2534

Email: info@artspsychotherapy.org

Website: www.artspsychotherapy.org

If you want to find a list of child or adolescent therapists and counsellors who work in the ways outlined in this book, go to the website and click on *Find a therapist*. Then enter your geographical area and whether you are needing a therapist for a teenager or a child.

Who to contact if you want to attend training days presented by Dr Margot Sunderland:

- how to have therapeutic conversations
- related child mental health topics
- tools and techniques
- neuroscience, child development and therapeutic interventions

The Centre for Child Mental Health

Address: 2-18 Britannia Row, Islington, London, N2 8PA

Tel: 020 7354 2913

Email: info@childmentalhealthcentre.org

Website: www.childmentalhealthcentre.org

Who to contact if you want to train as a child counsellor, parent-child relationship counsellor, or registered child psychotherapist: or if you need a supervisor

The Institute for Arts In Therapy and Education

(Academic Partner of University of East London)

Address: 2-18 Britannia Row, Islington, Lo ndon, N2 8PA

Tel: 020 7704 2534

Email: info@artspsychotherapy.org

Website: www.artspsychotherapy.org

From one day courses to four year Masters Degrees

Bibliography

Aldrich, R. (2008) cited in Claxton, G. (2008) *What's the Point of School? Rediscovering the heart of education* Oxford: Oneworld Publications

Anna Freud Centre (2013) *AMBIT manual,* [online] available at http://ambit.tiddlyspace.com [accessed 23.05.13]

Aram, D. & Aviram, S. (2009) Mother's storybook reading and kindergartner's socioemotional and literacy development, *Reading Psychology.* 2009; 30:175-194

Armstrong-Perlman, E.M. (2007) personal communication

Armstrong-Perlman, E.M. (2010) personal communication

Bar-Haim, Y., Fox, N.A., Van Meenen, K.M. & Marshall, P.J. (2004) Children's narratives and patterns of cardiac reactivity, *Developmental Psychobiology* 2004 May; 44(4): 238-49

Barrows, P.S. (Ed.) (2003) *Key Papers from the Journal of Child Psychotherapy* London: Brunner-Routledge

Batmanghelidjh, C. (2010) *Challenging Behaviour in Children and Teenagers: Understanding to Effective Intervention,* CCMH, unpublished

Ben-Ami Bartal, I., Decety, J. & Mason, P. (2011) Empathy and pro-social behavior in rats *Science,* 2011 Dec 9; 334(6061): 1427-30

Benson, H. (2013) *Let's Stick Together: The Relationship Book for New Parents* England: Lion Books

Berelowitz, S. (2013) *If Only Someone Had Listened* Office of the Children's Commissioner's Inquiry into Child Sexual Exploitation in Gangs and Groups, Final Report Nov 2013 London: Office of the Children's Commissioner

Bevington, D. *Lecture* 2013, London: The Centre for Child Mental Health

Bhavnagri, N.P. & Samuels, B. (1996) Children's literature and activities promoting social cognition of peer relationship in pre-schoolers *Early Childhood Research Quarterly,* 1996; 11, 307–331

Bion, W.R. (1959) Attacks on linking *International Journal of Psycho-Analysis,* Vol 40: Reprinted in *Second Thoughts,* (1967)

Bollas, C. (1987) *The Shadow of the Object: Psychoanalysis of the Unthought Known* London: Free Association Books

Booth, P.B. & Jerberg, A.M. (2010) *Theraplay: Helping parents and children build better relationships through attachment-based play,* New York: John Wiley & Sons Ltd

Bowlby, J. (1973) *Attachment and Loss: Volume 2 - Separation, Anxiety and Anger* London: Hogarth Press

Bowlby, J. (1978) *Attachment and Loss: Volume 3 - Loss, Sadness and Depression* Harmondsworth, Middx: Penguin

Bowlby, J. (1979) *The Making and Breaking of Affectional Bonds* London: Tavistock

Bowlby, J. (1988) *A Secure Base: Clinical applications of attachment theory* London: Routledge

Bremner, D.J. & Narayan, M. (1998) The effects of stress on memory and the hippocampus throughout the life cycle: implications for childhood development and aging *Development and Psychopathology* Volume Issue 04, December 1998, pp. 871-885

British Medical Association (2006) *Child and Adolescent Mental Health - A guide for healthcare professionals* London: BMA

Bushman, B. (1999) Does venting anger feed or extinguish the flame? Catharsis, rumination, distraction, anger and aggressive responding *Personality and Social Psychology Bulletin,* June 2002 Vol. 28 No. 6, pp.724-731

Canale, S.D., Louise, D.Z., Maio, V., Wang, X., Rossi, G., Hojat, M., & Gonnella, J.S (2012) The relationship between physician empathy and disease complications: an empirical study of primary care physicians and their diabetic patients in Parma, Italy *Academic Medicine,* Vol 87, No. 9 September 2012 2012;87(9):1243-1249

Casement, P. (1985) *On Learning from the Patient* Routledge: London

Centre For Social Justice Policy Group (2006) *Breakdown Britain: Interim report on the state of the nation* London: CSJ

Centre for Social Justice (2011) *Strengthening the Family and Tackling Family Breakdown* London: CSJ

Centre for Social Justice (2014) *Fully Committed? How government could reverse family breakdown* London: CSJ

Chamberlain, T., George, N., Golden, S., Walker, F. & Benton, T. (2010) *Tellus 4 National Report* London: DCFS

Chethik, M. (1989) *Techniques of Child Therapy: Psychodynamic Strategies* New York: The Guilford Press

Coan, J.A., Beckes, L. & Allen, J. P. (2013) Childhood maternal support and social capital moderate the regulatory impact of social relationships in adulthood', *Internal Journal of Psychophysiology,* 2013 Apr 29. p.ii: S0167-8760(13)00093-7

Comte, F. (1994) *The Wordsworth Dictionary of Mythology* (A. Goring, Trans) Wordsworth Editions: Ware (Original work published in French in 1988)

Copley, B. & Forryan B. (1997) *Therapeutic Work with Children and Young People* London: Cassell.

Cozolino, L.J. (2002) *The Neuroscience of Psychotherapy: Building and rebuilding the human brain* London: W.W. Norton and Company

Craig, A.D. (2009) How do you feel - now? The anterior insula and human awareness, *Nature Reviews Neuroscience* 2009; 10: 59-70

Decety, J. & Jackson, P.L. (2004) The functional architecture of human empathy, *Behavioural Cognitive Neuroscience,* Rev. 2004 Jun; 3(2): 71-100

Department for Education (2012) *Characteristics of Children in Need in England* London

Department for Education and Employment (1999) *National Healthy Schools Standard: Guidance* Nottingham

Department of Health (2004) *The Child Health Promotion Programme: Pregnancy and the first five years of life* London

Department of Health (2011) *No Health Without Mental Health: A cross-government mental health outcomes strategy for people of all ages* London

Department of Health (2012) *Too many young people suffering in silence with mental health problems,* [online] Available at https://www.gov.uk/government/news/too-many-young-people-suffering-in-silence-with-mental-health-problems [accessed 23.05.13]

Derksen, F., Bensing, J. & Lagro-Janssen, A. (2013) Effectiveness of empathy in general practice: a systematic review *British Journal of General Practice* 63 (606,e76-e84)

Dewey, J. (2009) *Art as Experience* USA: Perigee Books

Dinesen, I. (1957) *Talk With Isak Dinesen in The New York Times Book Review* by Mohn, B. [newspaper] November 3rd

Eisenberger, N.I., Lieberman, M.D. & Williams, K.D. (2003) Does rejection hurt? An FMRI study of social exclusion, *Science* Oct 10;302(5643): 290-2

Engen, H.G. & Singer, T. (2013) Empathy circuits *Current Opinion in Neurobiology*, 2013 Apr;23(2):275-82. Epub 2012 Dec

Field, T.M. (1994) The effects of mothers' physical and emotional unavailability on emotion regulation *Monographs of the Society for Research in Child Development* 59;(2-3): 208-27

Field, T.M., Hernandez-Reif, M. & Diego, M. (2006) Newborns of depressed mothers who received moderate versus light pressure massage during pregnancy *Infant Behavioural Development* 2006 Jan;29(1):54-8 Epub 2005 Oct 27

Fonagy, P. (2005) *Affect Regulation, Mentalisation and the Development of the Self* London: Other Press

Fonagy, P., Steele, M., Steele, H. & Target, M. (1997) *Reflective-functioning* Manual Version 4.1 London: University College London

Fosha, D. (2000) *The Transforming Power of Affect* New York: Basic Books

Fox, M. (1990) *Original Blessing* Lecture, St James Church London

Geddes, H. (2006) *Attachment in the Classroom: The links between children's early experience, emotional well-being and performance in school* London: Worth Publishing.

Gini, G. & al (2007) *The prevalence of bullying in schools is such a stark reminder for us all the lack of empathy in so many children,* [online] available at www.nspcc.org.uk/inform/resourcesfo,rprofessionals/bullying/bullying_statistics_wda85732.html [accessed 23.05.13]

Ginott, H.G. (1975) *Teacher and Child: A book for parents and teachers* New York: Macmillan

Gladstone, G.L., Parker, G.B. & Malhi, G.S. (2006) Do bullied children become anxious and depressed adults? A cross-sectional investigation of the correlates of bullying and anxious depression *Journal of Nervous and Mental Disease* 194, pp.201-208

Gottman, J., Katz, L. & Hoover, C. (1996) Parental meta-emotion philosophy and the emotional life of families: theoretical models and preliminary data *Journal of Family Psychology*, 1996; Vol. 10, No. 3, 243-268

Green, H., McGinnity, A., Meltzer, H., Ford, T. & Goodmand, R. (2004) *Mental Health of Children and Young People in Great Britain 2004* Palgrave Macmillan: London.

Greenberg, L. (2014) *Healing through Attachment and Emotion Conference*, London: The Centre for Child Mental Health (Nov)

Greenberg, L. & Bohart, A. (1997) *Empathy Reconsidered* New York: American Psychological Association

Grotstein, J. (2005) *Winnicott as a Precursor to Kohut and Stern: Psychotherapy and Creativity* Winnicott & British Object Relation Conference Lifespan Learning: Los Angeles (tape)

Gunnar, M.R. (2003) Integrating neuroscience and psychological approaches in the study of early experiences *The National Academy of Sciences of the United States of America* 1008: 238-247

Hauser, S., Allen, J. & Golden, E. (2006) *Out of the Woods: Tales of Resilient Teens* London: Harvard University Press
Hillman, J. & Pozzo, L. (1983) *Inter Views: Conversations with Laura Pozzo on psychotherapy, biography, love, soul, dreams, work, imagination and the state of the culture* New York: Spring Publications
Hillman, J. (1993) in Kidel, M. (1993) *Kind of Blue: An essay on melancholia and depression* Telluride Film Festival
Hillman, J. (2007) *The Art of Imagination Lecture* London: Institute for Arts in Therapy and Education
Howard, S. & Johnson, B. (2000) Resilient and non-resilient behaviour in adolescents *Trends and Issues in Crime and Justice, 183,* Australian Institute of Criminology
Hughes, D. (2006) *Building the Bonds of Attachment: Awakening love in deeply troubled children* New York: Jason Aronson
Hughes, D. (2007) *Attachment-Focused Family Therapy* New York: W.W.Norton & Co
Hughes, D. (2009) *Principles of Attachment-Focused Parenting: Effective strategies to care for children* London: W.W.Norton & Co
Hughes, D. (2011) *Attachment Focused Family Therapy Workbook* New York: W.W.Norton & Co
Hughes, D. (2012) *Why Empathy Heals Conference* London: Centre for Child Mental Health (May)
Hughes, D. (2014) *Dyadic Developmental Psychotherapy: Towards a comprehensive trauma informed treatment for developmental trauma disorder* www.ddpnetwork.org
Hunter, M. (2001) *Psychotherapy with Young People in Care: Lost and found* London: Routledge

Institute for Public Policy Research (2006) *Britain's Teenagers' Social Skills Gap Widens* London: IPPR

Johnson, S. (2004) *The Practice of Emotionally Focused Couple Therapy* London: Brunner-Routledge
Jung, C.G. (1982) *Aspects of the Feminine,* translated from German by R.F.C. Hull Princeton: Princeton University Press

Kaduson, H. & Schaefer, C. (1997) *101 Favourite Play Therapy Techniques* Jason Aronson: US
Kahn, M.M.R. (1997) *Between Therapist and Client: The new relationship* New York: W.H.Freeman
Kahr, B. (2006) *Lecture on Winnicott* London: Centre for Child Mental Health (June)
Kircanski, K., Lieberman, M.D. & Craske, M.G. (2012) Feelings into words: contributions of language to exposure therapy *Psychological Science* 23, 1086-1091
Kohut, H. & Wolf, E.S. (1978) The disorders of the self and their treatment *International Journal of Psycho-Analysis,* 59: 413-424
Kohut, H. (1977) *The Restoration of the Self* New York: International Universities Press

Lanyado, M. & Horne, A. (2006) *A Question of Technique (Independent Psychoanalytic Approaches with Children and Adolescents)* London: Routledge

Lanyado, M. & Horne, A. (Eds.) (1999) *Handbook of Child and Adolescent Psychotherapy: Psychoanalytic Approaches.* London: Routledge

Lewis, C.S. (1950) *The Lion, the Witch and the Wardrobe* London: Harper Collins

Lieberman, M.D. (2011) Why symbolic processing of affect can disrupt negative affect: Social cognitive and affective neuroscience investigation, in, Todorov, A., Fiske, S.T. & Prentice, D. (Eds.) *Social Neuroscience: Toward understanding the underpinnings of the social mind* (pp.188-209) Oxford, England: Oxford University Press

Lieberman, M.D., Inagaki, T.K., Tabibnia, G. & Crockett, M.J. (2011) Subjective responses to emotional stimuli during labeling, reappraisal, and distraction *Emotion* 2011; *3*, 468-480. doi: 10.1037/ a0023503

Lier, L. (1998) Mother-infant relationship in the first year of life *Acta Psychiatrica Scandinavica: Supplementum* 344:31-42

Lipton, B. (2011) *The Biology of Belief: Unleashing the power of consciousness, matter & miracles* London: Hay House UK

Lowenfeld, M. (1991) *Play in Childhood* London: MacKeith Press

Lowen, A. (1967) *The Betrayal of the Body* New York: Collier/Macmillan

Magagna, J. (2005) *Broken Hearts Conference* London: Centre for Child Mental Health (July)

Mahler, M. (1968) *On Human Symbiosis and the Vicissitudes of Individuation* New York: International Universities Press

Mar, R.A. (2011) The neural bases of social cognition and story comprehension *Annual Review of Psychology*, 2011; 62:103-34. doi: 10.1146

Mar, R.A., Tackett, J.L. & Moore, C. (2009) Exposure to media and theory-of-mind development in pre-schoolers, *Cognitive Development*. 2011 Nov; doi: 10.1016.

Mar, R.A., Oatley, K., Djikic, M. & Mullin, J. (2011) Emotion and narrative fiction: Interactive influences before, during, and after reading, *Cognition & Emotion* 2011 Aug; 25(5):818-33

McDougall, J. (1989) *Theatres of the Body: A psychoanalytical approach to psychosomatic illness* London: Free Association Press

McEwen, B.S. (1999) Stress and the ageing hippocampus *Journal of Neuroendocrinology* Jan;20(1):49-70

Meaney, M.J. (2001) Maternal care, gene expression, and the transmission of individual differences in stress reactivity across generations *Annual Review of Neuroscience* 24:1161-92

Mearns, D. & Cooper, M. (2005) *Working at Relational Depth in Counselling and Psychotherapy* London: Sage

Mellor, K. & Sigmund, E. (1975) Discounting *Transactional Analysis Journal* 5(3)295-302

Meltzer, D. (1969) The relation of aims to methodology in the treatment of children *Journal of Child Psychotherapy* 11(3) 1969: 57-61

Milton, J. (2003) *Paradise Lost* (Penguin Classics) Rev Ed edition Harmondsworth: Penguin

Mitchell, S. (2003) *Relationality: from Attachment to Intersubjectivity* London: The Analytic Press

Music, G. (2012) *Why Empathy Heals Lecture* London: The Centre for Child Mental Health (May) unpublished

National Healthy School Standard (2004) *Promoting Emotional Health and Wellbeing through the National Healthy School Standard* Wetherby: Health Development Agency

Nuffield Foundation (2013) *Social Trends and Mental Health: Introducing the main findings* London: Nuffield Foundation

Oaklander, V. (1978) *Windows to Our Children: A Gestalt approach to children and adolescents* Utah: Real People Press

Oaklander, V. (2006) *Hidden Treasure* London: Karnac Books

Office of National Statistics (2000) *Mental Health of Children and Adolescents in Great Britain* London: ONS

Office of National Statistics (2004) *The Health of Children and Young People: News Release* London: ONS March

Ofsted (2013) *Not Yet Good Enough: Personal, social, health and economic education in schools* No. 130065, London: Ofsted

Panksepp, J. (1998) *Affective Neuroscience: The foundations of human and animal emotions* Oxford: Oxford University Press

Panksepp, J. & Watt, D. (2011) Why does depression hurt? Ancestral primary-process separation-distress (PANIC/GRIEF) and diminished brain reward (SEEKING) processes in the genesis of depressive affect *Psychiatry* 2011 Spring;74(1):5-13

Pennebaker, J.W. (1993) Putting stress into words: health, linguistic, and therapeutic implications *Behavioural Research Therapy* Jul; 31(6): 539-48

Pennebaker, J.W. & Chung, C.K. (2011) Expressive writing: connections to physical and mental health *in* Friedman H. S. (Ed.) *The Oxford Handbook of Health Psychology* (pp. 417-437), New York: Oxford University Press

Penza, K.M., Heim, C. & Nemeroff, C.B. (2003) Neurobiological effects of childhood abuse: implications for the pathophysiology of depression and anxiety *Archives of Women's Mental Health* Feb;6(1):15-22

Perry, B.D. (2007) *The Boy Who Was Raised as a Dog* New York: Basic Books

Perry, B.D. (2008) *The Traumatised Child: Healing Brain, Mind and Body Conference* London: Centre for Child Mental Health (June)

Perry, B.D., Pollard, R., Blakely, T. & Baker, W. (1995) Childhood trauma; the neurobiology of adaptation and use-dependent development of the brain: how states become traits *Infant Mental Health Journal* 16: 271-91

Perry, B.D. & Ungar, M. (2012) Violence, trauma and resilience *in* Alaggia, R. & Vine, C. (Eds.) (2012) *Cruel But Not Unusual: Violence in Canadian families*, 2nd Edition, USA: Wilfred Laurier University Press

Petrash, J. (2003) *Understanding Waldorf Education: Teaching from the Inside Out* Maryland: Gryphon House

Radford, L., Corral, S., Bradley, C., Fisher, H., Bassett, C., Howat, N. & Collishaw, S. (2011) *Child Abuse and Neglect in the UK Today,* London: NSPCC

Rall, J. & Harris, P.L. (2000) In Cinderella's slippers? Story comprehension from the protagonist's point of view *Developmental Psychology,* 2000; 26, 202-208

Rosenblum, K. L., McDonough, S., Muzik, M., Miller, A. & Sameroff, A. (2002) Maternal representations of the infant: associations with infant response to the still face *Child Development,* 73, 999-105

Rottenberg, J., Wilhelm, F.H., Gross, J.J. & Gotlib, I.H. (2003) Vagal rebound during resolution of tearful crying among depressed and nondepressed individuals *Psychophysiology* Jan; 40(1): 1-6

Rowshan, A. (1997) *Telling Tales: how to use stories to help children deal with the challenges of life* Oxford, England: One World

Sambo, C.F., Howard, M., Kopelman, M., Williams, S. & Fotopoulou, A. (2010) Knowing you care: effects of perceived empathy and attachment style on pain perception *Pain* 151, 687-693

Scheff, T. J. (2001) *Catharsis in Healing, Ritual & Drama* Lincoln: iUniverse.com

Schmahmann, J.D. & Caplan, D. (2006) Cognition, emotion and the cerebellum *Brain,* Feb;129(2):290-2

Schore, A.N. (2005) *Repair of the Self: Psychotherapy for the 21st Century Conference:* London (Sept)

Segal, J. & Simkins, J. (1993) *My Mum Needs Me: Helping children with ill or disabled parents* Harmondsworth: Penguin Books

Sharples, J. (2008) *Early Years Commission Hearing* London: Centre for Social Justice, Westminster (March)

Siegel, D. J. (2012) (2nd Edition) *The Developing Mind* NYC: The Guildford Press

Sinason, V. (2008) The impact of child abuse and neglect, *Lecture,* London: Centre for Child Mental Health (Nov)

Singer, T., Seymour, B., O'Doherty, J., Kaube, H., Dolan, R.J. & Frith, C.D. (2004) Empathy for pain involves the affective but not sensory components of pain *Science* Feb 20;303(5661):1157-62

Sroufe, A., Collins, W., Carlson, E. & Egeland, B. (2005) *The Development of the Person* New York: Guildford Publications

Steele, M. Steele, H. & Johansson, M. (2002) Maternal predictors of children's social cognition: an attachment perspective *Journal of Child Psychology and Psychiatry, and Allied Disciplines* Oct;43 (7):861-72

Steinbeis, N., Bernhardt, B.C, & Singer, T. (2012) Impulse control and underlying functions of the left DLPFC mediate age-related and age-independent individual differences in strategic social behavior *Neuron* 2012 Mar 8;73(5):1040-51

Stern, D.N. (2004) *The Present Moment in Psychotherapy and Everyday Life* (Norton Series on Interpersonal Neurobiology) US: W.W.Norton & Co

Storr, A. (1972) *The Dynamics of Creation* Harmondsworth, Middx: Penguin

Stuart, T., Hauser, Allen, J.P. & Golden, E. (2006) *Out of the Woods: Tales of Resilient Teens* Cambridge, Massachusetts & London, England: Harvard University Press

Sunderland, M. (1997) *Draw on Your Emotions: A Practical Workbook* Oxford: Speechmark

Sunderland, M. (2001a) *A Wibble called Bipley* Oxford: Speechmark Press

Sunderland, M. (2001b) *A Nifflenoo called Nevermind* Oxford: Speechmark Press

Sunderland, M. (2001c) *Willie & the Wobbly House* Oxford: Speechmark Publishing

Sunderland, M. (2001d) *A Wibble Called Bipley* Oxford: Speechmark Publishing

Sunderland, M. (2001e) *The Frog who Longed for the Moon to Smile* Oxford: Speechmark Press

Sunderland, M. (2001) *A Pea called Mildred* Oxford: Speechmark Press

Sunderland, M. (2001) *Using Storytelling as a Therapeutic Tool with Children.* Oxford: Speechmark

Sunderland, M. (2002) *Helping Children with Loss* Oxford: Speechmark

Sunderland, M. (2002) *Helping Children Locked in Rage and Hate* Oxford: Speechmark

Sunderland, M. (2002) *Helping Children Who Think They Are Worthless* Oxford: Speechmark

Sunderland, M. (2002) *Helping Children with Anxiety* Oxford: Speechmark

Sunderland, M. (2003a) *The Day the Sea Went Out and Never Came Back* Oxford: Speechmark Press

Sunderland, M. (2003b) *How Hattie Hated Kindness* Oxford: Speechmark Press

Sunderland, M. (2003c) *Teenie Weenie in a Too Big World* Oxford: Speechmark Press

Sunderland, M. (2003d) *Ruby and the Rubbish Bin* Oxford: Speechmark Press

Sunderland, M. (2004) Theories of Causation of Child Mental Ill-health *The Neuroscience of Parenting Lecture* London: The Centre for Child Mental Health (Nov)

Sunderland, M. (2006) *The Science of Parenting* London: Dorling Kindersley

Sunderland, M. (2008) *Smasher! A story to help adolescents with anger and alienation* Bucks: Hinton House

Sunderland, M. (2008) *Draw on Your Relationships: A Practical Workbook* Oxford: Speechmark

Sunderland, M. (2010) *Monica Plum's Horrid Problem* Oxford: Speechmark

Teicher, M.H. (2008) *The Effect of Neglect and Abuse on the Brain Lecture* London: The Centre for Child Mental Health, (April)

Teicher, M.H., Samson, J.A., Polcari, A., McGreenery, C.E. (2006) Sticks, stones, and hurtful words: relative effects of various forms of childhood maltreatment *The American Journal of Psychiatry* Jun;163(6):993-1000

Theraplay (2004) *Theraplay Activities Flip Book* Vol 1 Illinois: The Theraplay Institute

Thomas, R.M., Hotsenpiller, G. & Peterson, D.A. (2007) Stress and neurogenesis in the rat *The Journal of Neuroscience* 2007 March, 27(11):1

Trop, J.L. & Stolorow, R.D. (1997) Therapeutic Empathy: An intersubjective perspective *in* Bohart, AC. & Greenberg, LS. (Eds) (1997) *Empathy Reconsidered: New Directions in Psychotherapy* Washington, DC: American Psychological Association, pp. 279-291

Vaillancourt, T., Duku, E., Becker, S., Schmidt, L.A., Nicol, J., Muir, C. & Macmillan, H. (2011) Peer victimization, depressive symptoms, and high salivary cortisol predict poorer memory in children *Brain Cognition* 2011 Nov; 77(2): 191-9

Van der Kolk, B.A. (2003) The neurobiology of childhood trauma and abuse *Child and Adolescent Psychiatric Clinics of North America* 12:293–317

Van der Kolk, B.A., Mcfarlane, C.A. & Weisaeth, L. (Eds.) (1999) *Traumatic Stress* NYC: The Guildford Press.

Vaughan, J. (2005) Attachment disordered Children *Children with Broken Hearts Conference,* London: The Centre for Child Mental Health, (July)

Vaughan, J. (2008) personal communication, unpublished

Vaughan, J. (2010) personal communication, unpublished

Wachtel, P.L. (2008) *Relational Theory and the Practice of Psychotherapy* New York: The Guildford Press

Walby, S. (2009) *The Cost of Domestic Violence: Up-date 2009,* UK: Lancaster University.

Winnicott, D.W. (1949) *World in Small Doses* London: Tavistock

YoungMinds (2011) *100,000 children and young people could be hospitalised due to self-harm by 2020 warns YoungMinds* London: YoungMinds

Zubieta, J.K, Ketter, T.A., Bueller, J.A., Yanjun, X.U., Kilbourn, M.R, Young, E.A. & Koeppe, R.A. (2003) Regulation of human affective responses by anterior cingulate and limbic and m-opioid Neurotransmission *Archives of General Psychiatry* 60:1145-1153

Index

A

Abandonment 27, 287, 323, 295
absence 206, 228, **233-5**
acknowledging 23, 42, 83, 111-2, 143, 165-8, 191, 228, 260, 263, 267, 271, 273, 278, 281, 289, 306, 318, 325, 341, **354**, 360, 369, 371, **396-7**
addictions 17, 61, 163, 350, 353, 388
affective magic 122
affect labelling 308, 326
aggression, aggressive 16, 17, 20, 25-26, 39, 46, 81, 83, 91, 100, 115, 127, 157, 186, 233, 253
alliance, *therapeutic*, 320: *working,* 80, 110, 113, 320-1
anger, adult's, 39, 48-9, 63-65, 111, 336:
child's, 7, 8, 15, 33, 34, 73, 84, 98, 113, 133, 139-40, 154, 170, 187-8, 202, 226, 238, 248, 279, 300, 321, 327, 330, 338-9, 345-6, 364, 375-7, 385
anxiety 3, 16, 20, 25, 26, 38, 40, 48, 115, 120, 146, 156-7, 185, 254, 300, 318, 337, 346, 349, 359
arousal 96, 308: *bodily,*157: *hyper-,* 26, 156-8, 307, 313, 390
art image 55, 124, 127, 238, 260
attachment figure 43, 310

B

Betrayal 123, 170, 218, 252, 295, 384, 398, 404
Big Empathy Drawing **79-95**, 96, 98, 101, 151, 153, 155, 184, 187, 203, 209, 272, 344, 358, 360, 363, 375
brain 33, **39**, 81, 84, 95, 99, 106, 121, 125, 138, **156-8**, 180, 187, 197, 238, 266, 303, 314, 336, 385, 406, 408, 410: *activity,* 39: *development,* 13, 14-16, **20, 40**, 128, 332: *negative effects on,* 24, 39, 125, 181, 188, 206, 231, 332, 396: *reptilian,* 33, 157: *science,* 6, 20, 24, **39**, 289, **293-4**: *state,* 24, 26, 131
bullying **40**, 75, 125, 174, 182, 197, 17, 247, 250, 268-9, 284, 313, **351**, 353: *cyber-,* 18, 351, 395

C

Can of worms 24-27
cerebellum 39, 95, 266
challenging behaviour 8, 14, 81, 96, **186-7**, 280, 342
clay 71, 99, 203, 231, 256, 288
co-created *empathy,* 222, 359: *meaning,* 96: *reflective process,* 184: *understanding,* 60. 66. 67 78
compassion 3, 4, 10, 8, 22-24, 27, 32, 40, 85, 114, 142, 153, 155, 280, 308, **315-6**, 321, 343, 345, 412
compliance 113, 179, 226, 269, 285
concentration 43, 128, 156, 297, 307, 311, 314
containing 40, **45**, 147, 263, 322
cortisol 131 156, 332
core feelings 80, 104-6, **168-71**, 190, 257, 73

counselling, *adult,* 32, 112, 114, 168, 255, 334, 336, 338: *child,* 5, 85, 258, 337, 347
curiousity 20, 31, 43, 64, 134-5, 142, 218, 231-2, 241, 332, 413

D

Defences **80**, 100 104, 114, **168**-70, 273, 313, 315, 317, 322-4, 345, **382**, 389: *adult's,* 336
depression 20: *adult's,* 44, 46, 76, 91, 131, 163, 192 196, 206, 216, 248, 271, 332, 405: *child's,*16-17, 25-26, **40**, 125, 169, 266, 269, 300-1, 306, 310, 349, **350**, 395
de-roling 277
dialoguing 217, 219, **245-48**, 260
direct communication 4, 6, **69-70, 73-77**: *passim*
distancing, see *psychological distancing*
divorce 11, 48, 90, 32, 353
domestic violence 54, 103, 286, 98, 351, 387
drum/triangle technique 51, 97, 200-1

E

Eating disorders 17, 33, 387
eleventh hour 70
emotion worksheets 145, **180-1, 326-9**
emotional, *baggage* 20-22, 114, 168, 254, 320, 334-8, 346, 349, 411, 413:
empowered anger 169, 354, **368-73**

empathic listening 31-33, *passim*
empathy *passim*
empty chair work 197, 201
enactment 274-85
envy 402-04
eye contact 133, 134, 158, 278

F
Family breakdown 3 , **350-1**, 387-8, 398
fantasies 14, 26, 32, 97, 147, 267, 324, 341, 357 fear 10, 15-16, 24, 25, 64, 80. 112, 121, 130, 147, 170-1, 176, 187, 229, 232, 255, 305, 307, 321, 327, 336, 338, 339, 345, 359, 361, 383, 401, 407, 410, 411
Feeling Rooms 114, 115, **412-3**
fight/flight/freeze 15, 33, 121, 157, 307
frontal lobes 33, 12, **156-7**, 266
frustration 133, 137, 248

G
Grief 18, 26, 47, 49, 87, 98, 105, 157, 170, 171, 206, 253, 263, 310, 336, 338, 373, **383-4**, 387, 396
guilt 4, 71, 92, 98, 02, 170, 259, 384, 406

H
Happy endings 24, **260-1**, 263, 314
'held in mind' 289, 331, 347, 384, 412
hope 289, 331, 347, 384, 412
hopelessness 111, 260, 263, 321, 336, 395

I
Identification **238-245**, 248, 260
illness 11, 16, 142, 184, 2006, 216, 357, 363, 405
indirect communication 4, 6, **69-73**: passim
insula 15, 39, 294
interviewing 55, 127, 134, 138, 219-20, **236-44**, 249

J
Jealousy 44, 50, 83, 196, 327, **385**, 407

K
Key psychological messages 191, 291, 297, 309-10, 313, **405-11**
kindness 40, 144, 405, 409, 412: *absence* of, 87, 89, 232-4, 385: *pain of receiving*, 317, 343

L
Language, *age appropriate*, 312, 339: *behaviour as*, 186, 342: *body*, 59, 324: *non-verbal*, 59: *of emotion*, 17, 64, 120, 123, 125, 158, 173, 186, 187: *of metaphor*, 123, 333: *of potency*, 264-5: *play*, 130: *processing centres*, 293
life story **6**, 31, 44, **48-52**, 58, 63, 64, 87, 88, 144, 181, 208, 232-3, 258, 261, 278-81, 287, 298, 300, 323, 336
loss *passim*

M
Meaning, *child's* 31, 53,

54-58, 65, 94, 96, 128, 32, 135, 202, 207, 236, 248
mentalising **78**, 199, 205, 294-5, 404
metaphor 6, 18, 64, 69, 70, **74-81**, 87, 90, 110, 123, 166, 184, 208, 211-2, 237, 247, 256, 258, 260, 286, 292, 323, 324, 333
miniatures 10, **222-5**, 254, 258, 273, 282
mirroring 107
misattunement 111-2, 119-23, 128-9, 134, 148, 260, 335

N
Negative self-referencing 79, 97, 149, 259, 306
neglect 141, 237, 260, 306, **352**
neuroscience 6, 84, 306, 332, 398
new baby 81, 84m 163, 229, 263, 410, 407
Nosy Seagull 251
numbing, *emotional* 15, 32, 157, 307-8, 358, 375, 382

O
Obsession 33, 38, 106, 339
opioids 81, 310, 366
oxytocin 60

P
Painting 52, 185, 223, 230, 236, 238-9, 252, 258-9, 271, 288
panic attacks 33, 38, 216
paraphrasing 136-7
parroting 107, 136
persecutory 233: *figure*, 248: *worlds*, 234
phobias 33, 38, 216, 339
platitudes 112, **139**

play *passim*
play story 6, 44, **48-52**, 58, 63-4, 85, 87, 88, 155, 177, 208, 232-3, 245, 248,
post-traumatic stress disorder 26, 158, **300-14**
pre-frontal cortex 14, 15, 39
protest 105, 169, 170, 179, 210, 268-8, 285, 291, 326, 368
psycho-education 50, **97**, 100, 102, 149, 179, 191, 196, 210, 218, 257, 259, 326, 344, 394, 397-8, 402
psychological, *distance*, 283, **285-6**: *journey*, 299: landscape, **225-7**, 233: safety, 6, 158, 215, 236, 283, **317-323**, 345, 398: *strengths*, 190, 262
puppets 10, 51, 182, **215-22**, 251, 260, 283, 392-5

Q
Questions, *open*, 132-36, 138, 142-3: *to an image/ puppet*, 220, 240

R
Reassurance 147, 149, 159, 363
reflective *adult*, 16, 18, 121, 277: *process*, 87, 182-4, 92, 283, 389, 397, 400: *skills*, 8, 389: *summaries*, 182: *time*, 256: *work*, 133
reflection 28, 48, 61, 108, 169, 199, 201, 212, 240, 256, 268, 271, **277**, 293, 297, **312-4**, 394-6, 404
regulation **28**: *dys-*, 146: *emotional*, 146, 166, 281, 310, 347, 413: *physiological*, 310: *stress*, 20 rejection 281, 399

relational depth, 79: *experience*, 18, 23, 115, 219, 333: *moments*, 218: *play*, 110, 134, 334-5: *poverty*, 114, 233, 237: *stress*, 114, 128, 233
repetitive play 272-3, 332,
re-traumatising 27, 157, 59, 280 283-4, 308

S
Safety 90, 156, 223, 236-8: *absence of*, 87, 232-3, 322, 325, 364: *psychological*, see psychological
sandplay *passim*
sandtray 222, 224, 229
school performance 16, 40
self *-acceptance*, 22: *-awareness*, 15, 2-2, 94, 334, 410: *-esteem*, 2, 24, 49, 87, 217, 382-3: *-harm*, 17, 27, 33, 272, 339, 350: *-states*, 217, 222, 236, 246 *sense of self* 24, 54, 101, 112, 113
sensory cortex 293
separation 11, 44, 166, 216, 353, 399
shame 26, 48, 64, 98, 113, 170, 217, 218, 268-9, 281, 289, 313, 317-321, 389
shock *passim*
"Show me" 0, 53, 173-5, 204, 256-9, 282-3, 286, 322
sibling, *abuse*, 67: *agony*, 83-84, **385**
silence 74, **145, 150**, 27
soothing 83, 128, 157-9, 367: *self-*, 157: *voice*, 59-60, 65, 145, 157, 334
'still face' 219, 332
story, *finish the - technique*:

189-95: *therapeutic use of*, **280-314**: *passim*
'suffering well' 17-18
summary, *end of session*, 182, 191, 256: *mid-session*, 182, 256: *reflective*, 156, 182, 195, 219, 240, 298,
supervision 100, 128, 136, 156, 170, 298, 314, 347, 390
sympathy 31, 107

T
Theraplay 331, 335
touch, *bad* 149, 406: *therapeutic effect of*, 157-9
trauma *passim*

U
Unfinished sentence technique **175-9**, 198, 202, 246, 369: *for anger*, 370-2; *for grief*, 373-5
'unthought known' 61, 96, 121

V
Vagal tone 16, 37
verbal abuse 125, 321
violence, *adult*, 144, 234, 253, 351-2: *child*, 21, 65, 121, 170, 253, 281, 286
voice, *child having a*, 23, 14, 137, 171, 238, 268-9, 354, 357, 369, 373, 405: *tone of*, 4, 43, **58-60**, 121, 197, 218, 258, 284, 296, 318, 334:

W
Wondering 51, 60, **71-74**, 122, 205, 343
worries 7, 10, 14, 38, 71, 322, 329, 383